Managing Disasters through Community and Local Government

Managing Disasters through Community and Local Government:

Indian and Global Experiences

Dr. Rajeev M.M.
Dr. C. Vinodan

KALPAZ

First Published, 2020

Published by

Kalpaz Publications
C-30, Satyawati Nagar,
Delhi – 110052
Ph.: 011-47034999, 9811692060
www.kalpazpublications.com
E-mail: kalpaz@hotmail.com

Printed at: Gyan Press, Delhi

Cataloging in Publication Data—DK
Courtesy: D.K. Agencies (P) Ltd. <docinfo@dkagencies.com>

Rajeev, M. M., 1976- **author.**
Managing disasters through community and local government : Indian and global experiences / Dr. Rajeev M.M., Dr. C. Vinodan.
pages cm
Includes bibliographical references and index.
ISBN 9789353242886 (HB)

1. Emergency management—India—Citizen participation. 2. Emergency management—Citizen participation. 3. Emergency management—Government policy—India. 4. Emergency management—Government policy. I. Vinodan, C., author. II. Title.

LCC HV551.5.I4R35 2020 | DDC 363.3480954 23

Contents

Preface

Disaster and Disaster Management has nowadays attained a lot of attention. The role of multiple stakeholders in disaster management, both pre and post-disaster phases, is very crucial. As a result of their vicinity to the emergency occasion and consciousness of the social, cultural, and economic milieu of the impacted community, local self-government can assume a notable role in structuring, planning, managing, networking and guiding community-based disaster relief efforts.

A robust community-based response system is fundamental in disaster relief efforts. It helps the affected area recoup from the social, political, and economic effects at a quicker movement. The research shows that deficient assets, helpless correspondence, and absence of coordination among legislative and non-administrative offices are probably the most repeating issues for hierarchical execution in disaster management projects.

Therefore, this book aims to identify the various social, political, and economic barriers that hindered local self-government's optimal participation in disaster relief operations, particularly concerning Alappadgram panchayat in Kerala following the 2004 tsunami. This book also attempts to review the various stakeholders' recovery and reconstruction activities concerning the disastrous tsunami that hit states of Kerala, Tamil Nadu, and the Andaman Islands.

Specifically, this book's primary focus is to understand and analyze Kerala's disaster management's formal and informal institutional mechanisms. Secondly, examine the problems and obstacles faced by local self-government in actively managing disaster response. Thirdly, this book outlines the social, political, and economic barriers that hindered local self-governments' optimal participation in disaster relief operations, incredibly natural disasters. The authors describe their experience and try to analyze the role of administration and the various other stakeholders in disaster recovery and reconstruction. This book also added a chapter on a research study carried out by the author and its findings.

The authors finally suggested the unavoidable elements needed to incorporate in the post-disaster response phase. This book recommended that, in disaster settings, the disaster management specialists can expect the position of power and help connect with local organizations to respond enough to catastrophes. The authors depict their experiences and attempt to examine the role of local administration and the different partners in catastrophe recuperation and reconstruction zones.

Dr. Rajeev MM
Dr. C. Vinodan

Chapter - 1

Disaster Management-Conceptual Framework

Disaster: Meaning, Concept and Explanation

Disaster implies a great or sudden misfortune that results in the loss of life and property or that is ruinous to an undertaking; calamity suggests a grave misfortune that brings deep distress or sorrow to an individual or to the people at large; catastrophe is specifically applied to a disastrous end or outcome; cataclysm suggests a great upheaval, especially a political or social one, that causes sudden and violent change with attending distress, and suffering *(Joseph F. Gustin, 2010)*. Disaster can also mean a catastrophic mishappening calamity of grave occurrence in any area, arising from natural or man-made causes, or by accident or negligence. Disasters are events that cause widespread damage, destruction and human sufferings. It requires immediate, coordinated and effective response by government, community, volunteers and corporate sector organizations *(Kumar, 2008)*.

Disasters are characterized by sudden onset, overwhelming severity, and mass destruction leading to property damage and resource loss. They cause injury and death, and they trigger emotional reactions in individuals. Disasters disrupt social networks and routines, and may affect the structure and functioning of the community itself (*Eranen & Liebkind, 1993*). *World Health Organization* defines disaster as a severe disruption, ecological and psychosocial, which greatly exceeds the coping capacity of the individual and the community *(WHO, 1992)*. Anything that exceeds one's personal ability to cope with a stressful event becomes a crisis. Disasters result from internal or external forces over which a community or system has no effective control. In such situations, external intervention is required to help people bounce back from the crisis. In line with the WHO definition, American College of Emergency Physicians (*2001*)[1] defines disasters as the destructive effects of natural or manmade force that exceeds the ability of a given area or community to meet the demand for health care. Social support may be mobilized or could deteriorate after a disaster, depending, in part, on the characteristics of the community, its members, and the disaster (*Kaniasty and Norris, 2004)*. Because the primary impact of disasters is on communities rather than society at large, the larger society may be relatively unaffected and remain available to assist the disaster-affected community by providing external aid for response and reconstruction.

The definition of a disaster adopted by the World Health Organization and the United Nations also indicate that, it is the damage that results from the impact on society that constitutes the disaster and not the disaster. The definitions used seem dependent upon the discipline using the term. No definition of "disaster" is accepted universally. Disaster is defined as "a situation resulting from an environmental phenomenon or armed conflict that produced stress, personal injury, physical damage, and economic disruption of great magnitude" *(Frederick C. Cuny, 1995)*. In another effort, *Perez and Thompson (2002)* in their series *on Natural Disasters*, define a disaster as: "the occurrence of widespread, severe damage, injury, or loss of life or property, with which the community cannot cope, and during which the affected society undergoes severe disruption." Both of these definitions note that a disaster disrupts the society stricken by the event. Furthermore, *Cuny* stresses that the event resulting in a disaster does not comprise the disaster: it is what results from the event that comprise the disaster, not the precipitating event itself.

In another seminal disaster pertinent literature, *Jerusalem and Colleagues (1995)* contend that stress at any level always begins with the individual. When individual and community resources are exhausted, the negative effects for the individual and/or for the community are increased while the capacity for coping generally decreases. Secondary adversities such as job loss or interruption of educational opportunity may also affect individuals and consequently reduce community capacity for coping. Community effects and the resultant impact on community capacity may extend to those who were not directly victimized. Resource loss at the community level exacerbates negative effects at the individual level as illustrated by the delayed and often averted return to New Orleans of residents displaced following Hurricane Katrina in 2005. As aptly noted by Jerusalem and Colleagues (1995), community vulnerability to stress is a function of "resource reserves" reflected in the relationship between depleted resources and remaining resources post-disaster. The future of

New Orleans Post-Katrina has been threatened, in part, by the dramatic decline in resource reserves *(Urasano & Blumenfield, 2005).*

The United States has a set of policy constructs that enable the federal government to assist state and local communities in the aftermath of a natural hazard or unexpected event. As defined in the legislation, "a major disaster means any natural catastrophe (including hurricane, tornado, storm, high water, wind driven water, tidal wave, tsunami, earthquake, volcanic eruption, landslide, mudslide, snowstorm, or drought), or, regardless of cause, any fire, flood, or explosion, in any part of the United States, causes damage of sufficient severity and magnitude to warrant major disaster assistance supplement the efforts and available resources of States, local governments, and disaster relief organizations in alleviating the damage, loss, hardship, or suffering caused thereby" *(FEMA, 2003)*[2].

In brief, from an in-depth conceptual analysis of the above given definitions of disasters, we can conclude that disasters are an extreme event, whether of natural or human origin, which overwhelm vulnerable populations and are characterized by some or all of the following: (a) they are disruptive to individuals and communities; (b)they are not part of the day-to-day experience and are outside normal life expectations; (c) they are often unpredictable in occurrence and effects; (d) they require a response for which normal local resources may be inadequate; (e) they have a wide range of effects and impacts on the human and physical environment; (f) there are complex needs in dealing with them; (g) they can be of sudden onset, like earthquakes; (h) they are destructive to human, animal and/or plant life, health, property and/or the environment; and (i) they overwhelm normal prudent protective measures *(David E. Hogan, Jonathan L. Burstein, 2007).*

Disaster: Occurrence and Cost

According to the Centre for Research on the Epidemiology of Disasters (CRED, 2018), In 2018, there were 315 natural disaster events recorded with 11,804 deaths, over 68million people affected, and US$131.7 billion1 in economic losses across the world. The burden was not shared equally as Asia suffered the highest impact and accounted for45% of disaster events, 80% of deaths, and 76% of people affected. Globally, Indonesia recorded nearly half the total deaths (47%), while India recorded the highest number of people affected (35%). Earthquakes were the deadliest type of disaster accounting for 45%of deaths, followed by flooding at 24%. Flooding affected the highest number of people ,accounting for 50% of the total affected, followed by storms which accounted for 28%.Given Asia's large land mass, higher population relative to other continents, and multiple hazard risks, the results are not surprising.

According to the Centre for Research on the Epidemiology of Disasters (CRED, 2011), 336 natural disasters and 234 technological disasters were reported worldwide in 2011. The number of natural disasters is the lowest of the decade and is 15 per cent below the decade's average. The number of technological disasters (234) is the second lowest of the decade, after 2009, far below the numbers reported during the first five years of the decade. The number of deaths caused by natural disasters (31,105) is the fourth lowest of the decade, much lower than the peaks of 2004 (242,010 deaths), 2008 (235,272) and 2010 (297,730). The deadliest natural disaster was the earthquake and the subsequent tsunami in Japan in March, which killed 19,846 people. The number of deaths is much lower than those caused by the Indian Ocean Tsunami in December 2004, (235,736 deaths) and the earthquake of January 2010 in Haiti (222,570 deaths). Tropical Storm Washi (Sendong), which killed 1,439 people in December in the Philippines, is the second deadliest natural disaster of 2011. The technological disaster that resulted in the highest number of deaths (203) was the sinking of a ferry in September in Tanzania. A total of 2,085 people died in 45 shipwrecks in 2011, accounting for 50 per cent of all deaths from transport accidents and almost one-third of all technological disasters. Among industrial accidents, an oil pipeline explosion caused 120 deaths in Kenya and the explosion of a fuel reserve led to the deaths of 100 people in Libya. The number of people reported to be affected by natural disasters (209 million) is the fourth lowest of the decade, but is much higher than the minimum of 2006 (147 million). In 2011, almost 70 per cent of people reported to be affected were victims of floods. The most severe occurred in June and September in China (68 and 20 million, respectively). Fifteen other floods affected 1 to 9 million people for a total of 45 million. Hailstorm affected 22 million people in China during the month of April and eight other storms in Asia, affected 1 to 3 million people for a total of 14 million. Seven droughts, of which five were in Africa, affected 1 to 4 million people for a total of 14 million *(CRED, 2011)*[4]. By comparison, the total number of people affected by earthquakes and tsunami (1.5 million) is the second lowest of the decade. The earthquake which affected the highest number of people (575,000) occurred in India in September 2011. The earthquake and tsunami in Japan, in March, affected 369,000 people and the February earthquake in New Zealand affected 300,000 people (*Center for Research on the Epidemiology of Disasters, 2011).*

Taking a close analysis of the five recent technological disasters that disrupted human life were fire outbreaks in slums which occurred four times. The two most ruthless ones occurred in the Philippines, affecting 20,000 and 10,000 people, and the two others in Kenya affecting 9,000 and 6,000 people. The explosion of an ammunition depot in Tanzania affected 1,500 people. In 2011, natural disaster losses (US$ 365.6 billion) were the highest of the decade, accounting for almost 1.5 times the direct losses reported in 2005 (US$ 248 billion, 2011 prices). The earthquake and tsunami in Japan cost US$ 210 billion and accounted for 57 per cent of all reported damages. Twenty-six other disasters accounted for another 48 per cent of all reported damages. Next to the gigantic damages caused by the tsunami, two earthquakes in New Zealand, in Christchurch and in South Island, cost US$ 15 billion and US$ 3 billion, respectively. An earthquake in Turkey in October cost US$ 1.5 billion. Damages from floods accounted for more than US$ 72 billion and were the highest reported for this type of disaster in the decade. The floods in Thailand cost US$ 40 billion. Ten other floods cost more than US$ 1 billion with a total of US$ 25 billion. These 11 disasters accounted for 87 per cent of damages reported for floods. Damages from storms accounted for almost US$ 51 billion, slightly lower than the decade's average of US$ 58 billion. Tornadoes in April and May in the United States cost US$ 11 billion and US$ 14 billion. Seven other storms, of which five occurred in the United States, each costs between US$ 1 to 7 billion, for a total of US$ 22 billion. These nine disasters accounted for 82 per cent of damages reported for storms. For three other natural disasters, reported costs exceeded US$ 1 billion: a drought in the United States (US$ 8 billion) and two forest fires, one in Canada in May (US$ 1.5 billion) and one in the United States in September (US$ 1 billion). For technological disasters, in 2011, the only damages reported were caused by two slum fires in the Philippines, which cost US$ 467,000 and US$ 234,000 *(World Disasters Report, 2012).*

The estimated economic losses from natural disasters in 2011 surpassed the last record year of 2005 (US$ 246.8 billion), and increased by 23.5% compared to the annual average damages from 2001 to 2010 (US$ 109.3 billion). Damages from geophysical disasters increased the most, from an annual average of US$ 24.1 billion during 2001-2010 to US$ 230.3 billion in 2011. Geophysical disasters represented a share of 62.9% of total damages caused by natural disasters in 2011. The number of reported natural disasters in 2011 was less when compared to the annual average occurrence from 2001 to 2010, mostly due to a smaller number of hydrological and meteorological disasters. Hydrological disasters still took by far the largest share in natural disaster occurrence in 2011 (52.1%), followed by meteorological disasters (25.3%), climatological disasters (11.7%) and geophysical disasters (10.8%), *(CRED, 2012).*

Looking at the geographical distribution of disasters, Asia was the continent which was most often hit by natural disasters in 2011 (44.0%), followed by the Americas (28.0%), Africa (19.3%), Europe (5.4%) and Oceania (3.3%). This regional distribution of disaster occurrence resembles the profile observed from 2001 to 2010. In 2011, Europe saw the largest decrease in disaster occurrence (68.7%), compared to the decade's annual average. In particular, Europe was less frequently hit by climatological and hydrological disasters *(CRED, 2012).*

In 2011, 86.3% of global disaster victims were from Asia, followed by Africa (9.2%). The number of victims in 2011 increased especially in Africa and Asia, but also in the Americas and Oceania, whereas fewer victims were reported in Europe, compared to the 2001-2010 annual averages. On a more detailed note, hydrological disasters in Asia caused many more victims in 2011, but climatological disasters made fewer victims, compared to the decade's annual averages. In Africa, it was climatological disasters, especially droughts in the Horn of Africa, which increased the number of victims. In 2011, Asia also suffered the most damages (75.4% of global disaster damages), followed by the Americas (18.4%) and Oceania (5.6%). For both Europe and Africa, a share of 0.3% of global disaster damages was reported. This distribution of disaster damages between continents differ from the distribution seen over the last decade, when the Americas experienced the most damages, followed by Asia and Europe. Damages in Asia increased the most in 2011 compared to the 2001-2010 annual average. In contrast, damages in Europe decreased. More precisely, geophysical and hydrological disasters contributed most to the increased damages in Asia, mainly due to the Tohoku earthquake and tsunami in Japan and the floods that affected Thailand from August to December *(CRED, 2012).*

According to the Centre for Research on the Epidemiology of Disasters (CRED), in 2010, 373 natural disasters were recorded globally. Events like earthquakes in Haiti, China and Chile, heat wave in Russia, floods in Pakistan and severe weather conditions in the U.S. had larger impact on human settlements. It is estimated that more than 2, 96,800 people were killed, 207 million people were affected and the economic loss was estimated to be over 109 billion US$ in the year 2010. In the year of 2010, 297,000 people died in natural disasters around the world and over 217 million others were affected by them (*Center for Research on the Epidemiology of*

Disasters, 2011). The year 2010 witnessed massive calamities including Japan's tsunami/nuclear emergency, which alone killed over 28,000 people, and the drought in the Horn of Africa, which has generated an intense food crisis for over 3 million *(Augustine & Kokkamadathil, 2011)*[6]. Beyond these calamities are hundreds of smaller disasters that failed to reach global headlines but dramatically upended the lives of those they touched. Such events are already on the rise and likely to continue to increase in the coming years due to the effects of climate change.

Natural Disasters World Wide 2000-2011

Disaster Statistics	*2000-2009 avg.*	*2009*	*2010*	*2011*
Number of recorded disasters	392	335	385	302
Fatalities	78,087	10655	297,000	29,782
Persons affected (millions)	227	119	217	206
Damage ($ billions)	89.3	41.3	123.9	366

Source: EM-DAT: The OFDA/CRED International Disaster Database, 2011.

The Haiti earthquake and floods in Pakistan and China helped make 2010 an exceptional year for natural disasters, killing 295,000 and costing $130 billion dollars. According to CRED (2011), 326 natural disasters and 259 technological disasters were reported worldwide in 2008 – the lowest figures for the decade in both cases. However, the number of people reported killed by natural disasters (235,736) was the second highest of the decade, close to the peak of 2004 (241,635, mostly attributable to the Indian Ocean tsunami). In 2008, Cyclone Nargis left 138,366 people dead or missing in Myanmar and the Sichuan earthquake killed 87,476 people in China. These two disasters account for 93 percent of all people considered dead or missing. The number of people killed in technological disasters (6,926) is, by contrast, the lowest of the decade and is, for 75 percent, attributable to transport accidents. The number of people reported affected by natural disasters (213 million) remained stable compared to the previous year and below the decade's average of 270 million. The extreme winter conditions that affected several Chinese provinces left 77 million people in difficulty, which represent more than one-third of all people affected by natural disasters. The Sichuan earthquake affected around 46 million people, a major flood in the United States affected 11 million people and a drought affected nearly 10 million people in Thailand. Another 19 other major natural disasters affected 1 to 8 million people. Eleven of these disasters occurred in Asia, five in Africa and three in the Americas. By comparison, technological disasters affected far fewer people – some 39,000, which is also the lowest of the decade. More than 50 percent were affected by miscellaneous accidents *(CRED, 2011).*

Natural disaster costs (US $181 billion) were the second highest of the decade and represent three-quarters of the record of 2005, when hurricane Katrina caused damage amounting to almost US $ 140 billion (2008 prices). The Sichuan earthquake (US$ 85 billion) accounts for almost half of 2008 costs. Damages from hurricane Ike cost US $31.5 billion (USA: US$ 30 billion; Cuba: US$ 1.5 billion), the cost of extreme winter conditions in China amounted to US $21 billion and a major flood in the United States cost US $10 billion. The cost of damage in 11 other disasters amounted to between US $1 and 9 billion: eight windstorms cost a total of US $20 billion; two floods cost US $3 billion and one wildfire- US $2 billion. Nine of the 15 natural disasters with damages equal or superior to US $1 billion occurred in North America and two in Europe; of the four that occurred in Asia, three hit China *(CRED, 2011).*

Globally Asia was the most badly affected continent caused by earthquake and flood. In 2009, out of 335 disasters, 135 occurred in Asia impacting 106.44 million people. In 2009, the proportion of economic damages from natural disasters was also the highest in Asia (38.5%), followed by the Americas (32.1%) and Europe (24.8%). The most recent disaster in Asia is an earthquake that struck off the coast of Japan churning up a devastating tsunami followed by nuclear emergency. According to National Police Agency, 14,416 people were killed, 5314 were injured and 11,889 went missing due the disaster *(Centre for Research on the Epidemiology of Disasters, 2011).*

Over the past two decades, the number of recorded disasters has doubled from approximately 200 to over 400 per year. Nine out of every ten of these disasters have been climate related. Current projections regarding climate change suggest that this trend is set to continue and that weather related hazard events would become more frequent and more volatile. Patterns of drought and desertification are also intensifying. In the absence of mitigation and preparedness efforts, vulnerability is also growing in many countries. Asia reported the maximum number of man-made disasters (174 disasters). Shipping disasters, mining accidents, stampedes and terrorism were identified as the major reasons for manmade disasters in 2008 *(William S. Kern, 2010)*[5]. Apart from direct financial losses, natural disasters have also led to indirect losses which may set back social investments aiming to ameliorate poverty and hunger, provide access to welfare services, or to protect economic investments that provide employment and income. It is interesting to note that only 11 percent of the population living in countries like Bangladesh, Afghanistan, Iran, Ethiopia, Sudan and so on account for more than 53 percent of total recorded deaths due to disasters (10 deaths per million population). This clearly establishes the fact that these countries have invested fewer resources in disaster mitigation and preparedness efforts *(UNDP, 2009)*. The levels of poverty in a country have a direct bearing on the levels of impacts of disasters. Though absolute levels of economic loss are greater in developed countries due to the far higher density and cost of infrastructure and production levels, less-developed countries suffer higher levels of relative loss when seen as a proportion of Gross Domestic Product (GDP).Women are made more vulnerable to disasters through their socially constructed roles. As per the WHO, women and children are particularly affected by disasters, accounting for more than seventy five percent of displaced persons. During disasters women are vulnerable to reproductive and sexual health problems, and increased rates of sexual and domestic violence. Women's vulnerability is further increased by the loss of men *(UNDP, 2009)*.

In India, between 1988 and 1997, disasters killed 5,116 people and directly or indirectly affected 24.79 million people. In the year 1998, 9,846 people died and 34.11 million people were affected by disasters *(CRED, 2011)*. Experience and study tells us that the actual figures greatly exceed the documented ones. India Disaster Reports explained that globally, natural disasters account for nearly 80 per cent of all disaster-affected people. The insurance industry estimates that natural disasters represent 85 per cent of insured catastrophe losses globally. In 1996, 40 million disaster-affected people depended on humanitarian assistance, a 60 per cent increase over the average figure of 25 million in the 1980s. In the first half of this decade, over 30 billion U.S. dollars was spent on humanitarian assistance. The average cost of natural disasters over the past 25 years stands at over 87 billion U.S. dollars a year. The average amount spent on humanitarian response is 3 billion U.S. dollars a year. Compared to expenditure on disaster mitigation, the average annual global military spending is around 780 billion U.S. dollars *(India Disasters Report, 2001)*[7].

The disturbing fact is that even in a region like South Asia, where poverty, deprivation, and death due to disasters are a common feature of life, India remains the worst-affected country in the region. In fact, the frequency of all categories of disasters, varying from epidemics to road accidents and perennial droughts and floods, is escalating, resulting in a multifold growth of injuries, disabilities, diseases, and deaths, disrupting life-supporting systems, and adding to the health, social, and economic burden of an already impoverished people. These disasters, large and small, strike people where they live. It is at the community level that disasters are felt and, frequently, it is also where risk reduction steps can make the biggest difference. As observed by the United Nations Development Programme

(UNDP, 2005)[8], disaster risk management at the local level is a key element in any viable national strategy to reduce disaster risks, building on the quality of community networks, the social fabric and effective municipal governance" *(UNDP,2005)*. All these geological disasters, biological and other man- made disasters, affect people of various regions or nations. There is a danger that these disasters might one or the other day destroys the earth or all the life forms on it. In such circumstances, every government has the responsibility to lay out plans on issues and strategies for ensuring the wellbeing of its citizens. It is of paramount importance for the United Nations to charter programmes and strategies, to guarantee the security and welfare of the inhabitants of the earth as such there is a need for a global policy to ensure coordination among various stake holders and also to provide International Disaster Management Plans (IDMP). For instance, capacity building and preparedness at global level needs to be further geared up. Disaster control and mitigation measures are gradually attaining momentum and could possibly be made subjects to be extensively taught or practiced. The UN General Assembly has declared the decade of the nineties (1990s) as the International Decade for Natural Disaster Reduction *(IDNDR)*.

UN and other associated agencies have called for a global concerted action for reduction of occurrences of natural disasters and for minimization of adverse impacts of such hazards of the maximum level. It is strongly being realized internationally that any attainment of local, national, regional or global sustainable development would be a misnomer without undertaking such measures at the earliest possible. Improved methods of prediction, proper risk assessment and efficient management plans could be the steps in the proper direction. Coordination among various governments and specialized agencies could reduce the damage, in particular during the post disaster phase to a great extent. Both national and international disaster management policies and programmes need to be complementary rather than being contradictory regarding prioritizing options *(UNDP, 2005)*. Developed societies such as Japan and the United States are the best resourced to deal with disasters. The more attention given to disaster preparedness before disaster strikes, the more efficiently, resources can be applied to ensuring the resilience of the nation and rapid recovery after a disaster *(The Heritage Foundation, 2011)*[9].

The Global Disaster Authority needs to review the different approaches that countries undertake to create national disaster management systems' diverse methods of transferring disaster risks; options available to governments in financing disaster recovery through risk- sharing tools; costs and benefits of policy options; methods of determining the financing needs for recovery using damage and reconstruction needs assessment. It is high time that a global policy on disaster for the welfare of the people on the earth is set. Unless the UN gathers considerable pace in framing a Global Policy on Disaster in the interest of the people on the earth to lead a decent and fulfilling life without the fear of disasters, the main objective of the UN will not be met. Thus the case for a global policy on disaster has been made *(UNDP, 2005).*

Disaster Management, which involves prevention, mitigation, preparedness, response and rehabilitation efforts, has been discussed for a long time. In short, such management stages can be classified into-before, during and after event activities. Disaster Preparedness can be referred to as, "all measures taken to prepare in advance aiming at reducing the impact of possible disasters". Although all preparedness activities aim at reducing the damage at community, on-site practicality, which concern the full utilization of the capacities particularly at the time of emergency, have not been well documented, possibly because of difficulties in visualizing emergency contexts to be faced by local communities *(R. Osti and K. Miyake, 2011).*

The role of Panchayati Raj Institutions in disaster management activities including both pre and post disaster response programmes have a significant place. The literature related to this study is comparatively less. So in this context, a study related to the effectiveness of local self-governments in disaster response programme is very significant. The investigator tries to understand and analyze the role and responsibilities of local self-government along with effective community participation in the context of tsunami 2004 in Kerala.

On December 26, 2004 an earth quake of an unprecedented magnitude of 9.3 on the Richter scale, as recorded by the Meteorological Department of India, occurred in the Indian Ocean generating giant "killer waves", called Tsunami, which struck the coastal areas of Indonesia, India, Maldives, Thailand, and Sri Lanka leaving hundreds of thousands of people dead, causing enormous destruction to properties, and leaving millions stranded without food, shelter, and safe drinking water. Estimates show that around 250,000 people died *(United Nations International Strategy for Disaster Reduction, 2005)*[10], 50,000 people were missing, 1.4 million people were displaced, and the economic loss incurred crossed billions of dollars. The waves, of height 2-3.5 meters, together with the increased level of seawater caused extensive damage to the coastal areas of several states of India including Kerala, Tamil Nadu, Andhra Pradesh, Pondicherry, and Andaman and Nicobar Islands *(UNISDR, 2005).*

In Kerala, though the relief, rescue, and rehabilitation activities of the government, non-governmental organizations, private welfare and charity institutions, and individuals were timely and appropriate, a closer analysis of these operations reveal several errors. One of the major errors was that the local democracies were not much involved in the relief, rescue, and rehabilitation efforts. The Panchayat Raj Bill clearly specifies the role of Panchayats/local democracies in effectively and efficiently managing any disaster situation. Though the "Kerala Model"[11] of development is considered as the ideal method of development in the country *(Richard W. Franke, 1999)*, the failure of the state to pull the local democracies in efficiently managing the disaster situations raises serious concerns among development professionals.

"The role of local communities and organizations particularly the Panchayat Raj bodies in managing natural disasters cannot be over emphasized. In the present situation the government agencies take full responsibility for disaster preparedness, rescue, relief and reconstruction activities without providing adequate scope for local participation. This has not only increased people's dependency on the government but has also waned the capacity of the local communities to cope up with the natural disasters. Moreover, due to lack of the disaster preparedness and mitigation planning at the local level, especially at the Gram Panchayat level causes considerable problems in the management of disasters" *(Madhava Rao & Hermon, 2004)*.

Type & Classification of Disasters

The rate of occurrence of events associated with natural hazards on earth may be increasing; this is probably due to variations in innate cycles, such as solar maxima, earthquakes, and volcanic activity. In addition, the earth is warming, which, at a minimum, is projected to increase severe storm activity in some areas and to cause drought in others. Other indications are that the range of diseases and disease-carrying vectors is expanding because of warming, bringing a number of infectious diseases to non-immune populations. In addition, changes in growing seasons, weather conditions, and ambient temperature and humidity are beginning to impact food supplies, allergen production, and other human health issues *(David E. Hogan, Jonathan L. Burstein – 2007)*.

Technological Hazards

The technological development of human society has resulted in the creation of an entirely new set of hazards, such as industrial waste and radiation and chemical disasters. Tons of hazardous materials are transported through densely populated areas each day, with each ton representing a latent disaster. Humankind's increasing development and dependence on a rather fragile industrial "technologic complex presents new possibilities for disaster. The information systems that operate our economic, transportation, and distribution systems and regulate our lives are relatively sensitive to disruption. Failure of these systems for even a short period may induce fear and injury into a population. Hurricanes Katrina and Rita have clearly demonstrated that even local destruction of such computer-based information systems adds substantially to the impact of such a natural disaster *(Disaster Medicine, 2007)*[3].

Human Conflict

"Humankind continues to be its own worst enemy". Will Rogers (1993) said it this way in his autobiography, One can't say civilization does not advance in every war they kill you in new ways. With wars both great and small occurring at regular frequency on earth, and now a global war against terrorism, ample opportunity is found for advancement. These activities create, both directly and indirectly, numerous casualties that require medical care, public health, and psychological management. The creation of weapons of mass destruction and the real and the potential use of these devices against human populations represent a new and increasingly complex problem for emergency health care providers.

The Nature of Disasters

Disasters are generally considered below probability high impact events. In fact, only a few disasters in the United States have resulted in more than 1,000 casualties. When disaster does strike, only 10 to 15 disasters a year result in more than 40 casualties. These statistics are often used to defer funding for disaster planning efforts in lieu of other projects. However, in fact, the impact of disaster in the United States and worldwide is much more significant than what these narrow statistics imply. For instance, although Hurricane Andrew killed only 44 individuals directly, it affected the lives of almost 3 million people, caused more than 3 billion dollars in damage, and involved significant national resources for rescue and recovery efforts. The disruption of the normal lives of the population measures the true impact of a disaster. Medical infrastructure may be totally disrupted during a disaster, thereby requiring time to reestablish normal function. Recovery efforts to repair a disaster-stricken community and the psycho emotional damage may last for years *(Disaster Medicine, 2007)*. Because of the multidisciplinary nature of disaster planning and response, the definition used for a disaster is often as varied as the discipline using it. Examples of disaster definitions are found in various sources. Usually each definition reflects the nature and focus of the organization or individuals defining it. The World Health Organization (WHO) defines a disaster as a sudden ecological phenomenon of sufficient magnitude to require external assistance. This broad focus definition may exclude some events that result in mass casualties. A more focused definition often used by practitioners of emergency medicine is when the number of patients presenting within a given time period are such that the emergency department cannot provide care for them without external assistance. This definition would exclude events such as aircraft crashes that result in mass death but place little or no stress on the medical system. Others may define disasters as an imbalance in the availability of medical care and a misdistribution of medical resources versus casualties within a community. Most emergency health care providers have some definition in mind regarding disasters, but more commonly the response is simply that they know a disaster when they see one *(David E. Hogan, Jonathan L. Burstein, 2007).*

Disasters are not defined by a specific number of casualties but rather by the event itself and the venue in which it occurs. A motor vehicle crash with five casualties in a metropolitan area will likely go unnoticed except as a footnote in the evening paper. The same crash casualties presenting to a rural community Emergency Department (ED) will probably require activation of the hospital disaster plan. In all definitions, disasters are something outside the normal experience of daily life that requires a change from daily management style and thinking *(Disaster Medicine, 2007).* The categorization of Disasters definitely helps to get the categorical wise understanding about the disasters in very detail. Disasters depending on their source have been classified into two main categories *(Sekar, 2005).*

Classification of Disasters

Natural Disasters

Major	*Minor*
Earthquake Flood Drought Cyclone	Heat wave Cold wave Landslide Avalanche Tornadoes Hailstorm

Human Made Disasters

Major	*Minor*
Communal riots Ethnic conflicts Refugee situations	Transport disasters Festival and pilgrimage disasters Food poisoning

CRED defines a disaster as "a situation or event which overwhelms local capacity, necessitating a request to a national or international level for external assistance; an unforeseen and often sudden event that causes great damage, destruction and human suffering". Table 1.1 shows the definitions of natural disaster subgroups and their main types. For a disaster to be entered into the database, at least one of the following criteria must be fulfilled:

- 10 or more people reported killed;
- 100 or more people reported affected;
- declaration of a state of emergency;
- call for international assistance.

Table 1.1: Disaster subgroup definition and classification,
EM-DAT: The OFDA/CRED International Disaster Database, 2011

Subgroup	*Definition*	*Disaster Main Types & Classification*
Geophysical	Events originating from solid earth	Earthquake, Volcano, Mass Movement (dry)
Meteorological	Events caused by short-lived/small to meso scale atmospheric processes (in the spectrum from minutes to days)	Storm
Hydrological	Events caused by deviations in the normal water cycle and/or overflow of bodies of water caused by wind set-up	Flood, Mass Movement (wet)
Climatological	Events caused by long-lived/meso to macro scale processes (in the spectrum from intra-seasonal to multi-decadal climate variability)	Extreme Temperature, Drought, Wildfire
Biological	Disaster caused by the exposure of living organisms to germs and toxic substances	Epidemic, Insect Infestation, Animal Stampede

Impact of Disasters

Another crucial area is the impact of the disasters among the affected population and the community. The following are the major impacts due to such kinds of calamity occurring in regular intervals upon the country to destruct the normal life of the human being *(Facilitation Manual for Trainers of Trainees in Natural Disasters, 2005)*[4].

Physical impact

Most disasters result in a lot of physical injuries. These vary depending upon the kind of disaster. For instance, in an earthquake you would find a lot of people with orthopedic problems, fractures, problems with mobility etc while in a communal strife there would be bullet injuries, stab wounds and results of physical assaults. In a chemical disaster there maybe aid burns or burns due to some explosive material so the physical impact of each disaster would differ in each case. Since people would be displaced and living in camps there would be problems arising out of the cramped living conditions like epidemics, allergies etc. Some others like fever, cough, colds, headaches, body aches and a general sense of illness would be common to all the disasters as these would be the manifestation of the trauma that people have undergone. If there were many expectant mothers there would be a spate of deliveries after a disaster. There could also be complications during childbirth for many women. Some people may lose their sense of hearing or speech for some time after going through a traumatic situation.

Economic impact

A disaster by definition affects large number of people and a vast region so the entire community would be experiencing its impact. Places of work maybe inaccessible or damaged. There may be total breakdown of communication and lack of basic supplies like food or raw material causing a breakdown in the normal lives that people have been leading. For some time people may be unable to return to work thus their source of living could be affected. If their work is land based, and due to the cyclone the land is inundated it may become totally worthless and the family may lose their source of income totally. For others it maybe a temporary loss; for instance, a communal riot may mean there is curfew so you cannot go to work for a few days *(Sekar.K .et.al, 2006)*.

Social impact

The living structures maybe damaged forcing people to live in camps with little or no privacy. There is discontinuity of normal life routines and things like education etc; that get totally affected. People face the problems of day-to-day living in difficult circumstances along with trying to pick up and rebuild their lives and get back to life as it was before the disaster. Family structure may undergo changes like becoming a single parent, losing the only earning member or a child becoming an orphan, losing life partners and becoming a widow or a widower. All this would bring about substantial life changes. There would be ceremonies that need to be completed and cultural rituals that need to be adhered to. People may need to shift in with extended family members or adjust to a life without the family members whom they have lost. Other aspects like domestic violence, exploitation, abuse and alcoholism become very prominent in the community affected by a disaster *(Sekar.K .et.al, 2006).*

Emotional impact

Any disaster affects people emotionally. The change it brings in life seems unbearable and people often feel helpless, hopeless and frustrated in the aftermath of a disaster. Often they seem unable to cope with the consequences of the loss they have experienced. They may have repeated thoughts about the events which sort of drain them of their energy, this is especially true when they have experienced some violence say in a riot or war, and it may leave them feeling very angry and irritable. Survivors may develop revengeful feelings *(Sekar.K .et.al, 2006).* Fear is another reaction seen among survivors of disaster. There is fear for its recurrence and this can lead to continued feelings of anxiety, sleeplessness and an inability to find strength to regain confidence to lead a normal life.

Disaster Management and Disaster Management Cycle

Nevertheless to say, Disaster management aims to reduce, or avoid, the potential losses from hazards, assure prompt and appropriate assistance to victims of disaster, and achieve rapid and effective recovery. The Disaster Management Cycle [5] illustrates the ongoing process by which governments, businesses, and civil society plan for and reduce the impact of disasters, react during and immediately following a disaster, and take steps to recover after a disaster. Appropriate actions at all points in the cycle lead to greater preparedness, better warnings, reduced vulnerability or the prevention of disasters during the next iteration of the cycle. The complete disaster management cycle includes the shaping of public policies and plans that either modify the causes of disasters or mitigate their effects on people, property, and infrastructure *(Corina Warfield, 2002).*

The mitigation and preparedness phases occur, as disaster management improvements are made in anticipation of a disaster event. Developmental considerations play a key role in contributing to the mitigation and preparation of a community to effectively confront a disaster. As a disaster occurs, disaster management actors, in particular humanitarian organizations become involved in the immediate response and long-term recovery phases. The four disaster management phases illustrated here does not always, or even generally, occurs in isolation or in this precise order. Often phases of the cycle overlap and the length of each phase greatly depends on the severity of the disaster *(WHO, 2002)*[6] Disaster management is defined as an applied science which seeks, by the systematic observation and analysis of disasters, to improve measure relating to prevention, mitigation, preparedness, emergency responses and recovery *(Carter, 1991)*. When public participation is integrated into disaster management planning and community planning, the result is sustainable hazard mitigation *(Pearce, 2003)*. It is well felt that community participation, local planning, development of self-reliance and manpower resource within the community itself can strengthen the effort of disaster preparedness and response *(Biswas et.al, 1997)*. Since the community bears the burden of disaster and is the first responder to the event, it is imperative to build the capacity of the community to enhance their coping mechanism and resilience to prepare for and face the disaster *(Biswas et.al, 1997)*.

Disaster Management as a practice and as profession is rapidly expanding and improving. Such change is necessarily driven by the modern needs of governments and non-governmental organizations involved in one or more of the four phases of emergency management-mitigation, preparedness, response, and recovery *(Coppola, 2007)*. Disaster Management processes depends on administrative as well as civil society actions. The role of the civil society becomes more prominent in states where governments do not have sufficient resources *(SEEDS, 2004)*[7].

Disaster Management, also called Disaster Risk Management, is the discipline that involves preparing, warning, supporting and rebuilding societies when natural or man-made disasters occur. It is the continuous process by which all individuals, groups and communities manage hazards in an effort to avoid or minimize the impact of disasters resulting from hazards. Effective disaster management relies on thorough integration of emergency plans at all levels of government and non-government involvement. Activities at each level (individual, group, community) affect the other levels *(SEEDS, 2004)*.

Disaster Management is the aggregate of all measures taken to reduce the likelihood of damage that will occur related to a hazard(s), and to minimize the damage once an event occurs or has occurred and to direct recovery from the damage. The effectiveness of disaster management determines the final result of the impact of the event on the environment and society impacted. Management of the damage/disaster either may be productive in minimizing the damage or it may be negative and, as such, contribute to the damage. The training of medical response personnel, as part of preparedness, and the actual responses of medical personnel to the persons injured by the event are both parts of management *(Coppola 2007)*. Events over the last two years have shown that there is no country that does not stand the threat of a disaster. Countries like China, Japan, Indonesia, Iran and Pakistan are prone to earthquakes. Small Island states in the Pacific region and countries like Maldives are prone to various types of threats from the sea. Bangladesh and parts of China and India experience floods each year. Therefore, disaster preparedness is no longer a choice; it is mandatory irrespective of where one lives *(ICT for Disaster Management, 2008)*[8].

According to Coppola (2007), Comprehensive Disaster Management is based upon four distinct components: Mitigation, Preparedness, Response and Recovery. According to the author, mitigation refers to the structural and non-structural measures undertaken to limit the adverse impact of natural hazards, environmental degradation and technological hazards. Disaster preparedness implies the activities and measures taken in advance to ensure effective response to the impact of hazards, including the issuance of timely and effective early warnings and the temporary evacuation of people and property from threatened locations. Disaster response denotes the provision of assistance or intervention during or immediately after a disaster to meet the life preservation and basic subsistence needs of those people affected. It can be of an immediate, short-term, or protracted duration. Recovery signifies the decisions and actions taken after a disaster with a view to restoring or improving the pre disaster living conditions of the stricken community, while encouraging and facilitating necessary adjustments to reduce disaster risk. Some other disaster scholars added two other terminologies to disaster literature: rehabilitation and reconstruction. Rehabilitation is the restoration of basic functions of the society which might take weeks to several months. And lastly, reconstruction indicates the full resumption or the improvement of the pre-disaster state including all preparedness, preventive, and mitigation measures *(International Disaster Management, 2007)*[9].

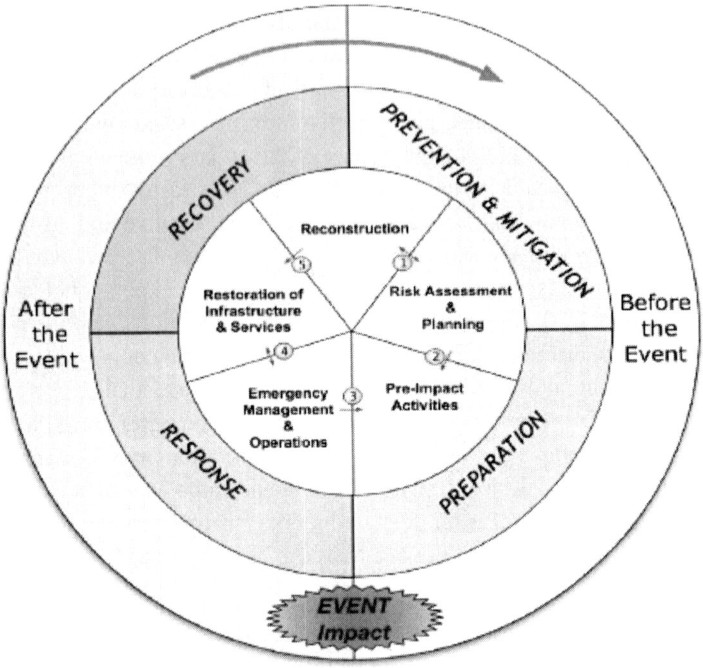

Source: Alexander, 2002.

The Disaster Management Cycle

The definition of a disaster can be well taken for granted, in that it is an event that brings in its trail several impacts such as on lives, properties, lifelines etc. Its management can be very naive to the extent we think about the immediate ways and means to stand up to it. One may tend to graft into it techniques and methods that rudiments of managing enterprises may provide *(Sinha, 2005)*. It has been acknowledged that the disaster management is nothing sort of being dynamic process in which the community participates along with several organizations. The ambit of such an endeavour is geared to work primarily on the adverse effects of a disaster. The dynamics of the ambit of the disaster management has preparedness, mitigation, relief, recovery and rehabilitation as its principal elements. The contours of disaster management should necessarily have several sub-areas of management depending basically on the phases of a disaster *(Sinha, 2005)*.

While proceeding with such exercise on discernible scores, the abiding but allied aspects of risks and vulnerabilities can in no way be ignored. Risk management, by itself is fast assuming evolutionary traits because of anticipatory acceptance, estimation characteristics etc. of a risk per se. Vulnerability management cannot obviously lag behind on account of the fundamental equation: Risk=Vulnerability+ Hazard. Such an approach has become all the more important because of emphasis being stressed by the World Conference on Disaster Reduction (WCDR) held from January 18-22, 2005, at Kobe, Japan (also called the *Hyogo Declaration, 2005)*[10]. Whatever be the complexion, the management of hazards acquires a pre-dominant character. Let us first dwell on this in general terms. Obviously key areas within the fold of hazard management should consist of (a) principles (b) practices(c) counter-disaster measures (d) other aspects conducive to socio economic and cultural facets of the community concerned. In any form of practices on hazard management, the main rationale should be to look for ways and means for disaster reduction or even elimination. Sensitizing the community on the cost and benefit, dominantly human, can emerge from the hazard management. Developing public awareness and influencing public perception hazard, should be a major objective of anything to do with management of hazards; hazard specific management practices should be identified. A vital element of this kind of management should be to devise plans as to how to go in for containing or in a way, altering hazards. Steps in this direction ought to aim at providing the takers' ability for acquisition of knowledge with wider horizons. Appropriately, strategies on any front of hazard management can hardly go by default, for familiarity with such strategies enabling mechanisms for the purpose *(WCDR, 2002).*

Having discussed some of the significant terminologies in disasters, it is important to lay emphasis on some of the emerging trends in disaster management nationally and internationally. One such effort is the increased emphasis on disaster risk reduction measures which will be the focus of the next section.

Disaster Risk Reduction

Disaster Risk Reduction (DRR) is a systematic approach to identifying, assessing and reducing the risks of disaster. It aims to reduce socio-economic vulnerabilities to disaster as well as dealing with the environmental and other hazards that trigger them. It has been strongly influenced by the mass of research on vulnerability that has appeared in print since the mid-1970s. It is the responsibility of development and relief agencies alike and it should be an integral part of the way such organizations do their work, not an add-on or one-off action. DRR is very wide-ranging, therefore its scope is much broader and deeper than conventional emergency management. There is potential for DRR initiatives in just about every sector of development and humanitarian work *(UNISDR, 2005).*

In India, at the national level, government has constituted a vast administrative mechanism to implement DRR measures. The organizational set-up consists of a cabinet committee on natural disaster management, a crisis management group presided by the Cabinet Secretary, and a Central Relief Commissioner for Disaster Relief Co-ordination. The State government typically has a Relief Commissioner and a Co-ordination committee. At the District level, the District Collector presides over the Relief Committee, which should consist of people's representatives. 'Disaster', under this rule designates only small-scale disaster, which occurs in the specific locations in the Panchayat due to natural calamities like flood or fire. This limits the scope for local bodies to get involved in natural disasters like tsunami. Capacity for disaster management intervention calls for perspective building through training and awareness programmes for elected representatives, officials and departmental staff, community organizations and the community at large, as well as the creation of an organizational set up for intervention. Moreover, an inventory of technical and technological manpower, financial and material resources should be kept updated *(UNISDR, 2005).*

Disasters are rationalized or interpreted according to the canons and preoccupations of the contemporary period. Modern interpretations are increasingly dominated by the new forms of symbolism constructed by the Mass Communication Industry *(Lombardi 1997).* These encourage a shallow view of history and strategic relationships, and thus a superficial approach to causality. Instead, one needs to search for the explanations of disaster in the global changes that are currently altering the scope and tenor of international relations *(Anderson 1997).* On aggregate, vulnerability to disaster is set to rise with the increasing polarization of a world in which two billion people have practically no access to modern technology and 800 million live in conditions of misery. As yet they have little collective voice, but that cannot be true forever, as present trends are unsustainable.

The foregoing discussion implies that disasters in the modern world are an artifact of two forces: commercialism and strategic hegemonies inherent in globalization. At the broadest scale that may be true, though it does not preclude more traditional interpretations based on primary vulnerability *(Blaikie et al. 1994),* or more optimistic ones based on globalism *(Kelman & Koukis 2000).* Perhaps one reason why "disaster" will probably never be completely, immutably defined is because the definition depends on shifting portrayals and perceptions of what is significant about the phenomenon. Some scholars would argue that it must be interpreted, and continually reinterpreted in the context of contemporary issues *(Perry & Quarantelli, 2005)*. The first is disaster as a duplication of war (catastrophe can be imputed to an external agent; human communities are entities that react globally against aggression). The second is disaster as an expression of social vulnerabilities (disaster is the result of underlying community logic, of an inward and social process). The third is disaster as an entrance into a state of uncertainty (disaster is tightly tied into the impossibility of defining real or supposed, especially after the upsetting of the mental frameworks we use to know and understand reality).

Disaster has been viewed in its extended scope and definition by taking into account all these perspectives and together these form the basis on which disaster vulnerability is understood and defined. The bottom line of all these paradigms is that disaster is supposed to represent total or near total breakdown of local systems. Ironically, the dilemma with all these paradigms is that while on one hand they define disaster as an objective reality, on the other hand, measures to reduce disaster seem to be so far from reality, that in most cases one finds that disaster vulnerability is increasing at a very fast pace (*Dombrowsky, 1998)* and rightly states that emancipation of the field from everyday knowledge and from the practical needs of disaster management has been neglected during the phase of its establishment.

Disaster is no longer bound by the physical boundaries; rather it extends deeper into human consciousness, extending much beyond physically perceived boundaries. The psychological impact of this is very deep. It is much deeper than one can expect, not only shaping the way people perceive the cause of disasters but also the way they respond to it. Interestingly, similar kinds of symbolical associations shape the perceptions and response actions as the ones, which give meaning to the space in the first place. However, there is always a limit to what our senses and the tools available can measure and these in fact pose a limit to individual ability of comprehension. "People have access to social and mental health services to reduce mental health morbidity, disability, and social problems" *(SPHERE, 2007)*[11]

Theoretical Framework for Disaster Management

Many humanitarian agencies have a dichotomous approach to emergency recovery and development efforts. They have emergency staffs who respond specifically to disasters and development staffs who step in once the crisis is under control. However, in the 1980s, experiences of major relief and development agencies have convinced them that emergency and development programmes are intertwined *(Johan Kieft and Aspian Nur, 2007)*. A second factor that plays a role in changing perceptions of effective assistance is the increasing emphasis on livelihood security for households affected by disasters. Calamities are the main threat to this security and reducing the communities' vulnerability to such hardships is a crucial response.

Based on these insights and through intensive discussions, disaster management has evolved to merge rescue and development plans, and several sophisticated approaches have been formulated. Within the context of disaster management, development is defined as a process that reduces vulnerabilities and increases capacities. For further clarity, vulnerabilities are generally defined as long-term factors that affect the ability of a community to respond to events or make it susceptible to calamities. They contribute to a disaster's severity, impede effective responses, present before disaster strikes and remain long after the event is over. In this respect, vulnerabilities differ from needs, which arise from the crisis and are often short term in nature (e.g. the need for relief food supplies immediately after a forest fire). Vulnerabilities to forest fires, however, are more enduring and have intensified in recent years because of increased conflicts, lack of law enforcement, and poor natural resource management. Nonetheless, their vulnerabilities, most communities still have capacities to rebuild their lives. From a disaster management's point of view, capacities are strengths on which future development can be built *(Johan Kieft and Aspian Nur, 2007)*.

During disasters, the community's vulnerabilities are more pronounced than their capacities. Recognizing the vulnerabilities and capacities of the affected population is essential for designing and implementing an effective disaster response. To identify these capacities and vulnerabilities, a Capacity and Vulnerability Analysis (CVA) matrix (Table 1.2) can be used to examine three aspects of information:

- Physical factors: what productive resources, skills and hazards (e.g. land, environment, health, skills and labour, infrastructure, food, housing, capital and technologies) are available?
- Social organization: What are the relationships among organizations of the communities (e.g. formal political structures and informal systems such as decision making, establishing leadership or organizing various socio-economic activities)? When prejudice or

conflict is present in a community, social and organizational vulnerabilities are inevitable.

- Attitudes: How does the community view its ability to adapt to changes? Strengths and weaknesses can make a significant difference in the communities' ability to rebuild and improve their material base and social institutions. A community is psychologically more vulnerable when its people feel victimized, fatalistic and dependent.

Table 1.2: Capacity and Vulnerability Analysis Matrix

	Vulnerabilities	*Capacities*
Physical factors	Geographical calamities (floods, earthquake) Economic misfortunes (drought) Poverty (insufficient resources) Lack of infrastructure Poor health	Skills to be productive Access to productive resources (land, forest, sea, capital, etc.) Technologies (agro-forestry/sustainable land management) Adequate infrastructure Good health
Social organization	Division according to religion, ethnicity, language, class or caste Prejudice Conflict Ineffective community organization	Social coping mechanism: family, group, community and/or area wide organizations
Attitudes	Superstition Fatalism (feeling that no body – Supporting them Dependence on external support	Fighting spirit Religion* Sense of purpose

* Religion can have a positive impact on attitudes, but can also divide the community and create conflict. In general there are two different disaster management models:

- The cyclic model in which emergency, recovery, development (preparedness, mitigation) and early warning are executed progressively, with each phase having its own particular approach (es).
- Expand and contract model in which all aspects of disaster management are addressed simultaneously, albeit with varying degrees of emphasis. For example, during the onset of a disaster, emphasis would be on emergency management and early warning

but recovery and mitigation are taken into account as well *(Johan Kieft and Aspian Nur, 2007).*

Some Lessons from the Tsunami disaster: *A Prelude to Future Strategies*

There are a lot of contrasts in the general public's view of the phenomenon with that of the technical community. Strategies should obviously seek for resolution of the technical, management and policy issues. The impact of life line failures in secondary and tertiary losses comes up as a major, if not common, concern while investigating the effect of natural disaster on regional and national economics. Losses due to tsunami waves, coming one after another through intervals, ought to be investigated, because of possible contrasting in losses, associated with an interruption of life line services. The recent tsunamis should provide us with data that might affect the future of lifelines *(Sinha.D.K, 2005).*

This assumes a distinctive character about tsunami mitigation. A "soft" mitigation is one of the educational programmes rather informative dissemination programmes about it. But the information seeks basically, in many ways, reduction of tsunamis. Yet, a harder phase of mitigation measure ensures which one goes in for estimating the cost of mitigation measures. If such measures are to balance against payoff, the need for analysis based on more of the other aspect of costs of the efforts, for purposes of analyzing cost effectiveness. A coastal process perspective and fragility, in particular, should be to devise a new strategy to reduce damages due to tsunamis. Various dimensions of recovery obviously warrant further consideration because of the character of the natural disaster which we haven't seen earlier. This gives rise to issues such as (a) how to find long-term recovery (b) mechanics for sharing lessons learnt from disasters. Considering the Andaman-Nicobar islands, the special character of needs; how to empower these special populations with capabilities and the backlash, as, well. There is a need for effective pre-disaster planning for coping with tsunamis and certainly, of course cost effective mitigation measures. The recovery and response of slow on-going phenomena of tsunamis and also that should be having financial support of one kind or the other, at the global level. The planning on logistics becomes then an integral part of the initial planning process for any operation *(D.K.Sinha, 2005).*

One of the tragic parts of the tsunami in the southern part of India is that so many children have become orphans. The realization is that there should be a full-time clinical consultant and trainer in disaster mental health.

There should be exposure for children, school teachers and other personnel such as mental health professionals and other concerned with assisting children in their emotional recovery from disaster; also, ways to make children learn techniques and tools in the classroom scenarios and having known these, equipping them with the ability to refer a child for additional assistance or counseling, videotape may be envisaged for the purpose of empowering children and the school personnel. In brief, steps, on a national level, are, called for educating children about disaster and preparation of age-appropriate materials and activities for the purpose *(D.K.Sinha, 2005).* Tsunami have brought to the fore the accounts of victims in low income groups of families despite all these disabilities, there are sparkling pockets of ethnicity whose possessors are remarkably well equipped with the wisdom on how to grapple with natural disasters like tsunamis. Despite fragilities of all kinds, resilience ought to assert itself organically, over and above, available relief, recovery and rehabilitation.

Tsunami has given rise to not merely problems of great complexities but also surprisingly those that have implications with far-ranging economic and social connotations. The global view continues to be relentless. Recently in the Indian ocean, the coastal vulnerability stands terribly exposed, and worse than what happened to be when tsunami hit the Pacific wreaking upon Chile and Japan there is always a propensity in case of a disaster like this, to draw several analogies, even though commonalities can hardly be precluded *(D.K.Sinha, 2005).* The World Conference on Disaster Reduction (WCDR) held at Kobe in January 2005 is not purely a rehash of what IDNDR stressed earlier. The tsunami in December 2004 obviously prevailed upon the deliberations of WCDR in that the vulnerability per se could come up as an area of vital concern, particularly in regard to coastal regions. The absence of forecasts and warnings, because of the lack of an approximate warning system, was keenly felt. The poignancy of the tsunami devastation was not simply confined to limits of emotion and feelings. WCDR really plunged itself into deliberation that covered vulnerability in the widest possible area. Spatial and temporal vulnerabilities were looked at new because of what occurred distressingly in Sumatra, Andaman and Nicobars, Sri Lanka. Here was a tsunami which didn't limit its destructive characteristics to preferred communities *(WCDR, 2005)*[12]

In recent years, international preoccupation with disasters and their impacts has intensified and raised closer to the top of the development agenda. For many years, response to disasters was largely confined to emergency relief and short term life-saving actions. But over the last two decades, the critical importance of disaster preparedness, mitigation, prevention, and adequate training of relief workers has been widely recognized. It has become increasingly apparent that a relatively small investment in disaster preparedness can save lives, reduce the number of people requiring emergency assistance and preserve vital economic assets, as well as reduce the cost of overall relief assistance to disaster-stricken countries. This fortuitous realization has largely contributed to the systematic decrease in the number of deaths due to natural disasters over the last two decades, despite the increase in the number of disaster events. Large donor programmes have dedicated substantial budget lines to disaster preparedness and prevention and have placed this issue higher on the agenda of development assistance *(Sinha, 2005).*

Disaster and Geographical Vulnerability

Asia and Africa are particularly vulnerable to disasters. Just as there are considerable differences in the number of people affected by natural disasters; there are also great differences in which continents are more affected by the different types of disasters. Asia and Africa bear a disproportionate burden of losses due to disasters. Over the last 30 years, approximately 88% of the total people reported killed and 96% of the people reported affected lived in these two regions alone. Of the total number of people killed by natural disasters worldwide over the last decade, more than 75% were in Asia. This figure rises above 98% for droughts and famines, 72% for earthquakes, 71% for avalanches and landslides and 56% for windstorms. Of the total of those reported killed by volcanic eruptions, Africa takes the lead with close to 62%. Only forest/ scrub fire fatalities are more or less evenly spread out across the continents, with 27% in Africa, 24% in the Americas, 25% in Asia and 22% in Europe. Looking at the data on the number of people affected worldwide by natural disasters over the same time period, Asia still leads with more than 75% of the total. For almost all disaster types, Asians are by far the most affected, with 88% for avalanches and landslides, 81% for droughts and famines, 84% for earthquakes, 89% for windstorms, 90% for forest/scrub fires and more than 97% for floods alone *(Guha-Sapir et.al, 2004).*

Notably, the Asian population represents about three-fifths of the world population and about one-third of total landmass. However, as we will see in the next chapter, it is possible to analyze the occurrence and impact of natural disasters taking into account the size of the population in a particular country and the size of the country itself. Among the top ten affected, India ranks first and second, again with droughts. In this instance, the large and dense population of the country contributes to the huge numbers affected by any natural event. The same holds true in China. Although the population density is not quite as high – tracts of China such as the Gobi Desert are practically uninhabitable - a flood in any inhabited area immediately affects millions *(Guha Sapir et.al, 2004).*

Significance of the Present Study

Natural disasters are the subjects of considerable study and international attention. Much of the literature on the topic addresses the causes and effects of natural disasters from multiple perspectives, including environmental studies, humanitarian assistance, disaster planning and hazard reduction, psychology, and public health. Little attention is paid to the impacts of natural disasters on individuals and communities from a human rights perspective. The response to the 2004 tsunami may be a turning point in this regard. Media coverage of the human rights dimensions of the tsunami relief and recovery phases has drawn attention to the relationship of natural disasters, community participation, and human rights. Lack of community participation is highly reported in almost all the places where the disaster strikes. Community participation rarely took place when decisions were made about reconstruction and rebuilding programs. In some cases, decision-makers discredited or ignored the views and opinions of local communities. Many survivors perceived the government as aloof and nonresponsive. Donors and aid agencies often prioritized timely outcomes over deliberative processes that allowed for community participation and discussion. Some agencies deliberately excluded certain groups because they were viewed as only serving "their own."

To rebuild communities that will be physically and socially resilient to the effects of natural disasters, tsunami survivors and their communities must be active and engaged participants—not merely acting as auxiliaries in resettlement and reconstruction efforts. The survivors of the regions affected by tsunami which were studied complained that decisions concerning relief, resettlement, and reconstruction aid were largely taking place without consultation with their communities, leading to frustration and despair. Survivors living in Internally Displaced Project (IDP) camps had little or no communication with government authorities about how long they could expect to remain housed there, whether and where they would be allowed to rebuild or be relocated, and the process for redevelopment planning in coastal areas.

Second, it is indeed needed to understand the role of local self-governments and the involvement of the affected community in managing the disasters. Because of their close proximity and knowledge of the community, local self-governments can play a critical role in disaster mitigation efforts. In addition, the affected people have the full right and the responsibility in participating in and facilitating the recovery process. Therefore, the vital role of the local self-government and the community in pre and post disaster context needs to be studied, documented, and evaluated. The present study is an attempt geared in this direction to understand various roles and responsibilities of the local self-government and the affected community in managing the natural disasters.

Notes

1. The American College of Emergency Physicians (ACEP) is the first and largest professional organization of emergency medicine physicians in the United States. It is headquartered in Irving, Texas. As of 2012, ACEP has more than 28,000 physician members. The college exists to support quality emergency medical care and the physicians who provide it. ACEP believes that "quality emergency care is a fundamental right and unobstructed access to emergency services should be available to all patients who perceive the need for emergency services." ACEP stands for Advancing Emergency Care during emergency situations.
2. The Federal Emergency Management Agency (FEMA) coordinates the federal government's role in preparing for, preventing, mitigating the effects of, responding to, and recovering from all domestic disasters, whether natural or man-made, including acts of terror. FEMA can trace its beginnings to the Congressional Act of 1803. This act, generally considered the first piece of disaster legislation, provided assistance to a New Hampshire town following an extensive fire. In the century that followed, ad hoc legislation was passed more than 100 times in response to hurricanes, earthquakes, floods and other natural disasters. FEMA's mission is to support our citizens and first responders to ensure that as a nation we work together to build, sustain, and improve our capability to prepare for, protect against, respond to, recover from, and mitigate all hazards. As of October 8, 2011, FEMA has 7,474 employees across the country – at Headquarters, the ten regional offices, the National Emergency Training Center, Center for Domestic Preparedness/Noble Training Center and other locations. FEMA is not the team, but part of a team. That team includes federal partners, state, tribal and local officials, the private sector, non-profits and faith-based groups and the general public. On March 1, 2003, the Federal Emergency Management Agency (FEMA) became part of the U.S. Department of Homeland Security (DHS), Federal Emergency Management Agency, U.S. Department of Homeland Security, 500 C Street SW, Washington.
3. Disaster Medicine- David E. Hogan, Jonathan L. Burstein, Written by more than 30 emergency physicians with first-hand experience handling medical care during disasters, this volume is the only single comprehensive reference on disaster medicine. It provides the information that every emergency department needs to prepare for and handle the challenges of natural and manmade disasters. The contributors present guidelines for assessing the affected population's health

care needs, establishing priorities, allocating resources, and treating individuals. Coverage encompasses a wide range of natural, industrial, technologic, transportation-related, and conflict-related disasters, with examples from around the world. This edition has more illustrations and more information on weapons of mass destruction and explosions.

4. Facilitation Manual for Trainers of Trainees in Natural Disasters, 2005. This manual is developed based on experiences and information, which has been documented in different information manuals for the survivor's in different disasters like the super cyclone in Orissa, killer earthquake in Gujarat and the Tsunami in South India. Specifically, the manual covers the basic concept of disaster and issues of psychosocial care in general. The presentation will be concentrating on two case studies, one natural and the other manmade disaster in India, and the psychosocial care provided in these two disasters as the background for development of community based psychosocial care model being provided in rescue, relief, rehabilitation and rebuilding phases. Prepared by Prepared by: Dr. K. Sekar, Professor, Department of Psychiatric Social Work, NIMHANS and team -Published by National Institute of Mental Health and Neuro sciences, Bangalore, Karnataka.
5. The Disaster Management Cycle illustrates the ongoing process by which governments, businesses, and civil society plan for and reduce the impact of disasters, react during and immediately following a disaster, and take steps to recover after a disaster has occurred. Appropriate actions at all points in the cycle lead to greater preparedness, better warnings, reduced vulnerability or the prevention of disasters during the next iteration of the cycle. The complete disaster management cycle includes the shaping of public policies and plans that either modify the causes of disasters or mitigate their effects on people, property, and infrastructure. The following references explained well about the DMC such as Environmental health in emergencies and disasters: A practical guide. WHO, 2002, Disaster Help, US Department of Homeland Security, Green Paper on Disaster Management, Department of Provincial and Local Government, South Africa & Coppola (2007), Comprehensive Disaster Management.
6. Environmental Health in Emergencies and Disasters: A Practical Guide. WHO, 2002. The WHO Guide to Sanitation in Natural disasters (Assar, 1971) summarized the essential aspects of environmental health management in disasters. These included the provision of emergency water and sanitation services; the burial or cremation of the dead; vector and pest control; food hygiene; and the assessment of the danger of epidemics following emergencies and disasters, etc. Thirty years later these aspects remain essential, though the needs, challenges and opportunities are greater. The present book deals not only with emergency response, but also with measures designed to reduce the impact of disasters on environmental health infrastructure, such as water supply and sanitation facilities. It also aims to strengthen the ability of people to withstand the disruption of their accustomed infrastructure and systems for environmental health (e.g. shelter, water supply, sanitation, vector control etc.) and to recover rapidly.
7. SEEDS Asia is a non-profit organization in Japan that takes an integrated approach to disaster management and environmental conservation to ensure safer communities in the Asia Pacific region. SEEDS Asia leverages the 17 years of

experience of its sister organization - SEEDS India. It is this foundation that enables it to expand the work to the Asia Pacific Region. Founded in 2006, SEEDS Asia comprises of individuals who a have wide range of experience in humanitarian response, particularly the Kobe Earthquake of 1995, community based disaster management and environmental education. In its short span of five years, it has actively engaged with communities across Asia namely Myanmar, Indonesia and Vietnam. It continues to draw from the best knowledge and practices in the region, particularly Japan, and contributes towards a collective vision of resilient communities.

8. ICT for Disaster Management (Disaster Prevention, Mitigation and Preparedness): The first important steps towards reducing disaster impact are to correctly analyze the potential risk and identify measures that can prevent, mitigate or prepare for emergencies. ICT can play a significant role in highlighting risk areas, vulnerabilities and potentially affected populations by producing geographically referenced analysis through, for example, a geographic information system (GIS). The importance of timely disaster warning in mitigating negative impacts can never be underestimated. For example, although damage to property cannot be avoided, developed countries have been able to reduce loss of life due to disasters much more effectively than their counterparts in the developing world. A key reason for this is the implementation of effective disaster warning systems and evacuation procedures used by the developed countries, and the absence of such measures in the developing world.
9. Introduction to International Disaster Management, Damon P. Coppola, Written from a global perspective on risk, hazards, and disasters. The book discusses special issues encountered in the management of international disasters, and explains the various private, non-governmental, national, and international agencies that assist in preparedness, mitigation, response and recovery during national and regional events. Concentrating on the four major phases of emergency management - mitigation, preparedness, response, and recovery - Introduction to International Disaster Management deals with such timely topics as Hurricane Katrina, the 2004 Asian tsunami, and SARS. It also serves as a reference to governmental and other agencies involved in international disaster management activities. This book is the first of its kind to take a global approach to the topic of international disaster management. This book serves as the first comprehensive resource dealing with the issues of international disaster management. It contains numerous case studies, examples of Best Practices in international disaster management, and a contact list of the governmental and nongovernmental agencies involved in international disaster management. And finally, this book provides a global perspective on risk, hazards, and disasters that is written both for students within disaster management programs and for professionals entering the field.
10. A global blueprint for disaster risk reduction efforts with a ten-year plan, adopted in January 2005 by 168 governments at the World Conference on Disaster Reduction. Governments around the world have committed to take action to reduce disaster risk, and have adopted a guideline to reduce vulnerabilities to natural hazards, called the Hyogo Framework for Action (HFA). The HFA assists the efforts of nations and communities to become more resilient to, and cope better with the hazards that threaten their development gains.

11. SPHERE Project: Humanitarian Charter & Minimum Standards in Disaster Response, 2007. The Sphere Project is a voluntary initiative that brings a wide range of humanitarian agencies together around a common aim - to improve the quality of humanitarian assistance and the accountability of humanitarian actors to their constituents, donors and affected populations. The Sphere Handbook, Humanitarian Charter and Minimum Standards in Humanitarian Response, is one of the most widely known and internationally recognized sets of common principles and universal minimum standards in life-saving areas of humanitarian response. Established in 1997, the Sphere Project is not a membership organization. Governed by a Board composed of representatives of global networks of humanitarian agencies, the Sphere Project today is a vibrant community of humanitarian response practitioners.
12. United Nations Inter-Agency Secretariat of the International Strategy for Disaster Reduction, This publication was prepared by the Inter-Agency Secretariat of the International Strategy for Disaster Reduction (UN/ISDR) to provide participants of the World Conference on Disaster Reduction (WCDR), held in Kobe, Hyogo, Japan, from 18 to 22 January 2005, and other interested readers with an easily accessible compendium of the main documents prepared for and agreed by the conference. It includes a compilation of the main preparatory and outcome documents, as well as a succinct summary on the thematic segment. A CDROM is included in the publication. It contains all the other relevant official and unofficial documents circulated at the plenary sessions and during the various clusters of the thematic segment of the WCDR. Information on the public forum and from civil society together with reference documents is also included.

Chapter – 2

Disaster Management at the Global Level

Overview

The International Response to Disasters is convoluted, at times chaotic, and always complex. Every country has its own hazard profile, vulnerability fluctuation, and evolution or demise of emergency management systems, as well as unique cultural, economic and political characteristics. Each of these qualities influences the country's interaction with international disaster management agencies and organizations (*Coppola, 2007).* It is a fact that natural disasters strike countries, both developed and developing, causing enormous destruction and creating human sufferings and producing negative impacts on national economies. Due to diverse geo-climatic conditions prevalent in different parts of the globe, different types of natural disasters like floods, droughts, earthquakes, cyclones, landslides, and volcanoes strike according to the vulnerability of the area *(Goel, 2010).* Typically, the poor are the worst hit for they have the least resources to cope with and rebuild *(Shah, 2011)*[1]. In this section, the researcher tries to evaluate the international response to some of the major disasters that occurred around the world in the last one decade.

The 2004 Asian tsunami led to the largest relief and recovery operation undertaken by the IFRC in living memory. Over 3 billion U.S. dollars was raised by their member national societies, 70 per cent of which came from the general public. On the fifth anniversary of the tsunami almost 5 million people received aid from Red Cross and Red Crescent partners. The various documents of the organization clearly demonstrate how those funds have helped communities to build back their lives and recover from the disaster *(Red Cross and Red Crescent Tsunami Operation, 2006).* In another major disaster, the Haiti Earthquake, the Red Cross Red Crescent took up the largest single country response in history *(IFRC, 2010).* In the emergency phase, the focus was firmly on urgently needed shelter, healthcare, relief items and water and sanitation. Ten months on, needs are still great and many people are still vulnerable. Non-food relief items continue to be distributed with a focus on replacing emergency shelter materials. Emphasis on recovery programmes is steadily increasing *(IFRC, 2010)*.

Disaster Relief Responses in Recent Major Disasters

(a) ***Haiti Earthquake***: Some have criticized the response by the international community in the actual delivery of humanitarian assistance is far too slow. For example, in the days following the earthquake some press reports commented on what they perceived to be a critical lack of food and water, insufficient medical care for the wounded, the slow pace of search and rescue, and the nonexistent presence of law and order. Others argue that there has been a great deal of unfair criticism about the slowness of the international aid effort. The weakened capacity of the Haitian government, critically damaged infrastructure, and logistical challenges posed by the influx of massive aid into a city largely destroyed by the earthquake all contributed to delay and difficulties on the ground. Still others have been concerned about bureaucratic red tape, lack of civil-military cooperation, and control by the U.S. military of flight priorities at the Port-au-Prince airport, and overall coordination issues. Evaluations of the relief response in Haiti would likely continue to be conducted and debated as the humanitarian effort moves ahead. A disaster of this scope is almost certain to run into many obstacles because the challenges on the ground are so daunting. While managing expectations of what is possible under these circumstances is important, so too, are the observations and lessons learned that with time and hindsight may benefit the actions and plans of those responding to future disasters *(Haiti Earthquake: Crisis and Response, 2010)*.

(b) ***Cyclone Nargis and the Sichuan Earthquake:*** The massive human loss and destruction caused by Cyclone Nargis and the Sichuan Earthquake once again revealed the failures of development that led to disaster risk and loss. On May 3, 2009, the coastal regions of Myanmar were devastated by Cyclone Nargis, which left more than 100,000 people dead. Less than two weeks later, an earthquake measuring 7.9 on the Richter scale struck the Sichuan region of China, killing more than 70,000 people. The events that followed highlight the importance of governance and local actors having a say in development and disaster risk reduction.

In Myanmar, the conversion of a mangrove delta ecosystem into commercial rice cultivation provided an important contribution to national GDP. However, it also created vulnerability leading to the Cyclone Nargis disaster. The unsustainable development of the Irrawaddy Delta manifested itself during the disaster in many ways: the loss of a natural buffer increased exposure to coastal storms, persistent poverty and inadequate provision of basic needs created a vulnerable population. In addition, the absence of effective local-, regional- and national-level early warning, public shelters and evacuation planning meant that disaster risk had not been mitigated. Cyclone Nargis was another in a long list of recent disasters waiting to happen *(ProVention Consortium, 2008)*[2] Governance failure was also at the root of the Sichuan earthquake disaster. In China, failure to regulate construction resulted in the deaths of many children as schools and residential buildings collapsed. The Chinese government estimates that 7,000 classrooms collapsed in the earthquake. As government investigators begin to examine the causes of so many building failures, parents have protested, calling for more urgent action.

Both disasters show how a lack of accountability to local populations and a lack of local participation in development decision-making have generated disaster risk. They also illustrate the great potential for disaster risk to be managed by interventions that are simple, but which rely on political will. As both disasters move into recovery mode, it is vitally important that local actors are involved. Where involvement is lacking, response can become a second disaster, eroding local economies, removing property rights and breaking up social capital *(ProVention Consortium, 2008).*

Country Level Disaster Management System- *An Analysis*

A closer analysis on the disaster management system prevailing or practicing in major countries would be valuable for interested professionals to learn what works and what doesn't work in times of major crises. The following paragraphs illustrate the world- wide mechanisms practiced in the management of disasters. Most would agree that the U.S. emergency management system is the most advanced and well-funded in the world. The equipment utilized, the training applied, and the dedication of its many practitioners to exercise and testing, are unequalled. Despite all these achievements, failures occur with regularity, as revealed in the hurricane Katrina response, thus proving in cruel fashion that the country does not yet possess all the answers to emergency management problems. When international disaster management is broached, what typically come to mind are the frail emergency management systems found in the developing world, rife with insufficient funding, poor training, corruption, and other obstacles. However, there is a great number of highly successful emergency management systems found in the many industrialized nations of the world, and a handful in the developing world, that we stand to learn from considerably. Their lessons become our lessons only when we pay attention. For example, the Netherlands, after fighting the encroachment of the North Sea for over 800 years, the country has developed a flood control system unrivaled by any other nation. U.S. planners often measure success in terms of resisting 100-year floods (as is currently employed in New Orleans) or 500-year floods. In the Netherlands, flood control systems are being updated to increase protection to 100,000-year flood events from the present 10,000-year flood defenses in place *(ProVention Consortium, 2008).*

An analysis of world-wide disaster management practices may remain incomplete, if one doesn't look into the emergency response system in Japan. The Japanese have been suffering from the effects of tsunamis for over a thousand years. Almost 200 major events have been recorded in the last 1300 years alone, or an average of one event per 6.7 years. The result of this experience is a remarkably diverse tsunami management system that combines widespread public education, advanced warning systems, and extensive mitigation countermeasures. The role of the government is very high in putting the disaster management activities in a more scientific and generic way. At the government level, Japan, a developed country, which is continuously losing much more in disasters, has launched a satellite- based alert system to speed up evacuations if earthquakes, tsunamis or missiles hit the country. Authorities, who earlier relied on low- tech ways to spread alerts, will now be able to send instant warnings via sirens of imminent tsunamis, volcano eruptions or other disasters. The new system known as *J-Alert's trial, (2004)* expanded to warn residents of approaching missiles and earthquakes, which Japanese meteorologists can *predict* seconds before they occur. The J-Alert's trail launch took place with some hiccups, in the western city of Kobe, which suffered a giant earthquake in 1995 that killed almost 6,500 people. In the drill, disaster authorities relayed news of a medium –size quake to Kobe's Ichikawacho area. On the second try, radio speakers installed in public places sounded a hypothetical alert to leave. Similarly, at an inter- governmental institutional level, an important part of the World Bank mission is providing assistance to prepare for and recover from natural or man-made disasters that can result in great human and economic losses. Indeed, developing countries suffer the greatest costs when a disaster hits- more than 95 percent of all deaths caused by disaster occur in developing countries; and losses due to natural disasters are 20 times greater (as a percentage of GDP) in developing countries than in industrialized countries *(Disaster Watch, 2004)*[3]

Countries such as Israel face a different form of emergency resulting from border dispute and violence. As a result of the Israeli/Palestinian conflict, the government of Israel has developed highly advanced systems of threat monitoring, detection, and prevention, and has improved their systems for dealing with the consequences when events actually occur. Following the September 11 terrorist attacks, officials from the Department of Homeland Security, and from many State and local government agencies, met with officials from the Government of Israel to learn from their experiences related to terrorism including anti-missile technology on commercial airliners, airline passenger security, monitoring of terrorist groups, and attack scene security *(Disaster Watch, 2004).*

With the help of the British colonialists, the Indian government solved centuries-old problems of drought and famine. Recognizing that the nation was never without sufficient resources, and that their only deficiency was in the movement of those resources to those in need, they developed the extensive railway system that reaches virtually every region of the country. Since its initiation, there has not been a single drought-related famine in India. Many researchers have theorized that the most significant failure in the response to Hurricane Katrina on the Gulf Coast in 2005 was a breakdown in the systems used to transport needed supplies to disaster-affected zones *(ProVention Consortium, 2008).*

Disaster response in the developing world (often referred to as the "Third World) has revolved around the recognition that central governments are unable to manage all the consequences of mega-disasters. These governments have compensated by forming pre- and post-disaster cooperative agreements and other arrangements with nongovernmental, nonprofit, and private organizations and businesses, which together provide the various components of the response that the beleaguered government is unable to manage on their own. Included in these services are mass care, transportation, re-supply, and case management, among others. These organizations are good at what they do, and they do it regularly, leaving them much more prepared and more able to deliver when called upon to do so *(ProVention Consortium, 2008).*

The insinuation that the US might be moving towards a "Third-World system evokes negative reactions – in response to assumptions that the speaker is claiming that the U.S. is regressing. However, the opposite may in fact be true – in a sense, the shift is a "correction" to assumptions that may have been the basis of flawed emergency management practices - as were evidenced in the response to hurricane Katrina in the Gulf Coast. Following Katrina, many of the shortfalls of the government response systems in the United States were exposed. Private and non-profit organizations stepped in to fill existing gaps, including businesses like Chevron and Walmart, international nonprofit organizations like Save the Children, local organizations like the Baton Rouge Community Foundation, and religious organizations like Southern Baptist Disaster Relief *(Disaster Watch, 2004)*.

When disasters occur in the developing world, much of the funding to support response and recovery is passed by the United Nations or the affected government directly to organizations that specialize in varying response and recovery tasks. Although the United States Government has worked with the American Red Cross for decades, it has little experience in more widespread application of this cooperative practice, and almost no experience exists at the State and local levels. Since Katrina, many changes have been made to accommodate such a system, and many new cooperative agreements have been made – a sign of the shift that is already occurring *(Disaster Watch, 2004)*.

Responsibility for disaster management ultimately rests with the local and national governments of the affected country or countries. Citizens expect their governments to provide both pre- and post-disaster assistance, regardless of the disaster's cause. But all too often, local and national governments are unable to manage the preparedness, mitigation, response, and recovery needs of large-scale disasters, and must turn to other governments for assistance. The mechanisms by which governments participate in international disaster management are diverse. Unfortunately, this support is not always sufficient. But where government assistance leaves off, multilateral and nongovernmental organizations pick up *(Coppola, 2007)*.

Disaster Management in the United States of America

Despite having responded to thousands of natural disasters and numerous terrorist attacks, at present the United States government at the federal, state, and local levels is exceedingly unprepared to handle the immediate aftereffects of disasters. The federal government has created numerous large bureaucracies and congressional panels as well as generated hundreds of official reports each of which purports to detail appropriate disaster response guidelines. Nonetheless, the improvement since the first disaster response plan was implemented during World War- I are not palpable *(Andrew S. Mener, 2007).*

During the most recent major Hurricanes – Katrina and Rita – despite having significant advanced notice of the impending natural disaster as well as years of investigative reports warning about the fragility of the New Orleans levy system, the disaster response system failed the citizens of Louisiana and the Gulf Coast and that the system requires repair is not debatable. The questions which remain are how the current system came to be, what our expectations of the system should be, and how we ought to shock the political bureaucracy into action to repair the obviously ailing system. Nonetheless, the improvements since the first disaster response plan was implemented during World War I are not palpable. Changes to this point have consistently stemmed from the conviction that failure was a result of poor leadership, poor individual decisions, and inexperience. These "improvements" stemmed from the obvious fact that the system would work better if each participating organization were better equipped, better trained, and more highly funded. However, while these shortcomings contribute to the inefficiencies, the consistent failure of the system under different personal leaderships, points to a systemic cause for the failure. Criticism must look at the overall system and the environment in which it functions to develop a practical, appropriate, and affordable strategic plan. The government must replace its tendency to fund "random acts of preparedness with a carefully outlined strategic plan that is sensitive to American political traditions, yet still effective *(Andrew S. Mener, 2007).*

In evaluating the effectiveness of the disaster system, it is critical to understand the secondary or even tertiary role of federal government in the response plan. When a disaster strikes a particular area, local authorities are the primary responders. While federal and state agencies are involved in training local responders and assuring adequate preparation, the system does not immediately involve them in the actual response efforts. The system assumes that most disasters can be handled entirely by local authorities *(Disaster Response in the United States of America, 2007).*

As criticism mounts in the wake of Hurricane Katrina over the inadequateness of the American disaster response system, it is important to look at other systems being used around the globe. This comparison process is complicated, however. The wealth of the United States inflates expectations of response capabilities, the size of the nation increases the scale and frequency of potential disasters, and the federalist system of government complicates the distribution of responsibility for disaster response. While one can look to Great Britain, Spain, Thailand, Israel, and other democratic nations which have experienced disasters in recent history, these nations do not share any of these characteristics. For that reason, the only two nations worthy of comparison are Australia and Canada, both of which are large and wealthy democratic nations which value the independence of their provinces *(Andrew S. Mener, 2007)*.

Disaster Management in Australia and Canada

In Australia and Canada, just as in the United States, emergency management agencies at the state, territory, province and local levels are primarily responsible for disaster relief. During most disasters, just as in the United States, the territory, province, state and local governments manage the disasters without federal intervention. However, when federal assistance is needed, unlike in the United States, there is no need for a formal disaster declaration. When Australian and Canadian disaster relief expenditures exceed a predetermined level, federal reimbursements begin; the process is automatic and thus depoliticized. In Australia, depending on the individual fiscal strength of the state or territory, 75%, 90%, or 100% of the response and relief costs are reimbursed. In Canada, federal reimbursement depends on the per capita expenditures and start when the province has spent $1 per capita; the reimbursement level increases on a sliding scale up to a maximum of 90% reimbursement when the province has spent more than $5 per capita. During large-scale disasters, the Canadian equivalent of FEMA, the Emergency Management and National Security Branch of Public Safety and Emergency Preparedness Canada (PSEPC) and the Australian equivalent of FEMA, Emergency Management Australia become involved. In general, any resources provided by Emergency Management Australia or PSEPC operate under the operational direction of the state and local governments. In Australia, even direct federal monetary assistance to citizens provided by Emergency Management Australia are administered through state or territory collection centers. In Canada, on rare occasions the federal government provides operational assistance through Health Canada or the military. Since there is no Canadian equivalent of the Posse Comitatus Law, the Canadian military is able to assist province law enforcement agencies when needed.

The Australian and Canadian systems of disaster response have been spared major criticism. The automatic and nonpolitical criterion for activating federal assistance moderates political tensions and staves off criticism. Although both governments place more confidence in the ability for states and territories to independently handle the operational aspects of disaster response, the overall system is not altogether different than that which exists in the United States. The state, territory, and province governments in Australia and Canada, however, are significantly more powerful within the overall governmental system and have proportionately more resources than American state governments. This enhances their abilities to handle disasters but does not demonstrate the overall effectiveness of the system during truly catastrophic disasters. Furthermore, in recent history Australia and Canada have been spared major disasters. Due to the low prevalence of major disaster and the increased reliance on local governments, Australia has only spent an average of $3 billion per year and Canada has spent less than $2 billion total over the course of the last 35 years on disaster response. This minimal involvement in disaster response activities makes it difficult to ascertain the overall effectiveness of the Australian and Canadian systems in comparison to the American system *(Miskel, 2007)*. The underlying structure of the American, Canadian, and Australian disaster response system is the same. State and local governments are given the primary responsibility for disaster response although in the United States the federal government maintains a larger operational role. The Australian and Canadian systems, however, are completely depoliticized. Regulations predetermine the exact extent and type of federal involvement. While one could argue that most significant disasters are declared without political debate and thus the politicization of the American system does not delay disaster relief, the American system may lead to irrationally lenient disaster declarations. Since most presidents do not want to be in the position of denying federal aid to states, the federal government frequently becomes entangled in disaster relief operations and reimbursements that could have been handled by the states. This involvement overwhelms the federal system and takes the focus from preparing for truly catastrophic disasters.

Integrated Disaster Risk Management of Japan

The failures in disaster response management came about through systemic weaknesses that were entirely predictable, and had been identified in previous similar events, including the 1995 Kobe-Hanshin earthquake *(Japan Earthquake Report, 2011)*[4] ———The events in Japan in March 2011, involving an earthquake and subsequent tsunami, fell exactly within the risk profile of Japan's disaster management programme, and there were no contributing factors to the disaster that could not or should not have been predicted and accounted for. The systemic failures of the Japanese government and disaster management system were not unique to Japan. They reflect almost completely the same weaknesses that were identified in America following Hurricane Katrina and 9/11. Japan's planning and construction laws have clearly made a difference to the ability of large buildings to survive even major earthquakes and this can be seen as a major success in their long-term earthquake management policy. Despite the fact that individual agencies have developed a high-level of expertise and capability (and often have world-class equipment and technology unavailable to other countries, including US), Japan still lacks a unified Disaster Management framework that allows the swift mobilization of separate agencies under a unified operational command *(Journal of Integrated Disaster Risk Management, 2011)*[5]

There needs to be a clear distinction made between 'Major Incidents' and 'National Disasters'. They require a different class of response, and as one USFEMA commentator noted, it is no use responding to a Class 5 Disaster with Class 1 frameworks. The failures at the tactical and operational level were reflected in, and in many ways caused by, a lack of leadership at the political level. Disaster management on a national level is a political issue, and responsibility for that needs to be accepted by national political leaders, whether in terms of long-term capability preparation or in the immediate post-incident response. Despite these failures, there is a clearly-defined development road-map that would allow Japan to use its existing technical, personnel and organization resources to create an appropriate, effective and integrated unified Disaster Management framework. None of the points above are new or unknown. They reflect almost completely the conclusions reached following the 1995 Kobe-Hanshin earthquake and the Hurricane Katrina (*JIDRM, 2011).*

Integrated Disaster Risk Management of China

Emergency Management System

In order to enhance emergency management and implement the governments' function entirely, the Emergency Management Office of State Council at the national level was established in April, 2006. It works as an operation hinge, which takes charge of the daily work of the national emergency management, responds to the public security events, collects the real-time information and harmonizes the related departments. Since the establishment in 2006, the Emergency Management Office of State Council has carried out some effective work to enhance the disaster emergency management: helped actualize and implement the Master State

Plan for Rapid Response to Public Emergencies of China; held the emergency management working meeting of State Council and the management working meeting of enterprise emergency work, deployed and unified the emergency management, and emphasized the governments of all levels to enhance emergency ability construction and get prepared for the prevention and dealing of the public security emergencies; started the Key Technologies R & D Program for the emergency platform construction to provide science and technology support for emergency management and increase the emergency treatment efficiency *(S.Pandey, 2008)*[6].

Emergency Response

During a disaster period, the emergency management[7] offices and the disaster reduction committees of all levels are in charge of the emergency response, together with the Civil Affairs departments, the Public Security departments, the arms, etc. Namely the bars and the blocks are combined together closely and rapidly to deal with the emergencies as soon as there is an emergency event. At present, a disaster emergency response system is set up and is running to guarantee that rescue taskforces, relief supplies, funds and information are on the ground and in place to address the immediate and real needs of the affected. According to disaster emergency management, the Chinese government has strengthened the emergency plan system construction. In the *Master State Plan for Rapid Response to Public Emergencies*, the public security events are divided into four kinds (natural disasters, industry accidents, public health and social security) according to their occurring process, characteristics and mechanism, and four grades (huge, bigger, big and ordinary grade). And it's prescribed that the huge and bigger grade emergencies must be reported to the State Council in 4 hours after the occurrence, and the local governments or related departments have to start the related emergency plan timely and effectively in to control further development. Besides, there have been several special plans and department plans for Rapid Response to Public Emergencies; and the plans for Rapid Response to Public Emergencies of national and local governments have also been compiled and accomplished, which makes the disaster risk management and disaster reduction more regular and systematic. Up to March 15th 2006, China has constituted 24,293 emergency response plans for unexpected public accidents, in which 1 national, 25 special, and 80 sectional, 971 from the sectors in the State Council (not including 80 sectional ones), 158 from central enterprises, 23058 regional ones. By now, the national emergency plan system has formed initiatively, and the emergency management system is under rapid construction *(Pandey, 2008)*.

Monitoring and Warning

During the disaster preparedness period, the mitigation and prevention work is taken by the professional technical departments, namely the bars. In the recent years, the Chinese government has increased the investment on natural disaster monitoring and warning system construction, and has established the natural disaster monitoring, warning and forecasting system primarily, including the meteorological disasters monitoring and forecast, the earthquake monitoring and forecast, the hydrological monitoring forest fire prevention, the forest and crop pests monitoring and forecasting, the marine environment monitoring, the geological disasters monitoring and early warning. This natural disaster monitoring, warning and forecasting system can monitor the disaster dynamic development, and provide the information for the disaster emergency decision-making *(UNCRD, 2010)*.

Relief Recovery and Reconstruction

During the post-disaster period, the disaster relief and recovery work is charged by the local disaster reduction committees, which work as a coordinator for the main departments to organize the people in disaster area to attain normal life, which includes the Civil Affairs departments, the Health departments, the Development and Deform Commission, the Finance departments, the Communications departments, the Construction departments, the Railway departments, etc. Namely, the blocks are the main responsibility body. Among these different departments, the Civil Affairs department takes the main responsibility for the disaster victims' life relief, and the insurance companies carry out the compensation for the disaster victims to help them to recover as soon as possible. With regard to the disaster relief work, the Ministry of civil affairs of China has set up the central system of material reserve for disaster relief since 1998. At present, the central stations of material reserve has been built in ten cities, which include Shenyang city, Ha'erbin city, Tianjin city, Zhengzhou city, Hefei city, Wuhan city, Changsha city, Nanning city, Chengdu city and Xi'an city. Some regions of high disaster frequencies, high vulnerability have also built the local storages of material reserve for disaster relief. Thus, the network of material reserve network for disaster relief which relies on the disaster relief storages has been established. At present, the central reserve bases store 135000 tents, and the local reserve bases store 236000 tents. If a severe disaster happens, the first tents for disaster relief would be sent out to the people in the 24 hours (*Pandey, 2008)*.

Another notable example is the recovery program employed in the Yunnan province in China *(Asian Disaster Preparedness Center, 2006)*[8].

Yunnan Province located in Southwest China where there is a fierce collision zone between the Indian Ocean tectonic plate and the Europe-Asia tectonic plate. Yunnan Province frequently suffers severe earthquakes, which often result in grave losses of life and property. A large number of dwelling houses have been destroyed and damaged due to earthquakes in Yunnan. Thus, lots of dwelling houses will be reconstructed or repaired to resettle victims by local governments during post-disaster activities. Usually, there are not enough considerations on disaster reduction in the project of reconstruction due to the limit of reconstruction funds, and the newly-built houses are probably still vulnerable to earthquake, especially in the rural areas *(UNCRD, 2010)*.

Usually, in the aftermath of a severe earthquake, the local governments find it difficult to find enough safe shelters to resettle the victims. The central government may dispatch some tents to the local governments to alleviate this problem, but the transportation of tents takes much time. Sometimes, the tents are quite difficult to reach the disaster-hit areas in time due to the road's damage and the rugged landform. So the local governments need an effective and efficient resolution project *(UNCRD, 2010)*. Yunnan province is a region of underdeveloped, ethnic minorities' and also a region prone to earthquakes. Abundant bamboo resources are distributed in this region and bamboo is used as a major building material by local residents, especially ethnic minorities. Bamboo can be used as a better quakeproof material for its good toughness and light weight, owing to its cheap price and short growth period, bamboo is widely used to build and reinforce the dwelling houses in earthquake prone areas so as to improve the earthquake resistance of local dwelling houses (S.*Pandey, 2008)*. In order to improve the effectiveness and efficiency of the emergency relief system of local governments, the Recovery and Reconstruction Management Office as the key management unit on the recovery and reconstruction work at the national level, proposes a research project aimed at facilitating the development and construction of bamboo dwelling houses and bamboo shelters in the earthquake prone rural areas, Yunnan. This project is funded by the ProVention Consortium's programme for Applied Grants for Disaster Risk Reduction. Asian Disaster Preparedness Center is responsible for managing the grant and the research progress of the project. Through this project, some on-site surveys were conducted and research report was delivered to the local governmental stakeholders and the community leaders in earthquake prone areas of Yunnan. It would encourage and guide them to build more seismic-resistant bamboo dwelling houses in the post-disaster reconstruction and bamboo shelters in pre-disaster efforts as part of the disaster preparedness efforts, so as to timely provide the victims enough safer shelters to protect themselves from the aftershock, and reduce the loss of life and property to the minimum *(UNCRD, 2010)*[9]

At the same time, the Chinese government encourages the public social donation activities from the whole society and the NGO's to be an important force in the post-disaster period, including the endowment activity for the severe disaster, the mutual support activity between the eastern area and ten provinces in the west, and the disaster relief activity of the social organization. There are nearly 30 thousand urban donation receiving stations in China, carrying out regular social donation activities perennially, especially in the period when some natural disaster occurs *(UNCRD, 2010)*. This social mobilization mechanism provides a solid material supporting for disaster management, and help the people in the less-developed area to recover rapidly after disasters.

Efficacy of the Chinese Space Assets in Disaster Management

The People's Republic of China (PRC) has consistently been improving its space based infrastructure *(Pandey, 2008)*[10]. In 28 years since the first successful launch of Dong Fang Hong-1 Satellite into orbit on 24 April 1970, the PRC has demonstrably scaled many a reckonable technological step. The space missions that the PRC launches today include: recovery capsules and non-capsule remote sensing satellites; communication/ broadcasting satellites; metrological satellites; science satellites; engineering test satellites; positioning satellites; and, manned space satellites. China's goals and objectives for going into orbit with a variety of space assets including manned are predictably similar to those that drove the Russian and the US- to gain national prestige, and to signal wealth, commitments and technological prowess quite apparently, as the foregoing discussions boil down, the existing Chinese space based infra structure then did not produce worthwhile imagery for any of the three phases of disaster management efforts. The system did not have much to contribute for disaster prevention and mitigation works for future either. Prediction of earthquake would remain an enigma not until a system is in place to take cognizance of terrestrial geophysics and geology related precursors with space based cognition and identification parameters *(Pandey, 2008)*.

The role of Chinese photogrammetry and remote sensing professionals has been quite reckonable. In the company of foreign professionals, they got deep insights. In phase- I of the disaster management efforts, the Chinese photogrammetry and remote sensing professionals received on-ground-exposure of the latest techniques of interpretation of high resolution imagery that helped in locating buildings that collapsed in the worst hit areas. In phase-II of the disaster management efforts, which sought to meet out and cater prevention and preparedness for secondary disasters, the Chinese photogrammetric and remote sensing professionals got through with the system mechanism of handling airborne and space borne optical imagery and radar data that were used for identifying, assessing and formulating decisions in areas prone to secondary disasters like landslides and mudslides, especially those in and around the quake lakes or barrier lakes that were formed when a land slide plugged a river. They have benefited greatly in the third phase, which has now gone to focus on disaster assessment and reconstruction. It relates to high skills of topographic mapping at 1:10000 scales in the region with an aerial extent of 120000 kms based on the techniques of aerial photogrammetric survey without ground control points, generating information products such as DEM, DOQs and DLGs *(Pandey, 2008).*

Much of the lacuna in the Chinese system came for discussions in the emergency session of Xiangshan Science Conference (XSSC) in Beijing on 19thMay 08, where 40 top experts in seismology and geophysics got to discuss threadbare different shades of the issue. The top Chinese minds in the field included Prof. Zhang Peizhen from the State Bureau of Seismology (SBS), Prof. Xu Zhiqin from the China Academy of Earth Science (CAES) and Prof Wang Guanqian from Qinghua University. They came out with a wide range of recommendations, some of which speak of the process and system that the Chinese approach hitherto lacked to handle the issue. The gloat over China lacking reckonable system for forecasting deadly earthquakes as large as 8 in magnitude is understandable. This is besides the fact that the Chinese did not have a worthwhile and dependable imagery interpretation system in place to support post-quake rescue, relief and rehabilitation as well *(Pandey, 2008).*

The United Nations Disaster Management Team

The United Nations General Assembly believes that the objectives of team management are applicable to the UN agencies oriented to emergencies. They have mandated that standing UN Disaster Management Team (UN-DMT) be formed in each disaster-prone country, convened and chaired by the UN resident coordinator. The composition of the UN-DMT is determined by taking into account the types of disaster to which the country is prone and the organizations present, but should normally include a core group consisting of the country-level representatives of FAO, UNDP/UNDRO,

UNICEF, WFP, WHO and, where present, UNHCR. It may be enlarged to include additional representatives or project personnel from other relevant agencies when an emergency arises *(UNDP- UNDRO, 1992)*[11]

The original and primary purpose of the UN-DMT is to ensure a prompt, effective and concerted response by the UN system at country level in the event of a disaster. The team should also ensure similar coordination of UN assistance to the Government with respect to post-disaster rehabilitation and reconstruction, and relevant disaster mitigation measures through long-term development programs. It should be emphasized that in all aspects of disaster management, the UN-DMT alerts the government. The UN-DMT recognizes and in no way supersedes the mandates and specific functions of the various organizations in the exercise of those mandates. It supports and assists the office of the resident coordinator in the exercise of its system-wide functions. In line with General Assembly resolution 46/182, the latter will maintain close contact with, and receive leadership from the Emergency Relief Coordinator *(UNDP- UNDRO, 1992).*

Country Disaster Management Team

Most disaster prone countries already have a formal or informal disaster management team. It is typically headed by a National Disaster Focal Point Body. This body functions in liaison with the Office of the President or Prime Minister, with civil defense organizations, key government ministries, the Red Cross/Red Crescent, and other NGOs and major donors. Where national officials do not participate in UN-DMT meetings or activities, the resident coordinator should ensure that they are consulted and briefed on all relevant matters. In practice it is vital that the policies of the DMT relate to those approved by the Government even under the pressure of the event *(UNDP- UNDRO, 1992).*

Tasks, Roles and Resources of the UN: Organizational Tasks and General Roles

The UNDP/UNDRO Disaster Management Manual *(DMM, 1992)* describes in detail the role of the UN system and its agencies in disaster management. As per the manual, primary responsibility for all aspects of disaster management rests with the Government of the affected country. This includes: planning and implementing long-term risk reduction and preparedness measures; requesting and administering disaster relief and rehabilitation operations, requesting international assistance if required; and coordinating all disaster-related assistance programs, both nationally and internationally funded *(UNDRO, 1992).*

Each UN organization or agency is responsible for providing advice and assistance to the Government of a disaster-prone or disaster-affected country, in accordance with its mandate and the resources available to it. In doing so, each agency is accountable to its own governing body, but it is also called upon to act as a member of a united team. In the case of refugee emergencies, UNHCR remains responsible for their protection and the coordination of international assistance for the refugees. In relation to disaster relief and other post-disaster assistance, each organization and agency of the UN system is called on to: (a) mobilize and provide timely technical assistance and material support to disaster-affected countries, according to its own mandate and the resources available to it; and, (b) co-operate with the UN resident coordinator, UNDRO, or any other coordination mechanism established by the Secretary-General to ensure appropriate, coordinated UN system assistance in the context of a concerted plan and program *(UNDP- UNDRO, 1992).*

Roles and Resources of UNDP, UNDRO, and other UN agencies -The Role of UNDP

UNDP focuses primarily on the development-related aspects of disaster risks and occurrences, and on providing technical assistance to institution-building in relation to all aspects of disaster management. Its emphasis is therefore on: (a) incorporating long-term risk reduction and preparedness measures in normal development planning and programs, including support for specific mitigation measures where required; (b) assisting in the planning and implementation of post-disaster rehabilitation and reconstruction, including the definition of new development strategies that incorporate risk reduction measures relevant to the affected area; (c) reviewing the impact of large settlements of refugees or displaced persons on development and seeking ways to incorporate the refugees and displaced persons in development strategies; and, (d) providing technical assistance to the authorities managing major emergency assistance operations of extended duration (especially in relation to displaced persons and the possibilities for achieving durable solutions in such cases). In addition, UNDP provides administrative and operational support to the resident coordinator function, particularly at country level, but also at the headquarters *(UNDP-UNDRO, 1992).*

In the event of a disaster, UNDP may grant a maximum of $50,000 from SPR funds to provide immediate relief. UNDP is not otherwise involved in the provision of "relief" using any of its own resources or other funds administered by the Program. Where a major emergency substantially affects the whole development process within a country, IPF resources may be used to provide technical assistance to plan and manage the operation, with the agreement of the Government. Technical and material assistance in support of long-term risk reduction and preparedness measures is included in the country program, and may be funded from IPF resources or from other UNDP-administered funds. The same can also be used to assist rehabilitation and reconstruction. Special additional grants (up to $1.1 million) may be made from SPR funds for technical assistance to such post-disaster recovery efforts following natural disasters. The particular responsibilities of the UNDP resident representative are summarized in the following panel *(UNDP- UNDRO, 1992)*.

Disaster Management Responsibilities of the UNDP Resident Representative

The resident representative is responsible for: (a) ensuring that all concerned in planning development programs are aware of any known or potential hazards and their likely effects, and that these are appropriately taken into account in the country program; (b) designating a "disaster focal point", and ensuring that the field office is adequately prepared to respond to an emergency; and, (c) in the event of a disaster Mobilizing UNDP staff and technical assistance personnel and other resources that meet the needs of the situation, particularly those needed for the initial assessment and immediate response and ensuring that UNDP assistance is used for good effect and the capacity of the office is strengthened if necessary to ensure effective response (*UNDP, 1992)*.

In all disaster-prone country field offices, a Senior National Officer is designated a "*disaster focal point*" for all disaster-related matters including mitigation, response and international UN/ UNDP preparedness. Section 3A and appendix 3A of the UNDP/ UNDRO Disaster Manual provide in detail the duties and qualifications of the disaster focal point. In a major or complex emergency of extended duration (typically involving displaced populations), UNDP may temporarily assign an additional deputy resident representative. That deputy may either manage normal UNDP business while the resident representative concentrates on the resident coordinator functions, or may take day-today responsibility for matters relating to the emergency which are within the UNDP mandate. In the countries with the most severe or prolonged emergencies UNDP has established UN Emergency Units. These units are able to focus exclusively on addressing the emergency and are often staffed by persons seconded from sister UN agencies that are operational in that country. In the event of a sudden influx of refugees into a country in which there is no UNHCR representation, the resident representative immediately notifies UNHCR and initiates the assessment process on behalf of the UNHCR (*UNDP- UNDRO, 1992).*

The Role of UNDRO

UNDRO is the focal point for disaster management in the UN system (except in those countries where a UN Emergency Unit is established). In relief, it provides a framework for coordination of assistance by the UN agencies and helps to coordinate such assistance with that from other sources. In addition, UNDRO has an important role in mobilizing external assistance and serving as a clearing house for information concerning disasters. In the area of mitigation, UNDRO promotes long-term measures to reduce disaster-related risks and enhance preparedness in disaster-prone countries. UNDRO is represented at the country level on a permanent basis by the resident coordinator/representative. Coordination at the headquarters level is often effected by contacts between the Head of Agencies concerned at the beginning of a relief operation, and through frequent ongoing contacts between the relevant focal points. At the country level, coordination is undertaken by the resident coordinator who is also the UNDRO representative. Whenever possible and required, UNDRO supports the resident coordinator by dispatching an UNDRO delegate or emergency assistance team *(UNDP- UNDRO, 1992).*

UNDRO concentrates on problems related to natural hazards and sudden disasters, but as its mandate covers all kinds of emergencies UNDRO may also offer its services and advice in situations including droughts, and cases of war and civil conflicts, unless and until the Secretary-General makes other arrangements. Following a disaster, UNDRO, acting on behalf of the Secretary-General, offers its services to the Government of the disaster-stricken state in assessing the need for external relief assistance, and communicating that information to prospective donors and others concerned. (Contacts with the Government are conducted through the resident coordinator /representative and the country's mission in Geneva or New York). Where international assistance is required or requested, UNDRO: (a) helps to identify priority needs on the basis of information from the Government, the resident coordinator/representative, UN-DMT, and other competent bodies; (b) issues international appeals and acts as a clearing house for information on needs and contributions, the assistance extended or planned by all donors, and the progress of relief operations; and, (c) seeks to mobilize resources and coordinate relief assistance by various UN organizations and agencies, bilateral donors, and inter-and non-govern mental organizations and administers funds channeled through it *(UNDP, 1992).*

Depending on the particular situation after consultations, wherever possible, with the Government or the resident coordinator/ representative, UNDRO may: (a) assign one or more delegates on mission to assist the national authorities in organizing the assessment and administering relief operations, and assisting the resident coordinator/representative in information management, the local coordination of international relief assistance, and in his reporting responsibilities to UNDRO; and, (b) provide logistic support to ensure the timely arrival of relief supplies and their prompt delivery to the affected population. This may include organizing shared or joint relief flights. The Coordinator may approve a grant of up to US$50,000 per disaster from funds available to UNDRO, subject to certain conditions. In some situations, UNDRO can release supplies from the emergency stockpile it administers in Pisa, Italy *(UNDP- UNDRO, 1992).*

UNDP/UNDRO Collaboration

UNDP and UNDRO complement each other. UNDP has a wealth of experience in development planning and administration, and well-established field offices. UNDRO has specific knowledge and experience in disaster management, and established contacts with relevant specialist bodies. The fact that the UNDP resident representative also represents UNDRO helps to ensure fruitful cooperation between the organizations. At the country level UNDP field offices generally administer funds and resources channeled through UNDRO, following normal inter-agency procedures. This includes the local procurement of supplies and services, and the recruitment and appointment of temporary staff *(UNDP- UNDRO, 1992).*

Disaster-Related Roles of the Core Members of the UN-DMTs

Provides technical advice in reducing vulnerability and helps in the rehabilitation of agriculture, livestock, and fisheries, with emphasis on local food production. Monitors food production, exports and imports, and forecasts any requirements of exceptional food assistance. UN- DMT members promote the incorporation of disaster mitigation in development planning, and funds technical assistance for all aspects of disaster management. The team provides administrative support to the resident coordinator and UN-DMT. Mobilizes and coordinates international emergency relief assistance, issuing consolidated appeals, assists in assessments and relief management if required. It provides advice and guidance on risk assessments and in planning and implementing mitigation measures. Assures the protection of refugees and seeks durable solutions to their problems. Helps to mobilize and assure the delivery of necessary assistance in the country of asylum if it is a developing country and attends to the well-being of children and women, especially child health and nutrition. Assistance activities may include: social programs; child feeding (in collaboration with WFP); water supplies, sanitation and direct health interventions (in collaboration with W.H.O). The team provides related management and logistical support. Provides "targeted" food aid for humanitarian relief, and to support rehabilitation, reconstruction, and risk-reducing development programs. Mobilizes and coordinates the delivery of complementary emergency and food supply from bilateral and other sources. Finally, the team provides advice and assistance in all aspects of preventive and curative health care, including the preparedness of health services for rapid response to disaster *(UNDP- UNDRO, 1992).*

Role and Coordination of the UN Resident Coordinator and the UN-DMT

The National Government is ultimately responsible for requesting and coordinating all international assistance. It also approves all programs and emergency work in the country. However, the UN system stands ready to assist upon request. At the country level, the resident coordinator/representative and the UN disaster Management Team (UN-DMT) are the essential UN coordinating institutions. Their responsibilities apply to all situations which require significant interventions from more than one UN organization or agency. At the international level, UNDRO promotes the coordination of responses to particular disaster situations, both within the UN system and in the wider international community, essentially through information-sharing *(UNDP- UNDRO, 1992).* The resident coordinator, also representing UNDRO, is both the UN system team leader at country level, and chairman of the UN-DMT. Following the occurrence of a major disaster, the resident coordinator/representative must be ready to give absolute priority to this coordination role, which also includes helping to ensure the coordination of all international emergency assistance.

Role of Other UN Organizations and Agencies

A number of other UN organizations and agencies have specific responsibilities, organizational arrangements, and capabilities relating to disaster mitigation, and/or relief or recovery assistance. UNDP, UNDRO, and resident coordinators must respect the mandates and skills of these agencies, and seek to ensure that all work together in harmony. All should use their expertise and resources to the best effect in helping people in disaster-prone and disaster-affected areas. Some of the relief programs include: (a) UN system resources available to initiate responses to disasters and emergency needs up to $20,000 at the discretion of FAOR within the context of an ongoing emergency or long-term aid project; (b) up to $50,000 per occurrence for immediate relief; approved by the Director DOF following a request from the resident representative; (c) up to $1.1 million for technical assistance for rehabilitation and reconstruction approved by the Administrator or Governing Council; (d) IPF funds for technical assistance to emergency management is major operations agreed with Government; approved by Director PCO; and, (e) up to $50,000 per disaster, subject to the availability of resources approved by the UNDRO coordinator following a request by the Government and proposal by the resident representative or other UN organization or agency. In addition there are allocations from a global emergency reserve for assistance to refugees, approved by the High Commissioner. For instance, up to $25,000 diversion of existing programme funds or in-country supplies at discretion of the country representative in agreement with the Government. Larger amounts from global emergency reserve ($4 million per year) are available once approved by Executive Director following a specific proposal by the country representative. There is also a possibility of borrowing food aid commodities from ongoing WFP-assisted development projects, governmental or other donor stocks, subject to headquarters approval to assure replacement. In some instances, up to $50,000 for local purchases of commodities at the discretion of the Director of Operations where there are no other means of arranging timely deliveries. Allocations primarily from the International Emergency Food Reserve (IEFR), managed by WFP, and from WFP general resources ($45 million annually). Global reserve from which allocations can be made for priority medical needs in anticipation of special donor contributions; approved by the Director ERO *(UNDP, 1992).*

Disaster Management: *Experiences and Experiments at the Grass Root* Level

This section will focus primarily on the disaster risk reduction at the grass root level highlighting practice examples from around the globe. In a seminal work, Christopher Hartnady of Umvoto Africa in Cape Town *(2009)* said the technical tools he had described for assessing vulnerability – the characteristics of building materials and building harmonics – are very useful for reducing earthquake risk. He said his organization worked on disaster reduction risk in South Africa and Africa more broadly. Christopher said that there was a low awareness of earthquake risk in South Africa, even though Cape Town had an earthquake in 1809 and there had been another about 135km from the city in 1969. Scenario planning based on the 1809 earthquake suggested that a one in 300–500 year earthquake event in Cape Town would cause 20000–25000 deaths and significant property losses. His organization was working with the provincial government to mitigate risk and do disaster management planning. Speaking of seismic risk in other parts of Africa, he said an earthquake measuring 6.8 on the Richter scale struck Lake Tanganyika in 2005. The rates of seismic movement in Algiers are in the order of 5–6mm per year, and the rates of motion near Dar es Salaam are 2–3mm per year. In February 2006, two people were killed in an earthquake in Beira, Mozambique. Christopher reports that community action was a key factor in ensuring that authorities respond to earthquake threat *(Christopher, 2005).* Another striking model was the MANDISA database system developed by Ailsa Holloway and Leigh Sonn of DiMP in Cape Town. With a focus on fires in informal settlements in Cape Town, the authors spoke about the MANDISA database. MANDISA database records small and large disaster events such as fires and floods in Greater Cape Town. The current emphasis of MANDISA is on recording fire events in informal settlements where there has been damage to a structure, based on official fire services records. The project aims to systematically characterize the determinants and consequences of informal fire risk in Cape Town in order to inform better informal fire risk management. It also aims to strategically communicate its risk research outcomes to inform transversal mainstreaming of risk reduction *(Christopher, 2005).*

The authors indicated that in the period 1990–2004 about 41,000 informal dwellings had been destroyed or damaged and about 164,000 people lost their household assets and their homes. The data indicate that fire events are concentrated in informal settlements, and these seem to be on the increase. There is a cyclical trend in informal fire events – once a large-scale event has taken place, people are more careful for a time, but then the number of incidents increases again. An analysis of informal fire occurrence and fire severity in five at-risk areas of Cape Town shows the risk varies from place to place. In one informal settlement, a clear link can be seen between increasing population density and fire risk. In another area the fire data show an accumulation of fire risk, and this is an early warning of increasing household livelihood stress *(UNDP, 1992).*

DiMP's presenters reported on two ways in which MANDISA had impacted on government action. Data about economic loss from informal fires had provided South Africa's National Treasury with good reason to fund the National Disaster Management Framework. Mapped evidence of significant fire loss in the Cape Town metropolitan area had resulted in risk management being made an explicit priority in the Strategic Infrastructure Plan for the Western Cape provincial government. The authors argued that a major challenge in mainstreaming risk reduction is to bridge the gap between strategic risk reduction sectors/ disciplines and firefighting/ emergency responders. Strategic risk reducing disciplines have strong analytic capability, but limited disaster risk content knowledge (economics and planning). Disaster management and firefighting disciplines have strong fire risk knowledge, but limited analytic/ strategic risk communication capability. A second challenge is to overcome the obstacles in interdisciplinary risk reduction planning and resource allocation. In addition, DiMP contributes more broadly to risk reduction by training young professionals with interdisciplinary communication skills, risk assessment and monitoring capabilities. It runs a formal graduate programme in disaster risk science at the University of Cape Town, as well as professional Summary report on the African Urban Risk Analysis Network (AURAN) international workshop, 7–9 March 2006, Cape Town workshops in disaster risk reduction. DiMP also does applied disaster risk research (for example, investigating the link between climate change and fire risk and investigating the relevance of actuarial science).

GAMA Project in Ghana

Ben Brown of the National Disaster Management Organization (NADMO) discussed the GAMA project that would generate information that is useful for disaster management in Ghana as a whole. NADMO works with government agencies responsible for meteorology, hydrology, geology, agriculture, information, police, the defense force and health. He said his organization has come to realize that it is not possible to prevent disasters, that they must be managed when they come. It is not possible to immediately move people living in parts of Accra that are subject to annual flooding, but an early warning system of community assisted by telecommunications infrastructure could assist people to move to higher ground in time. A major storm water drain was built to mitigate flooding in the city. The last earthquake in Accra took place in 1939, and it is expected that another one will occur at some time in the future. NADMO is working with communities on how to respond to earthquakes – for example, moving into safer places like the corners of buildings where there are pillars, sheltering under tables, and having escape routes which can be found even when there is a power failure *(UNDP, 1992).*

Ben said the current structure of NADMO is geared towards preparing for major disasters, but the work of Jacob's team had raised awareness of how important it is for disaster management structures to also respond to everyday risks. Ben said most risk management workshops focus on major natural and human-made disasters, but this one was useful to look at the smaller factors that contribute to a risk accumulation which are actually more likely to cause problems. For example, people throw their garbage into the drains alongside the Odore River in Accra. This blocks the drains, contributing to the risk of flooding when it rains. There is a need, he said, to change the behaviour of individual citizens by making them aware of the consequences of throwing rubbish into the drains. But the authorities have a critical role to play too. If they do not remove the garbage, the temptation will remain for people to put it in the drain rather than keep it in the home until it can be removed. In some locations, there is a destructive cycle in which street cleaners move rubbish into the drain so that the streets are clean, and drain cleaners put the rubbish back on the road so that the drains are clean. The authorities do not take responsibility for taking the rubbish away from the site *(United Nations Development Programme, 1992).*

Recommendations at the 2008 PROVENTION FORUM Panama City, Panama

Previous ProVention forum discussions examined the potential for reconstruction to provide a window of opportunity to promote disaster risk reduction. It is hoped that local, national and international actors can build partnerships during the relief and recovery stages in order to promote risk reduction and the provision of basic needs, as well as local participation to reduce future vulnerability. The further development and application of lessons learned during the 2008 forum is made all the more urgent by these events. The issues range from the involvement of indigenous and women's groups in risk reduction, to the role of the media, and integrating climate change adaptation into disaster risk management *(The Provention Forum, 2008).*

According to the consortium, people centered Disaster Risk Reduction should be the major focus of global disaster management institutions. The role and power of indigenous people and women's groups in managing disaster risk need to be highlighted and strengthened. Local actors are the primary agents in local disaster risk reduction and disaster response. No one understands better the local culture, needs and capacity. Very often, the historical repositories of local knowledge on risk are indigenous groups. A failure to recognize this alienates local actors and leads to reduced efficiency in risk reduction investments. Women are often described as the glue that holds local society together, but they can also be marginalized from decision-making processes. Engaging women, indigenous people and other marginalized groups is not easy. Unexpected harmful social change can arise from well-intended interaction. Even greater harm may be caused by inaction. As we move forward with discussions and experience on how local actors may organize to participate in local disaster risk reduction, these groups can strengthen disaster risk reduction efforts, making them both more transparent and effective from the bottom to top. Grassroots-driven disaster risk reduction should not only be a right for affected communities, but also demanded by governments *(The Provention Forum, 2008).*

Communicating Risk and the Power of Visual Media, as one of today's most powerful communication tools, the effective use of visual media has enormous potential in risk communication, whether from one community to another or from one organization to an international audience. Using visual media effectively at a community level means partner organizations must be willing to relinquish control of the process, allowing local participants to own the task. Visual media on disaster risk is most effective as an advocacy tool when it speaks from the context and culture of those at risk. It is also effective when it goes beyond the reporting of project aims and outcomes to examine the deeper processes at work in generating risk, and in shaping capacity and action for risk reduction. Local involvement in media production – while requiring the development of a media culture – can be a powerful tool of community empowerment as well as a means of transferring knowledge and lessons learned. Organizations can also learn to use visual media in order to increase understanding of the complex process of disaster risk production and reduction *(UNCRD, 2010).*

Another prominent suggestion was to encourage Public–Private Partnerships and Risk Financing in order to bring together resources for Effective Risk Reduction. There is much scope for public–private partnerships across infrastructure development, reconstruction and risk financing. The evidence from risk financing shows that public–private partnerships are growing rapidly in popularity, and range from crop insurance to the underwriting of disaster funds. As capacity increases, so do questions on community involvement, from a partnership's inception onwards. Where commercial interests are involved, a careful balance has to be struck between this and the extraction of resources from the vulnerable. When successfully established, public–private partnerships for risk financing are indeed political in nature. However, they are also powerful and can be beneficial to all actors involved, particularly when it comes to highlighting issues such as risk mitigation that require long-term engagement *(The Provention Forum, 2008).*

Upscaling Grassroots Efforts: Opportunities and Challenges

In order to effectively build community perspectives, the reproduction of community based disaster risk management initiatives need to be supported by open and strong systems of governance. Where such systems do not exist, grassroots efforts may be replicated horizontally, or scaled across. Indeed, replication through horizontal learning can also be a strategy where inclusive governance is strong. Both strategies face challenges in terms of finding actors to mobilize joint actions, as well as a lack of long-term financial, political and social support for learning. However, it is thought that the benefits are greatly enhanced once the capacity to communicate information on, and react to, risk are increased *(The Provention Forum, 2008).* Ways forward include gathering data on the past benefits of scaling-up or -across, and lessons learned on techniques for achieving and maintaining these goals. Experience shows that success is most likely when communities and governments work together, sometimes assisted by external actors, or where strong community-based networks are in place.

Developing a New Generation of Disaster Risk Reduction Champions

A new generation of disaster risk reduction champions is emerging as a result of increased awareness of disaster risk and the availability of supporting programs, which develop interest and knowledge in the field. Despite the evolving nature of the disaster risk reduction field, new actors face challenges when it comes to integrating their interests and ideas into the current disaster risk reduction debate. More opportunities are needed for new actors to become involved with established actors and organizations, be it on the ground, within academia, or in professional, public, private and civil society organizations. This provides a wider opportunity to integrate thinking between academia and practice around the world *(The Provention Forum, 2008).* Conversations on the fringes of meetings can be as informative as program sessions, and the ProVention Forum is no exception. This section tries to capture the gist of these conversations through interviews with participants. There was broad support for greater engagement with local actors in disaster risk reduction and, more broadly, for cultural sensitivity in planning and implementing disaster risk reduction programs. However, it was also recognized that this requires political will. One participant noted that governments should pay communities to promote disaster risk reduction efforts, if it can be proved that activities effectively reduce risk. Attendees noted a clear change of direction in the disaster risk reduction discourse, which is beginning to reflect the needs and involvement of the South, the building of bottom-up initiatives, and actions being taken not just to disseminate information to communities, but also to stimulate debate on risk at a local level around the world. Challenges facing the disaster risk reduction agenda include the proliferation of jargon. However, as one participant noted, if we understand the culture and values of the communities in which we are working, we will always find ways to communicate. Other concerns include how to make disaster risk reduction more fashionable and how to hold media attention beyond the emergency phase. Future challenges include the growing synergy between conflict, displacement and environmental change.

The 2008 forum continued in the tradition of ProVention to seek ways of extending access to all stakeholders. The location in Panama was particularly significant when it came to incorporating representatives from indigenous groups. As in previous years, local government and national government were less represented than donor governments. ProVention was challenged to continue to lead the way on research and policy development by opening up new agendas for disaster risk reduction. It was also asked to make the most of its reputation as a bridge between stakeholders. This would enable it to engage with emerging interests in disaster risk reduction such as the military and new themes such as changes to mechanisms used in the disbursement and management of bilateral and multilateral aid *(The Provention Forum, 2008).*

Conclusion

This significant chapter addresses the international perspectives of different disasters, its impacts and also its management aspects. Nevertheless to say that, every disaster leaves larger volume of effects in various spheres of social and economic life. And it is inevitable to understand how the international community is responding to disasters, the strategies and actions carried out to fight or survive or reduce the impact of the disasters. Each country has its own wings to tackle humanitarian crisis. The entire sessions of this chapter clearly reveals the role of different stake holders in responding during disasters and post disaster context. The case studies and experiences of the various agencies and the role of international communities are well mentioned in the chapter. No doubt, disasters keep on occurring around the globe without any discrimination, the coordinated, systematical and participatory actions are necessary to tackle this crisis which largely affects the most deprived sections of the society as well as the general community. Past experiences especially related to a country like Japan proved well-coordinated efforts from all the major stakeholders helped to control the situation and improve the quality of the life of the affected population.

We need to take a common-sense, practical approach to reducing the risks we face and protecting our citizens and our communities. "We need to identify our risks, educate and communicate to our people about those risks, prepare as best we can for the risks, and then, together, form partnerships to take action to reduce those risks. This approach applies whether we are dealing with flood, a tornado, a hazardous materials spill, a wildfire, a potential suicide bomb explosion, or a pandemic flu outbreak" *(Federal Emergency Management Agency (FEMA).*

Notes

1. Natural disasters such as earthquakes, tsunamis, and floods can often come at the least expected time. Others, such as hurricanes and cyclones are increasing in severity and destruction. Typically, the poor are the worst hit for they have the least resources to cope and rebuild. This part of the globalissues.org web site looks at some of these issues. Shah, Anup. "Natural Disasters." Global Issues. 06 Apr. 2011. Web. 06 Jun. 2012.
2. The ProVention Consortium is a global partnership of governments, international organizations, academic organizations, the private sector and civil society. Its goal is to support developing countries to reduce the risk and social, economic and environmental impacts of natural hazards on vulnerable populations. The ProVention Forum 2008 had the theme of 'From Grassroots to Global: People-Centered Disaster Risk Reduction'. The forum was held in Panama City between April 8 and 10, 2008 and brought together 170 partners. The ProVention Forum is designed to allow free talking and frank exchange of ideas, challenges and innovation on disaster risk reduction. The aim of this forum report is to record the energy, ideas and views resulting from discussions and presentations in the formal sessions and also in the corridors of the event.
3. Global Disasters Watch: Monitoring natural disasters: climate change, cyclones, drought, earthquakes, flooding, freak waves, hurricanes, landslides, meteor strikes, mystery booms/sky-quakes, pandemics, record-breaking disasters, solar flares, space weather, tropical storms, tsunamis, volcanoes, unusual animal behavior, weather extremes, wildfires; disaster archives from 1998-present.
4. Japan Earthquake Report, July 28, 2011, Japan Earthquake Report was written by a British private firm. It is 38 pages. The subtitle is "A Preliminary Briefing on the Japanese Government's Disaster Response Management." The events in

Japan in March 2011, involving an earthquake and subsequent tsunami, fell exactly within the risk profile of Japan's disaster management programme, and there were no contributing factors to the disaster that could not or should not have been predicted and accounted for. The current document clearly describes some observations of the disaster response programmes of Japan subsequent to the recent earthquake disaster (Long-term recovery from disasters, Recovery Diva).

5. Journal of Integrated Disaster Risk Management- The IDRiM Journal builds upon the existing international and interdisciplinary network fostered by the IDRiM Forum attracting high quality manuscripts of validated, real world cases of successful integrated disaster risk management practices and research. Currently there is an open call for manuscripts on research and implementation cases studies on Integrated Disaster Risk Management from researchers and practitioners from around the world (Vol 1, No 2 (2011).
6. Dr. Sheonandan Pandey is a China watcher with a long stint in the Government of India and finally retied from National Technical Research Organization. Guest Column by the author, Paper No: 2922, Meteorological and Seismological Disasters and the Chinese Emergency Response Mechanism. This article, in its perspective, delves into the working of the Chinese Disaster Management Mechanism, and would crystallize, in particular, the efficacy of the system in the emergency response phase. The broad assumptions include: First, China is prone to natural and manmade disasters; Second, China has of late put in place a nearly comprehensive disaster management system; and, the latest events of natural disaster have put the efficacy of the system to litmus test. The hypothesis includes: the Chinese system, while well-articulated and orchestrated, it lacked vital hinge of broad based people participation; the Chinese system, put to ground test in 2008, showed a measure of fragility and indecisiveness at middle and lower levels of bureaucratic and political management even though high level bureaucratic and political management exhibited strong and determined bid to tide over the scenario; and, the Chinese system, in overall perspective, borders on traditional pattern. Applying an eclectic methodological option, the paper goes to present a mirror view of the efficacy of the Chinese disaster management system, as deduced from on ground scenario in the management of first, the '2008 Snow Disaster' and second, the '2008 Wenchuan Earthquake Disaster'. The paper is sequenced to focus: the Decision Matrix; the 2008 Snow Disaster and the Working of the System; the 2008 Wenchuan Earthquake and the Working of the System.
7. Emergency Management is the generic name of an interdisciplinary field dealing with the strategic organizational management processes used to protect critical assets of an organization from hazard risks that can cause events like disasters or catastrophes and to ensure the resiliency of the organization within their planned lifetime. Haddow, George D. Jane A Bullock (2003), Introduction to Emergency Management. Amsterdam: Butterworth-Heinemann, ISBN 0-7506-7689-2.
8. Asian Disaster Preparedness Center (ADPC): As a leading regional resource center, ADPC works towards the realization of disaster reduction for safer communities and sustainable development in Asia and the Pacific. Since its inception in 1986, ADPC has been recognized as the major independent center

in the region for promoting disaster awareness and the development of local capabilities to foster institutionalized disaster management and mitigation policies. Bangkok, Thailand. At the recommendation of UN Disaster Relief Organization (UNDRO) - now known as UN Office for the Coordination of Humanitarian Affairs (UN-OCHA) - ADPC was established in 1986 as an outreach activity of the Asian Institute of Technology in Bangkok, Thailand, with the aim of strengthening the national disaster risk management systems in the region. In 1999, ADPC became an independent entity, which is governed and guided by a Board of Trustees (21 members representing 15 countries) and advised by a Regional Consultative Committee (32 members from 26 countries) and Advisory Council (55 members from a wide range of agencies).

9. United Nations Centre for Regional Development (UNCRD), which was established in 1971 based on an agreement between the Government of Japan and the United Nations, strives to promote sustainable regional development in developing countries with a focus on development planning and management in the context of globalization and decentralization trends, and the growing concern towards global environmental issues and their impacts. UNCRD, which was established in 1971 based on an agreement between the Government of Japan and the United Nations, strives to promote sustainable regional development in developing countries with a focus on development planning and management in the context of globalization and decentralization trends, and the growing concern towards global environmental issues and their impacts.

10. China's Space Infrastructure: Ground Test of China's Space Based Infrastructure and Wenchuan Earthquake Management, Ó Dr. Sheo Nandan Pandey 2009.This paper is part of a series to focus working efficacy of Chinese state machinery in different fields. The People's Republic of China (PRC) has consistently been improving its space based infrastructure. In 28 years since the first successful launch of Dong Fang Hong-1 Satellite into orbit on 24 April 1970, the PRC has demonstrably scaled many a reckonable technological steps. The space missions that the PRC launches today include: recovery capsules and non-capsule remote sensing satellites; communication/broadcasting satellites; metrological satellites; science satellites; engineering test satellites; positioning satellites; and, manned space satellites. China's goals and objectives for going into orbit with a variety of space assets including manned are predictably similar to those that drove the Russian and the US to gain national prestige, and to signal wealth, commitments and technological prowess. Development of space infrastructure has wide ranging applications, which includes meeting environmental challenges. The People's Republic of China (PRC) is deepening reforms; transforming its economic structure; and rebalancing growth toward a consumption-driven, service-oriented, and environmentally sustainable economy. The country's growing importance in the global economy and increased emphasis on rebalancing growth require ADB to ensure its operations are relevant and responsive to the country's needs and add value to its future development.

11. An Overview of Disaster Management: 2nd edition. This training module has been produced for the UNDP/UNDRO Disaster Management Training Programme by the University of Wisconsin Disaster Management Center. The Technical Operational Partners for the DMTP provided valuable advice on the

format and content. The principal sources for the content include the UNDP/UNDRO Disaster Manual and six complementary training modules prepared for the DMTP. Intersect Training Services has edited the material and prepared the educational components. An Overview of Disaster Management: 2nd edition. This training module has been produced for the UNDP/UNDRO Disaster Management Training Programme by the University of Wisconsin Disaster Management Center. The Technical Operational Partners for the DMTP provided valuable advice on the format and content. The principal sources for the content include the UNDP/UNDRO Disaster Manual and six complementary training modules prepared for the DMTP. Intersect Training Services has edited the material and prepared the educational components.

Chapter – 3

Disaster Management in India

(1) Overview

India has been traditionally vulnerable to natural disasters on account of its unique geo-climatic conditions. Floods, droughts, cyclones, earthquakes and landslides have been recurrent phenomena. About 60% of the landmass is prone to earthquakes of various intensities; over 40 million hectares is prone to floods; about 8% of the total area is prone to cyclones and 68% of the area is susceptible to drought. Along with China, Indonesia and Bangladesh in 2009, India occupied the fourth position in ranking of regular occurrence of natural disasters. Since 1900 to 2011, India has faced 590 natural disasters. In 2009, 1806 people were killed, 9.0 million people were affected by 15 natural disasters that occurred in India. Economic losses due to disasters in the year 2009 in India were estimated to be 2.7 billion USD *(Social Work Chronicle, 2012)*[1]. According to Disaster Mitigation Institute (DMI), India suffers considerably due to disasters, as about two per cent of its gross domestic product (GDP) is lost due to natural disaster. Of the 35 States and Union Territories in India, 27 are disaster prone areas (*Govt of India, Natural Disasters in India, 1900 to 2011)*. The unique geo-climatic conditions have made India highly vulnerable to natural disasters. Floods, droughts cyclones, earthquakes and landslides have been recurrent hazardous phenomena in India. Rajasthan is the most drought prone state of India. Cyclones are other hazards in India that generally strike the East Coast. However, some of the Arabian Sea Cyclones strike the west coast of India, mainly the Gujarat and North Maharashtra coast. Out of the storms that develop in the Bay of Bengal, more than half approach or cross the east coast in October and November. The Himalayan and sub-Himalayan regions, Kutch and the Andaman and Nicobar Islands are particularly earthquake hazard prone (*Gupta, K, 2009).*

Apart from natural disasters, human made disasters like conflicts, communal riots and refugee situations, road accidents and other disasters like fire, epidemics, industrial and transport disasters leave a long trail of mortality and morbidity *(Dutt B, 2007)*. Nevertheless, more recently urban India is facing major crisis with the increasing incidences of manmade disasters. Horrifying events like blasts that shattered Delhi, the capital city in 2005 leading to 62 casualties, series of bomb blasts in local trains in Mumbai in 2006 killing 209 lives and the terrorist attacks in 2008 have caused an economic loss of nearly Rs 40,000 million *(Social Work Chronicle, 2012)*.

(2) Natural Disasters in India (1900-2011) Statistical Analysis

The occurrence of natural disasters increased after 2002, as out of 590 disasters 27% (159) disasters struck post 2002 *(The International Disaster Database (EMDAT, 2010,* India)[2] Climate change, increasing urbanization, including growing concentrations of people in unplanned and unsafe urban settlements and exposed coastal areas, poverty, HIV prevalence, and inadequate attention to changing risk patterns, are placing more and more people in disaster-prone locations. In addition to this absence of disaster preparedness is seen as a major reason for larger number and greater impact of natural disasters.

Table 3.1: Disaster Statistic

Disasters	*Number of Events*	*Number of people killed*	*Total Affected*	*Damage in (000 US$)*
Drought	14	42, 50, 320	106,18,41,000	24,41,122
Earthquake (seismic activity)	26	78,094	2,79,19,695	51,02,700
Epidemic	68	45,43,874	4,21,473	NA
Extreme temperature	47	13.801	250	5,44,000
Insect infestation	235	60,188	79,86,54,220	3,41,45,188
Mass movement dry	1	45	0	0
Mass Movement wet	42	4762	38,39,116	54,500
Storm	154	1,64,179	9,32,94,512	1,10,51,900
Wildfire	2	6	0	2000
Total	***590***	***91,15,269***	***198,59,70,266***	***5,33,41,410***

Source: EM-DAT: The OFDA/CRED International Disaster Database, 2011.

Situation in Maharashtra

According to Vulnerability Atlas of India, in Maharashtra, 14 districts and 7 cities have been identified as disaster prone. The State is prone to various natural disasters such as drought, floods, cyclones, earthquake and accidents. While low rainfall areas of the state are under the constant risk of droughts, high rainfall zones of eastern and western Maharashtra are prone to flash floods and landslides. Many areas of the State have faced droughts for consecutive years, which damaged agriculture and caused water shortage in more than 20,000 villages. Floods, though, are not a regular phenomenon, took 180 lives in 1996 and, more recently, in July 2005, about 900 people died in the Konkan Region due heavy rainfall of about 37 inches.

Mumbai is India's most populous conurbation and the third most populous agglomeration in the world *(UNFPA, 2006)*. The population has increased from 11.9 million (Census 2001) to 18.84 million in 2006 (UNFPA). Though Mumbai contributes the largest share of GDP (6.16%) 31, more than half of its inhabitants (54.5%) live in slums *(Singh, D.P., 2009)*. Certain regions in Mumbai are identified for high fire risk due to old timber framed buildings and also because establishment of oil refineries in the area. Chembur-Trombay belt of almost 10 kms has concentration of hazardous industries which is highly prone to industrial accidents (33Relief and Rehabilitation, Government of Maharashtra, 2007). Hence, geographic conditions, industrial growth, increasing population density and squatter settlements have increased Mumbai's vulnerability to disasters. Fire and industrial accidents, floods, chemical (transport and handling), biological, and nuclear hazards, earthquake, cyclones, landslides, bomb blasts, terrorism, riots and tidal surge have been identified as major hazards in Mumbai *(Social Work Chronicle, 2012)*.

The United Nations Intergovernmental Panel on Climate Change (IPCC) recently announced Mumbai being at the risk zone for disasters. According to Shaw (2009), the overall climate-disaster resilience is relatively low for Mumbai City. Gaps in the early warning system and evacuation, internal road network, solid waste disposal and water supply will have tremendous effects on the city's resilience to disasters. Being the commercial capital of the country, Mumbai faces major challenges of manmade disasters. The city has witnessed a couple of terrorist attacks since 1993, which have led to serious social and economic disruptions in addition to loss of life and property. It can be surmised from the above discussion that disasters undermine development achievements, impoverishing people and nations. Destruction of social and economic assets, loss of production capacity, livelihood, damage to transport, communications, erosion of physical as well as social capital, limit the development process. Recurrent occurrence of disasters in under developed countries forces diversion of development funds and investment to handle the emergencies. In the absence of concerned efforts to address root causes, disasters represent an increasingly serious obstacle to the achievement of the Millennium Development Goals (MDGs). For instance, displacement of population further interrupts schooling which can be seen as direct impact of disasters. Reduction in household assets could also lead to less affordability to avail educational facilities. This creates hindrance in attaining MDG of achieving universal primary education *(Social Work Chronicle, 2012).*

In the decade 1990-2000, an average of about 4344 people lost their lives and about 30 million people were affected by disasters every year. The loss in terms of private, community and public assets has been astronomical *(Ministry of Home Affairs, Government of India, 2004).* In contrast, between 1988 and 1997, disasters killed 5,116 people and affected 24.79 million every year. In 1988, 11.2 % of total land area was flood prone, but in 1998 floods inundated 37% geographical area *(Reports, GOI, 2004).*

The Indian sub continent is highly prone to natural disasters. Floods, droughts, cyclones and earthquakes are a recurrent phenomenon in India. Susceptibility to disasters is compounded by frequent occurrences of manmade disasters such as fire and epidemics. Frequent disasters lead to erosion of development gains and restricted options for the disaster victims. Physical safety-especially that of the vulnerable groups-is routinely threatened by hazards. The super cyclone in Orissa in October, 1999 and the Bhuj earthquake in Gujarat in January, 2001 underscored the need to adopt a multi-dimensional endeavour involving diverse scientific, engineering, financial and social processes; the need to adopt multi disciplinary and multi-sectoral approach and incorporation of risk reduction in the developmental plans and strategies. These two major disasters have very clearly illustrated that we need multi-hazard prevention, response and recovery plans for natural hazards so that threat to human life and property is minimized *(Reports, GOI, 2004).*

The natural and man-made disasters and crises create hardships for the poor, who are chronically vulnerable in terms of their access to resources, entitlements and livelihood support. In fact, the lives of people in the hazard-prone regions, particularly the poor, are almost completely insecure *(Dreze & Sen*, 1988). Irrespective of the type of disaster, it is mostly the poor who are the worst sufferers. According to a study *(Sudhir, 2001)* conducted in the 2001 earthquake-affected areas in Gujarat, most of the victims of the quake were the poor, comprising the landless households, rural artisans, and SC and ST people. Therefore, the poor should be the focal target group for disaster management. Effective disaster management requires a multi-sectoral, multi-disciplinary, and holistic approach, encompassing pre-disaster preparedness initiatives, disaster response, and post-disaster rehabilitation, all with active participation of local people living in hazard-prone regions *(Singh & Ballabh, 2004).*

It is an irony that in many parts of India, we have droughts and in many others, we have floods occurring almost concurrently every year. Yet, this kind of risk is not even recognized in India's policies and plans, not to speak of the absence of any national policy for disaster management. It is a sad commentary that despite several programmes launched by the Government of India (GOI) from time to time for minimizing their adverse impacts, natural disasters such as droughts, floods, and cyclones continue to haunt almost every year affecting millions of people living in disaster-prone areas of India and unfortunately, there is no national policy on disaster management. Irrespective of the type of disaster, it is mostly the poor who are the worst sufferers *(Reports, Government of India, 2004).* Disaster risk management is essentially a developmental problem and thus any preparedness and mitigation planning will have to be taken up in tandem with environmental concerns that the country is facing today.

Disasters disrupt progress and destroy the hard-earned fruits of painstaking developmental efforts, often pushing nations, in quest for progress, back by several decades. Thus, efficient management of disasters, rather than mere response to their occurrence has, in recent times, received increased attention both within India and abroad. This is as much a result of the recognition of the increasing frequency and intensity of disasters as it is an acknowledgement that good governance, in a caring and civilized society, needs to deal effectively with the devastating impact of disasters *(NPDM, 2005).*

The Government of India has set up a National Committee on Disaster Management (NCDM) under the Chairmanship of the Prime Minister. The recommendations of this National Committee would form the basis of national disaster risk management programme and strengthening the natural disaster management and response mechanisms. The High Powered Committee [HPC] on Disaster Management was earlier constituted in August 1999. The mandate of the HPC was to prepare Disaster Management Plans at National, State and District level and also suggest strengthening of existing arrangements. The recommendations of the HPC relating to the distribution of relief and human resource development that primarily concerns the States have been communicated to the States for appropriate action *(Reports, GOI, 2004)*.

The Ministry of Home Affairs in the National Government is the new nodal ministry for disaster management. In addition, disaster management is deemed to be a 'state subject' and different states have initiated efforts to strengthen their agencies responsible for disaster management. Orissa State Disaster Mitigation Authority (OSDMA)[3] and Gujarat State Disaster Management Authority (GSDMA)[4] were constituted after two major disasters that the respective states experienced. At present, the majority of states and union territories have set up their own disaster management authority to manage and monitor disasters in their respective regions. The programmes formulated by the disaster management authority essentially aims at strengthening community, local self-governments and district administrations' response, preparedness and mitigation measures in some of the most vulnerable districts *(Vulnerability Atlas, Govt of India, 2007)* along with states' and national response. The key element of this programme is establishing linkages between the Government and civil society response plans and capacity building of government institutions and the local self-governments in disaster mitigation, preparedness and recovery (*Vulnerability Atlas, Govt of India, 2007)*[5].

Over the past couple of years, the Government of India has brought about a paradigm shift in the approach to disaster management. The new approach proceeds from the conviction that development cannot be sustainable unless disaster mitigation is built into the development process. Another corner stone of the approach is that mitigation has to be multi-disciplinary spanning across all sectors of development. The new policy also emanates from the belief that investments in mitigation are much more cost effective than expenditure on relief and rehabilitation. The present disaster management program envisioned by the government of India reflects this paradigm shift. Panchayati Raj and Urban Planning Institutions at all levels in the selected districts would be directly involved in the planning process to ensure sustainability of these initiatives. A wide representation of women is envisaged in this project during the planning process. Self help groups of women in the programme areas would be directly involved in the disaster risk management programme. This project will work closely with the relevant Government departments and institutions at the national and State levels. Learning from this programme will feed into the national capacity building programmes of the Government of India, and the global knowledge base on disaster risk management *(Disaster Information's, GOI, 2007).*

Disaster management occupies an important place in this country's policy framework as it is the poor and the under-privileged who are the worst affected on account of calamities/disasters. The steps being taken by the Government emanate from the approach outlined above. The approach has been translated into a National Disaster Framework [a roadmap] covering institutional mechanisms, disaster prevention strategy, early warning system, disaster mitigation, preparedness and response and human resource development. The expected inputs, areas of intervention and agencies to be involved at the National, State and district levels have been identified and listed in the roadmap. This roadmap has been shared with all the State Governments and Union Territory Administrations. Ministries and Departments of Government of India, and the State Governments/UT Administrations have been advised to develop their respective roadmaps taking the national roadmap as a broad guideline. There is, therefore, now a common strategy underpinning the action being taken by all the participating organizations/stakeholders *(Disaster Reports, GOI, 2007).* However, critics *(Muricken & Kumar, 2007)* of India's disaster management plan argues that lessons are learnt at great cost in India, as the knowledge attained from previous disasters is seldom reflected in the overall policy framework or in planning.

The lessons learnt from the Orissa Super cyclone of 1999, the Latur and Gujarat earthquakes of 1993 and 2001, respectively, and other similar disasters have failed to induce a paradigm shift in our approach to disaster mitigation. Nor have we learnt lessons as to how to cope well with the disaster demands- of regulating communities for safety, protecting the vulnerable people especially in the areas exposed to disaster, empowering people's organizations for transparency and decision- making, and the right of the affected communities to necessary information *(Reports, GOI, 2007).*

(3) Paradigm Shift in Disaster Management in India

India was, until recently, reactive and only responded to disasters and provided relief from calamity. The recurrent occurrences of different types of disasters compelled Government of India to take cognizance of the objectives of International Decade for Natural Disaster Reduction (1990-2000), Yokohama Strategy for safer world (1994)[6] and the Plan of Action for Safer World (Istanbul, 1996)[7], and set up a High Power Committee on

Disaster Management (HPC) in 1999 to recommend strategies for preparation of Disaster Management plans. The High Power Committee gave its recommendations in October 2001 including a draft of the Disaster Management Act, a National Response Plan, and establishment of National Disaster Management Authority. Following one of the HPC recommendations, the Disaster Management function was transferred from Ministry of Agriculture to Ministry of Home Affairs.

The occurrence of tsunami in the Indian Ocean in 2004 and its consequential impact heightened the level of awareness of the Government about the importance of integrating disaster risk reduction into national development planning and the need for aligning and coordinating with UN agencies and other UN Member States to respond to the threat of disasters. Based on the recommendations of HPC, UN agencies and Hyogo Framework of Action 39, the Government of India has brought about a paradigm shift in its relief centric to responsive and preparedness approach to disaster management.

The new approach proceeds from the conviction that development cannot be sustainable unless disaster mitigation is built into the development process. The focus is now more on disaster risk assessment, preparedness and mitigation. This paradigm shift reinforces that disasters can be managed through adequate planning and preparedness for response *(Guzman, 2005)*.

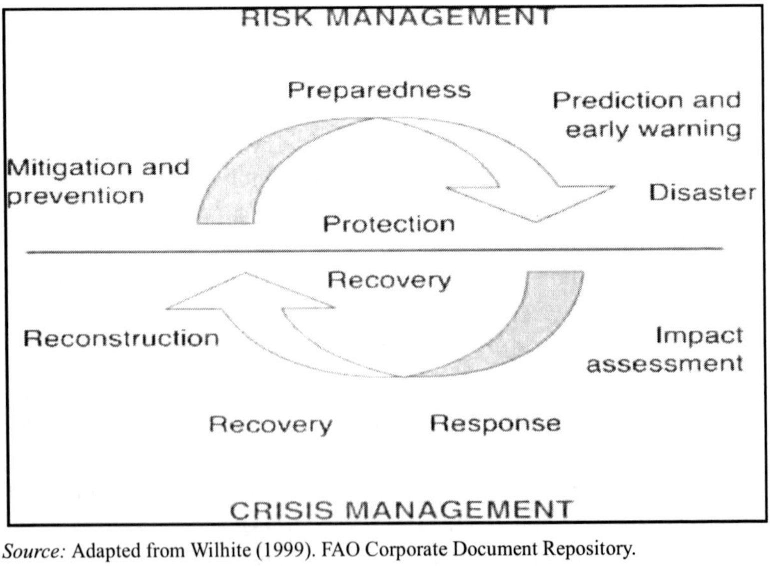

Source: Adapted from Wilhite (1999). FAO Corporate Document Repository.

Disaster, Risk and Crisis Management Cycle

The new approach also emanates from the belief that investments in mitigation are much more cost effective than expenditure on relief and rehabilitation. The most noteworthy step in this direction has been the passage of the National Disaster Management Act. The National Disaster Management Authority (NDMA) instituted under the Act work's in accordance with all other institutions spread across the country to anticipate the disaster and prevent it from causing huge damage. In keeping with this shift, new institutional mechanisms are being put in place at the State and District levels as well. The changed approach is being put into effect through:

- Institutional changes
- Enunciation of policy
- Legal and techno-legal framework
- Mainstreaming Mitigation into Development process
- Funding mechanism
- Specific schemes addressing mitigation
- Preparedness measures
- Capacity building
- Human Resource Development
- Community participation

The lessons learnt from the past clearly bring out the fact that no State/ Central Government can meet the disaster management challenges alone. The Governments' efforts have to be strengthened by a host of private sector organizations and communities themselves getting involved in the emergency response system *(Social Work Chronicle, 2012).*

(4) Institutional and Policy Framework / Mechanisms

The Historical Backdrop

Government intervention in the form of relief measures in the years of droughts and famines are a long history in India going back to the late 19th century, when the then British Government of India formulated a Famine Code specifying what is to be done by whom and under what circumstances. Following the Famine Code, every State (then Provincial) government formulated its own relief manual. The relief manuals of the states provide for provision of employment or relief only on a spasmodic basis. Yet even the colonial rulers recognized that there was a continuum of agricultural distress and that the timing of such intervention could not be accurately determined. They specified that this distress directly related to the fact that the wages offered did not command the purchasing power necessary for the sustenance of the affected people. They acknowledged that the present system of relief could only be looked upon as a temporary measure, which would have to be set aside later and replaced by more systematic measures. However, the ad hoc nature of relief has persisted. Since the Indian state provides no social security or unemployment relief, the official declaration of drought or flood continues to be the sole means of mitigating their harmful effects.

Current Policies and Strategies

However, despite its importance, the subject of disaster management does not find any mention in any of the three lists included in the 7th Schedule of the Constitution of India, i.e., List I: the Union List, List II: the State List, and List III: the Concurrent List. As per Entry 97 of the Union List, the Union government should deal with this subject. However, in practice, it is a state subject. In view of this dichotomy, a lot of confusion exists when it comes to pinpointing specific responsibilities for dealing with various problems. Recently, the Constitutional Review Committee has recommended that disaster management be included in the Concurrent List of the Constitution (List III). Besides, there is no specific legislation to provide an appropriate legal framework for disaster management, and the existing codes/regulations are not enforced strictly and the adoption of various standards and guidelines is not mandatory. In view of this, it is necessary to review the existing laws/codes/regulations relating to various aspects of disaster management and evolve a suitable mechanism for their strict enforcement preferably through a Central Act and State Acts as recommended by the High Powered Committee on Disaster Management.

Furthermore, there is no integrated programme for disaster management. What we have is an assortment of several projects and programmes that aim at reducing the vulnerability of people to disasters. Some of those programmes are: Integrated Rural Development Programme (IADP), Drought Prone Area programme (DPAP), Integrated Wastelands Development Programme (IWDP), Desert Development Programme (DDP), Flood Control Programmes, National Afforestation and Eco-development Programme (NA&ED), Accelerated Rural Water Supply Programme (ARWSP), Indira Awas Yojana (IAY), National Agricultural Insurance Scheme, Crop Insurance Scheme, Sampoorna Grameen Rozgar Yojana (SGRY), and Disaster Risk Management Programme. Most of these programmes have the rural poor as their main target group and hence they may be called pro-poor. Until recently, disaster management was not conceptually linked with developmental planning in India. It was only in the 10th Five Year Plan that it was mainstreamed into the planning process and a separate chapter on Disaster Management was included in it. But even now, there is no long-term strategy for mitigation and development of hazard prone areas for disaster reduction. The Eleventh Finance Commission has suggested that this task needs to be addressed by the Planning Commission, which in consultation with the state governments, and the concerned ministries of Government of India should identify works of capital nature to prevent the recurrence of specific calamities, to be financed under planned funds *(Reports, Govt of India, 2009).*

Institutional and policy mechanisms for carrying out response, relief and rehabilitation have been well-established since Independence. These mechanisms have proved to be robust and effective as response, relief and rehabilitation are concerned. At the national level, the Ministry of Home Affairs is the nodal Ministry for all matters concerning disaster management. The Central Relief Commissioner (CRC) in the Ministry of Home Affairs is the nodal officer to coordinate relief operations for natural disasters. The CRC receives information relating to forecasting/warning of a natural calamity from India Meteorological Department (IMD) or from Central Water Commission of Ministry of Water Resources on a continuing basis. The Ministries/Departments/ Organizations concerned with the primary and secondary functions relating to the management of disasters include: India Meteorological Department, Central Water Commission, Ministry of Home Affairs, Ministry of Defense, Ministry of Finance, Ministry of Rural Development, Ministry of Urban Development, Department of Communications, Ministry of Health, Ministry of Water Resources, Ministry of Petroleum, Department of Agriculture & Cooperation. Ministry of Power, Department of Civil Supplies, Ministry of Railways, Ministry of Information and Broadcasting, Planning Commission, Cabinet Secretariat, Department of Surface Transport, Ministry of Social Justice, Department of Women and Child Development, Ministry of Environment and Forest, Department of Food. Each Ministry/Department/Organization nominates their nodal officer to the Crisis Management Group chaired by Central Relief Commissioner. The nodal officer is responsible for preparing sectoral Action Plan/Emergency Support Function Plan for managing disasters *(Reports, Govt of India, 2009).*

Disaster Management Framework in India

The National Institute of Disaster Management (NIDM) is set up by GOI in order to develop specially trained personnel to develop capacities of

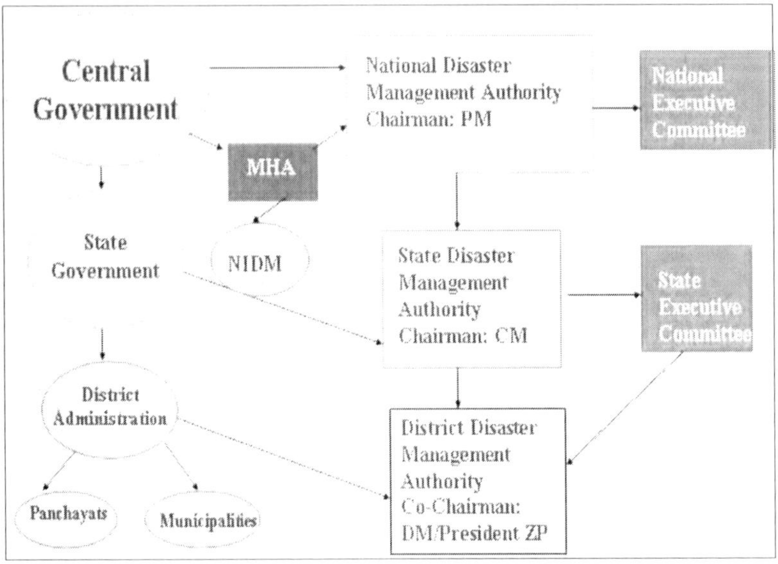

Source: Kumar, S. (2007). Disaster Management Framework, India.

communities and organizations to build a culture of disaster preparedness through training programmes and research. In this context the Eleventh Five Year Plan gives impetus on addressing disaster risk reduction through education at various levels as one of the priority of all development programmes. An allocation of Rs 2,13,880/- million towards disaster management has been incorporated in the Eleventh Plan.

National Crisis Management Committee (NCMC): Cabinet Secretary, who is the highest executive officer, heads the NCMC. Secretaries of all the concerned Ministries /Departments as well as organizations are the members of the Committee. The NCMC gives direction to the Crisis Management Group as deemed necessary. The Secretary, Ministry of Home Affairs is responsible for ensuring that all developments are brought to the notice of the NCMC promptly. The NCMC can give directions to any Ministry/Department/Organization for specific action needed for meeting the crisis situation *(Disaster Management in India, 2004)*[8]

Crisis Management Group (CMG): The Central Relief Commissioner in the Ministry of Home Affairs is the Chairman of the CMG, consisting of senior officers (called nodal officer's) from various concerned Ministries. The CMG's functions are to review every year contingency plans formulated by various Ministries/Departments/Organizations in their respective sectors, measures required for dealing with natural disasters, coordinate the activities of the Central Ministries and the State Governments in relation to disaster preparedness and relief and to obtain information from the nodal officers on measures relating to above. The CMG, in the event of a natural disaster, meets frequently to review the relief operations and extend all possible assistance required by the affected States to overcome the situation effectively. The Resident Commissioner of the affected State is also associated with such meetings.

Control Room (Emergency Operation Room): An Emergency Operations Center (Control Room) exists in the nodal Ministry of Home Affairs, which functions round the clock, to assist the Central Relief Commissioner in the discharge of his duties. The activities of the Control Room include collection and transmission of information concerning natural calamity and relief, keeping close contact with governments of the affected States, interaction with other Central Ministries/ Departments/ Organizations in connection with disaster relief, maintaining records containing all relevant information relating to action points and contact points in Central Ministries etc., and keeping up-to-date details of all concerned officers at the Central and State levels *(Status Reports, 2004).*

Contingency Action Plan: A National Contingency Action Plan (CAP) for dealing with contingencies arising in the wake of natural disasters has been formulated by the Government of India and it had been periodically updated. It facilitates the launching of relief operations without delay. The CAP identifies the initiatives required to be taken by various Central Ministries/Departments in the wake of natural calamities, sets down the procedure and determines the focal points in the administrative machinery.

State Relief Manuals: Each State Government has relief manuals/ codes which identify that role of each officer in the State for managing the natural disasters. These are reviewed and updated periodically based on the experience of managing the disasters and the need of the State *(Disaster Management in India, 2004).*

Funding Mechanisms: The policy and the funding mechanism for provision of relief assistance to those affected by natural calamities are clearly laid down. These are reviewed by the Finance Commission appointed by the Government of India every five years. The Finance Commission makes recommendation regarding the division of tax and non-tax revenues between the Central and the State Governments and also regarding policy for provision of relief assistance and their share of expenditure thereon. A Calamity Relief Fund (CRF) has been set up in each State as per the recommendations of the Eleventh Finance Commission. The size of the Calamity Relief Fund has been fixed by the Finance Commission after taking into account the expenditure on relief and rehabilitation over the past 10 years. The Government of India contributes 75% of the corpus of the Calamity Relief Fund in each State. Twenty five percent is contributed to by the State. Relief assistance to those affected by natural calamities is granted from the CRF. Overall norms for relief assistance are laid down by a national committee with representatives of States as members. Different States can have State specific norms to be recommended by State level committee under the Chief Secretary. Where the calamity is of such proportion that the funds available in the CRF will not be sufficient for provision of relief, the State seeks assistance from the National Calamity Contingency Fund (NCCF) - a fund created at the Central Government level. When such requests are received, the requirements are assessed by a team from the Central Government and thereafter the assessed requirements are cleared by a High Level Committee chaired by the Deputy Prime Minister. In brief, the institutional arrangements for response and relief are well established and have proved to be robust and effective *(Disaster Management in India, 2004).*

In the federal set up of India, the basic responsibility for undertaking rescue, relief and rehabilitation measures in the event of a disaster is that of the State Government concerned. At the State level, response, relief and rehabilitation are handled by Departments of Relief & Rehabilitation. The State Crisis Management Committee set up under the Chairmanship of Chief Secretary who is the highest executive functionary in the State. All the concerned Departments and organizations of the State and Central Government Departments located in the State are represented in this Committee. This Committee reviews the action taken for response and relief and gives guidelines/directions as necessary. A control room is established under the Relief Commissioner. The control room is in constant touch with the climate monitoring/forecasting agencies and monitors the action being taken by various agencies in performing their responsibilities. The district level is the key level for disaster management and relief activities. The Collector/Dy. Commissioner is the chief administrator in the district. He is the focal point in the preparation of district plans and in directing, supervising and monitoring calamities for relief. A District Level Coordination and Relief Committee is constituted and is headed by the Collector as Chairman with participation of all other related government and non-governmental agencies and departments in addition to the elected representatives *(Disaster Management in India, 2004).*

The Collector is required to maintain close liaison with the district and the State Governments as well as the nearest units of Armed Forces/Central police organizations and other relevant Central Government organizations like Ministries of Communications, Water Resources, Drinking Water, and Surface Transport, who could supplement the efforts of the district administration in the rescue and relief operations. The efforts of the Government and non-governmental organisations for response and relief and coordinated by the Collector/Dy. Commissioner. The District Magistrate/ Collector and Coordination Committee under him reviews preparedness measures prior to an impending hazard and coordinate response when the hazard strikes. As all the Departments of the State Government and district level report to the Collector, there is an effective coordination mechanism ensuring holistic response *(National Disaster Management Division, 2004).*

New Institutional Mechanisms

As has been made clear above, the existing mechanisms are based on post-disaster relief and rehabilitation and have proved to be robust and effective mechanisms in addressing these requirements. The changed policy/approach, however, mandates a priority to full disaster aspects of mitigation, prevention and preparedness and new institutional and policy mechanisms are being put in place to address the policy change. The importance of establishing a National Emergency Management Authority at the National level was the need of the hour. Therefore, the High Powered Committee on Disaster Management which was set up in August, 1999 and submitted its Report in October, 2001, had inter alia recommended that a separate Department of Disaster Management be set up in the Government of India. It was, however, felt that conventional Ministries/Departments have the drawback of not being flexible enough especially in terms of the sanction procedures. The organization at the Apex level will have to be multi-disciplinary with experts covering a large number of branches. The National Emergency Management Authority has, therefore, been proposed as a combined Secretariat/ Directorate structure – a structure which will be an integral part of the Government and, therefore, will work with the full authority of the Government while, at the same time, retaining the flexibility of a field organization. The National Emergency Management Authority will be headed by an officer of the rank of Secretary/Special Secretary to the Government in the Ministry of Home Affairs with Special Secretaries/ Additional Secretaries from the Ministries/Departments of Health, Water Resources, Environment & Forests, Agriculture, Railways, Atomic Energy, Defense, Chemicals, Science & Technology, Telecommunications, Urban

Employment and Poverty Alleviation, Rural Development and India Meteorological Department as Members of the Authority. The Authority would meet as often as required and review the status of warning systems, mitigation measures and disaster preparedness. When a disaster strikes, the Authority will coordinate disaster management activities. The Authority will be responsible for: (a) coordinating/mandating Government's policies for disaster reduction/mitigation; (b) ensuring adequate preparedness at all levels in order to meet disasters; (c) coordinating response to a disaster when it strikes; and (d), coordination of post disaster relief and rehabilitation *(National Disaster Management Division, 2004).*

At the State level, disaster management is being handled by the Departments of Relief & Rehabilitation. As the name suggests, the focus was almost entirely on post-calamity relief. The Government of India is working with the State Governments to convert the Departments of Relief & Rehabilitation into Departments of Disaster Management with an enhanced area of responsibility to include mitigation and preparedness apart from their present responsibilities of relief and rehabilitation. The changeover has already happened in eight State Governments/Union Territory Administrations. The change could also be felt in other States. The States have also been asked to set up Disaster Management Authorities under the Chief Minister with Ministers of relevant Departments [Water Resources, Agriculture, Drinking Water Supply, Environment & Forests, Urban Development, Home, Rural Development etc.] as members. The objective of setting up an Authority is to ensure that mitigation and preparedness is seen as the joint responsibility of all the Departments concerned and disaster management concerns are mainstreamed into their programmes. This holistic and multidisciplinary approach is the key to effective mitigation. At the district level, the District Magistrate who is the chief coordinator will be the focal point for coordinating all activities relating to prevention, mitigation and preparedness apart from his existing responsibilities pertaining to response and relief. The District Coordination and Relief Committee is being reconstituted/ re-designated into Disaster Management Committees with officers from relevant departments being added as members. Because of its enhanced mandate of mitigation and prevention, the district heads and departments engaged in development will now be added to the Committee so that mitigation and prevention is mainstreamed into the district plan. The existing system of drawing up preparedness and response plans will continue. There will, however, also be a long term mitigation plan. District Disaster Management Committees have already been constituted in several districts and are in the process of being constituted in the remaining multi-hazard prone districts *(National Disaster Management Division, 2004).*

Similarly, the government is in the process of creating Block/Taluk Disaster Management Committees in these 169 multi-hazard prone districts in 17 States. At the village level, in 169 multi-hazard prone districts, Disaster Management Committees and Disaster Management Teams are being constituted. Each village will have a Disaster Management Plan. The process of drafting the plan has already begun. The Disaster Management Committee which draws up the plans consists of elected representatives at the village level, local authorities, government functionaries including doctors/ paramedics of primary health centers located in the village, and primary school teachers. The plan encompasses prevention, mitigation and preparedness measures. The Disaster Management Teams at the village level will consist of members of voluntary organisations such as Nehru Yuvak Kendra and other non-governmental organisations as well as able bodied volunteers from the village. The teams are provided basic training in evacuation, search, rescue, and various other aspects of disaster management. The Disaster Management Committee will review the disaster management plan at least once in a year. It would also generate awareness among the people in the village about dos' and don'ts for specific hazards depending on the vulnerability of the village. A large number of village level Disaster Management Committees and Disaster Management Teams have already been constituted. The States have been advised to enact Disaster Management Acts. These Acts provide for adequate powers for authorities coordinating mitigation, preparedness and response as well as for mitigation/ prevention measures required to be undertaken. Two States [Gujarat & Madhya Pradesh] have already enacted such a law. Other States are in the process. The State Governments have also been advised to convert their Relief Codes into Disaster Management Codes by including aspects of prevention, mitigation and preparedness.

In order to further institutionalize the new approach, the Government of India have decided to enunciate a National Policy on Disaster Management. A draft policy has accordingly been formulated and is expected to be put in place shortly. The policy shall inform all spheres of Central Government activity and shall take precedence over all existing sectoral policies. The broad objectives of the policy are to minimize the loss of lives and social, private and community assets because of natural or manmade disasters and contribute to sustainable development and better standards of living for all, more specifically for the poor and vulnerable sections by ensuring that the development gains are not lost through natural calamities/disasters *(National Disaster Management Division, 2004).*

The policy notes that State Governments are primarily responsible for disaster management including prevention and mitigation, while the Government of India provides assistance where necessary as per the norms laid down from time to time and proposes that this overall framework may continue. However, since response to a disaster requires coordination of resources available across all the Departments of the Government, the policy mandates that the Central Government will, in conjunction with the State Governments, seek to ensure that such a coordination mechanism is laid down through an appropriate chain of command so that mobilization of resources is facilitated. The broad features of the draft national policy on disaster management are enunciated below:

(i) A holistic and pro-active approach for prevention, mitigation and preparedness will be adopted for disaster management.

(ii) Each Ministry/Department of the Central/State Government will set apart an appropriate quantum of funds under the Plan for specific schemes/projects addressing vulnerability reduction and preparedness.

(iii) Where there is a shelf of projects, projects addressing mitigation will be given priority. Mitigation measures shall be built into the on-going schemes/programmes

(iv) Each project in a hazard prone area will have mitigation as an essential term of reference. The project report will include a statement as to how the project addresses vulnerability reduction.

(v) Community involvement and awareness generation, particularly that of the vulnerable segments of population and women has been emphasized as necessary for sustainable disaster risk reduction. This is a critical component of the policy since communities are the first responders to disasters and, therefore, unless they are empowered and made capable of managing disasters, any amount of external support cannot lead to optimal results.

(vi) There will be close interaction with the corporate sector, non-governmental organizations and the media in the national efforts for disaster prevention/vulnerability reduction.

(vii) Institutional structures/appropriate chain of command will be built up and appropriate training imparted to disaster managers at various levels to ensure coordinated and quick response at all levels; and development of inter-State arrangements for sharing of resources during emergencies.

(viii) A culture of planning and preparedness is to be inculcated at all levels for capacity building measures.

(ix) Standard operating procedures and disaster management plans at state and district levels as well as by relevant central government departments for handling specific disasters will be lay down.

(x) Construction designs must correspond to the requirements as laid down in relevant Indian Standards.

(xi) All lifeline buildings in seismic zones III, IV & V – hospitals, railway stations, airports/airport control towers, fire station buildings, bus stands, major administrative centers will need to be evaluated and, if necessary, retro-fitted.

(xii) The existing relief codes in the States will be revised to develop them into disaster management codes/manuals for institutionalizing the planning process with particular attention to mitigation and preparedness.

With the above mentioned institutional mechanism and policy framework in position and the actions taken to implement the policy guidelines, it is expected that the task of moving towards vulnerability reduction will be greatly facilitated *(Status Reports, 2004).*

Disaster Management Act

The Government decided to enact a law on disaster management to provide for requisite institutional mechanism for drawing up and monitoring the implementation of the disaster management plans, ensuring measures by various wings of Government for prevention and mitigating effects of disasters and for undertaking a holistic, coordinated and prompt response to any disaster situation. The Disaster Management Act, 2005 [9] was enacted and notified on December 26, 2005. The salient features of the act include:

(i) Setting up of a National Disaster Management Authority under the Chairmanship of the Prime Minister (PM) with such other Ministers not exceeding nine, as may be nominated by the PM. One of the Members may be designated as Vice-Chairpersons of NDMA by the Prime Minister. The Authority shall be assisted by an Executive Committee of Secretaries to be constituted by the Central Government. The National Authority may set up all Advisory Committee of Experts and The National Authority will have the responsibility for laying down the policies, plans and guidelines for disaster management.

(ii) There shall be a State Disaster Management Authority in each State/UT under the Chairmanship of Chief Minister/Lt. Governor, Administrator, as the case may be the Vice-Chairperson and Members, of the State Disaster Management. Authority will be nominated by the Chief Minister/Lt. Governor/ Administrator, as the case may be the State Authority shall be responsible for laying down the policies and plans for disaster management in the State. It shall be assisted by a State Executive Committee. The State Authority may constitute an Advisory Committee of Experts as and when it is considered necessary. It will be mandatory for relevant Ministries/ Department to draw up department wise plans in accordance with the National Disaster Management Plan.

(iii) The State Government shall constitute District Disaster Management Authority with District Magistrate as Chairperson and President, Zila Parishad or Chief Executive Member, District Autonomous Council as the case may be, as Co-Chairperson and the District Authority shall act as the District planning, coordinating and implementing body for disaster management. Appropriate provisions will be made for taking mitigation and preparedness measures in accordance with the National, State and District Plans at National, State and District levels *(National Disaster Management Authority)*[10].

(iv) The Central Government shall be responsible for coordinating action by Ministries/Departments of the Central Government, National Authority and State Authority, Governmental and nongovernmental organizations. The local authority shall ensure training of its officers and employees and maintaining all resources so as to be readily available for use in the event of a disaster. The local authority shall also ensure that construction projects under them conform to the standards and specifications lay down. The local authority shall carry out relief, rehabilitation and reconstruction activities in the affected area within its jurisdiction.

(v) The Central Government shall constitute the National Institute of Disaster Management *(NIDM)*[11]. NIDM shall plan and promote training and research in disaster management, documentation and development of National level information base relating to disaster management policies, prevention mechanism and mitigation measures A National Disaster Response Force shall be constituted for specialist response *(National Disaster Management Authority).*

(vi) The Central Government shall constitute a National Disaster Response Fund for emergency response.

In addition, the Central Government may constitute a National Disaster Mitigation Fund for mitigation projects. The State Government shall establish Disaster Response Fund and Disaster Mitigation Fund at State and District Level Every Ministry/Department of Central and State Governments shall make provision in its annual budget for funds to carry out the activities set out in its Disaster Management Plan. There is provision in the Bill for punishment for obstructing response, false claims, mis-appropriation of money or materials and issuing of false warning. No prosecution for offences shall be instituted except with the previous sanction of the Central Government or State Government. There shall be no discrimination on the grounds of sex, caste, community, descent or religion while providing compensation on relief to the victims. The Central Government has the power to issue directions to the Government Authorities/Organizations/statutory bodies to facilitate or assist in disaster management. Action taken in good faith by any officer or employee of the Central Government, National Authority, State Government, State Authority, District Authority and Local authority shall be protected and no prosecution or suit will lie in any Court. The Officers shall be immune from legal process in regard to any warning communicated or disseminated in their official capacity. The Central Government and the State Government may make rules to carry out the provision of the Act NIDM and may make regulations to carry out its objectives as laid down in the Act *(National Disaster Management Division, 2004).*

State Disaster Management Act

Respective States have made legislative provisions to enact the Disaster Management Act. The act provides for effective management of disaster, for mitigation of the effects of disaster, for administering, facilitating, coordinating and monitoring emergency relief during and after occurrence of disasters and for implementing, monitoring and coordinating measures for reconstruction and rehabilitation in the aftermath of disasters, in the State Governments for these purposes to establish the State Disaster Management Authority and to specify other agencies and for matters connected therewith or incidental thereto.

State Government of Gujarat was the first state to enact its State Disaster Management Act in 2003. While other States of Governments of Maharashtra, Uttarakhand, Bihar, Uttar Pradesh and Sikkim have enacted the DM act in subsequent years of 2004, 2005 and 2006. National Policies and Programmes which relate to Disaster Risk Reduction over the years have been instituted. The Government of India has initiated a wide array of programmes and activities for holistic disaster management by changing its orientation from a relief centric approach to a pro-active approach towards disaster management and by adopting a multi-disciplinary and cross-sectoral approach. A National Disaster Management Framework/Roadmap addressing institutional, legislative and policy frameworks, disaster prevention and mitigation, preparedness and response, networking of emergency operations centers, early warning systems, human resource development and capacity building and research and knowledge management has been formulated.

The National Disaster Management Authority (NDMA)

The NDMA has been set-up to lay down the policies, plans, and guidelines for disaster management and a complementary structure is also envisaged at the State and District level. The Authority aims to integrate disaster prevention and mitigation in development plans and projects and to formulate projects and schemes for mitigation and earmark funds. Enactment of Disaster Management Act, 2005 confers legislative sanction to the institutional and coordination mechanisms to ensure holistic and coordinated disaster management measures. In addition to providing for institutional framework to cater to mitigation and preparedness efforts, the Act mandates constitution of the Disaster Response Fund and Disaster Mitigation Fund at the national, state and district levels and assigns an important role to urban local bodies and Panchayati Raj institutions (*National Disaster Management Division, 2004).*

A national disaster management policy is being presently formulated. A large number of hazard-specific projects and programmes aimed at risk reduction have been initiated. Separate National Core Groups on Earthquake, Cyclone and Landslides have been constituted to assist in risk assessment and mitigation planning, developing a techno-legal regime, land-use zonation etc. Specific programmes for addressing earthquake and cyclone risk mitigation have been formulated along with training of engineers, architects and masons in hazard-resistant construction practices and inclusion of elements of earthquake engineering in undergraduate engineering and architectural courses. Simultaneous efforts at assessing and retrofitting the existing lifeline infrastructure and the critical establishments have also been initiated. The guidelines of various development schemes relating to construction of housing, community assets and other physical infrastructure have been reviewed to make them disaster-resilient. To address the need for developing a trained cadre of human resource for DRM, the National Institute of Disaster Management (NIDM) has formulated a national HRD Plan for Disaster Management. It also undertakes training and capacity building programmes along with assisting the national and state level training institutions in developing training modules and curricula for various sectors and stakeholders *(Status Reports, 2004).*

The Government, in partnership with UN and other national and International agencies has launched community-based disaster preparedness (CBDP) and planning initiatives. The CBDP process is being institutionalized in the administrative structures especially the three-tier Panchayati Raj system in the most multi hazard prone areas. Alongside, earthquake vulnerabilities in urban cities lying in seismic zones III, IV and V are also being addressed. Disaster management has also been included in the school curricula to build a generation sensitive to disaster risk reduction concerns. This is accompanied by training of teachers for building aptitude and skills in the subject. As envisaged in the National Disaster Management Framework, a multi-stakeholder approach involving the corporate sector, the youth voluntary organizations, construction industry, professional and sectoral organizations for dissemination of disaster risk reduction is being implemented (*National Disaster Management Division, 2004).*

Specific work plans addressing the concerns and needs of each sector have been drawn up and are being operationalized through their respective nodal agencies/organizations. The UN agencies in India have constituted a UN Disaster Management Team which facilitates coordinated support to the national and state governments in various stages of DM cycle, as well as facilitate information sharing with other partners. For far too long, disaster management in India was marginalized as an issue of providing relief and rehabilitation to the people affected by natural calamities. In the Central Government it occupied a place in the Ministry of Agriculture, in the States it was a concern of the Revenue or Relief Departments, while in the districts it was one of the many crisis management functions of the Collectors. There was hardly any attempt to look into the impact of disasters on the economy and development and to examine how at times development itself can lead to disasters as the recent urban floods in various parts of India has demonstrated. The significant issues of disaster risk reduction in the policies and programming of various plan schemes on poverty alleviation, environment, micro-credit, social and economic vulnerabilities, etc., have hardly been deliberated in the apex planning body of the country. The country's commitment to mainstream disaster risk reduction into the process of development planning at all levels for sustainable development, as stated in Hyogo Framework of Action 2005-15: Building the Resilience of Nations and Communities to Disasters have not been carried forward across sectors for actionable programmes for achieving the desired results *(Status Reports, 2004).*

Tenth Plan Formulations

The Tenth Five Year Plan, prepared in the backdrop of Orissa super cyclone, Gujarat earthquake and end of International Decade of Natural Disaster Reduction (IDNDR), for the first time, recognized disaster management as a development issue. The Plan document not only included a separate chapter on Disaster Management, it made a number of important prescriptions to mainstream disaster risk reduction into the process of development.

The Tenth Plan prescriptions on disaster Management can broadly be divided into three categories: (a) policy guidelines at the macro level that would inform and guide the preparation and implementation of development plans across sectors, (b) operational guidelines of integrating disaster management practices into development, and (c) specific developmental schemes for prevention and mitigation of disasters. At the macro level, the Plan emphasized that "while hazards, both natural or otherwise, are inevitable, the disasters that follow need not be so and the society can be prepared to cope with them effectively whenever they occur" and called for a "multi-pronged strategy for total risk management, comprising prevention, preparedness, response and recovery, on the one hand, and for initiating development efforts aimed towards risk reduction and mitigation, on the other". It stated that only then we can look forward to "sustainable development." At the operational level, the Plan made a number of very important prescriptions as given below;

(a) Institutional arrangements for disaster response should be streamlined by an integrated approach involving civilian and military resources, setting up a modern permanent national command center or operations room with abundant communications and data links to all State capitals, establishing a quick response team particularly for search and rescue operations, developing standard operating system for dealing with humanitarian and relief assistance from non-government sources and formulating a unified legislation for dealing with all types of disasters *(National Disaster Management Division, 2004).*

(b) Disaster prevention and preparedness should be built into development planning by introducing a rigorous process of vulnerability analysis and risk assessment, maintaining comprehensive database and resource inventories at all levels, developing state-of-the-art infrastructure for mitigation planning and establishing a Disaster Knowledge Network for the use of disaster managers, decision makers, and community *(National Disaster Management Division, 2004).*

(c) A nationwide culture of prevention should be developed by introducing disaster management in school curriculum, including relevant aspects of disaster management in professional courses, enhancing the capacity of disaster managers by better training facilities and creating a massive awareness at all levels.

(d) Community level initiatives for disaster preparedness should be encouraged by involving people at the grassroots, particularly those who are more vulnerable, for better preparedness and response.

(e) Appropriate zonal regulations, design standards, building codes and performance\specifications should be developed for safe constructions.

(f) All development schemes in vulnerable areas should include a disaster mitigation analysis, whereby the feasibility of a project is assessed with respect to vulnerability of the area.

(g) Disaster mitigation components should be built into all development projects, financed under the Plan, as part of approved project costs. Given the pervasive nature of disasters and the wide spread havoc caused by some of them, the Tenth Plan felt that "planned expenditure on disaster mitigation and prevention measures, in addition to the Calamity Relief Fund (CRF), is required *(Disaster Management in India - A Status Report, 2004).*

Critical Reflections Towards Disaster Management Act

The disaster management act opens a lot of analysis especially in the areas of people's participation. India needs a disaster response policy that puts people first. A major noted point is that the bill misses the point of mitigating effects of a disaster; that is the rehabilitation or relocation and reconstruction. There is no clear-cut definition of relief but general guidelines for minimum standards of relief. The bill does envisage the establishment of a National

Disaster Management Authority along with state and district authorities but they are not accorded any well- defined legal status. The bill also states that the actions of the national, state and district authorities cannot be challenged except in the Supreme Court or the High Court's having respective jurisdiction. Another major gap that was pointed out was the non-inclusion of community participation in the areas of disaster control. Recent disaster situations have effectively proved that it is only community participation that brings about effective implementation. Also the formation of district level authorities alone will not take care of the actions at the ground level. The officials in charge need to be given specific guidelines in terms of actions to be taken in cases of disasters. Also their emergency powers and duties need to be defined more clearly *(Action Aid 2007)*[12] The bill has proposed to create series of funds but the authorities under the Bill do not have independent budgets. The various departments to be used in disasters will be providing the money. This again ties the hands of the authorities. The observations on the bill made here are not meant to take attention away from the positive steps taken. The wetting up of a national authority with a response force and a policy which covers all spheres of disaster response right from the center to the district level is commendable.

(5) Disaster Management in Kerala

The State's geographical location, weather pattern and high population density makes it prone to severe natural as well as human-induced disasters which can be countered only through organized mitigate actions. Most of the districts of Kerala are multi-hazard prone. In Kerala lightning, landslides (debris flows) and floods are the most commonly occurring natural hazards. Droughts and minor earth tremors also occur occasionally. The recent Tsunami of 26 December 2004 added a new dimension to the disaster profile of the state. Kerala is prone to high incidence of lightning, especially during the months of April, May, October and November. It is estimated that about 70 people die every year due to lightning. About 14.8% of the state is prone to flooding *(CESS, 2010)*. Apart from floods the mountain regions of the state experience several landslides during the monsoon season. It is known that a total of 65 fatal landslides occurred between 1961 and 2009 causing the death of 257 individuals *(Kuriakose, 2010)*. Between 1871-2000, the state experienced 12 moderate drought years. The 570 km long coast line of Kerala is prone to erosion, monsoon storm surges and sea level rise. Land subsidence due to tunnel erosion or soil piping which is a slow hazard, is recently noticed to be affecting the hilly areas in the state. This often goes unnoticed and is a hazard with potential of causing landslides, infrastructural damages and crop loss covering vast areas in the high land regions of the state *(Kuriakose, 2009)*. Kerala is also prone to several anthropogenic disasters such as road accidents, rail accidents, boat capsizing, industrial accidents, epidemics, pest infestation, stampedes, building collapses and fire accidents. As many of the dams in the state have exceeded their design life, they are potentially disastrous to people living in the downstream. Population pressure and unsustainable land use practices prevailing in the state are the main reason for many of the hazards to turn into disaster events. Lack of proper infrastructure facilities and exceeding of carrying capacity are the cause of many of the anthropogenic hazards *(State Disaster Management Authority, 2005)*.

The Kerala State Disaster Management Authority was formed as stipulated in the National Disaster Management Authority Act of 2005 with the Chief Minister as Chairman and the Revenue Minister as Vice-Chairman. It has a State Executive Committee. Formulation of a state policy, identification of disaster -prone areas and planning of disaster management programmes incorporating the services of various departments comes under the purview of the State Executive Committee. District Disaster Management Authority was constituted with the District Collector as Chairman in each district.

- ***Kerala State Disaster Management Policy***

The Disaster Management policy acts as the guiding principle of the State for disaster management and manifests the vision of the State. It aims to establish an optimal system for dealing with disasters, ensuring continuity in developmental activities without damaging the environment and avoiding disruption of economic activity. The policy framework is structured in such a way that Kerala State Disaster Management Authority provides the overall direction and guidance to various entities leveraging the resources and capability of existing entities and building new capabilities without treating disaster management as a separate sector or discipline *(State Disaster Management Authority, 2005)*.

- ***Kerala State Disaster Management Act***

Kerala State Disaster Management Authority[13] is the apex decision-making body to facilitate, co-ordinate, review and monitor all disaster management related activities in Kerala State Disaster Management Policy. The State authority has drafted the State disaster management policy and guidelines to be followed by the State government departments and districts. The Authority prepared the State Disaster Management Plan and endorses departmental plans and district plans. The Authority is provided with statutory powers to facilitate, coordinate and monitor the activities related to disaster management utilizing the resources and expertise of relevant government departments, district administrations, local authorities, non-governmental organizations, public sector, international development agencies, donors and community. It exercises the powers and functions as laid down in the notification of Kerala State as per National Disaster Management Act, 2005.

The State government, by notification, has established and constituted District Disaster Management Authorities in all 14 districts as per the provisions of National Disaster Management Act, 2005. The district authority act as the district planning, coordinating and implementing body for disaster management and take all measures for the purposes of disaster management in the district in accordance with the guidelines laid down by the National Authority and the State Authority *(State Disaster Management Authority, 2005)*.The State Government ensures an appropriate chain of command whereby the Kerala State Disaster Management Authority at the State level and District Disaster Management Authorities headed by District Collectors at the district level are empowered to coordinate disaster management activities and mobilize resources of all relevant Departments at their level. Similar institutional arrangements fixing responsibilities, administrative mechanism and procedures is made at Taluk and Village levels.

• ***Kerala State Nodal Departments***

The Department of Revenue and Disaster Management is the nodal department for management of all types of natural disasters that include water and climate related disasters and geological disasters. The scope of Department of Revenue has been enhanced to include prevention, mitigation and preparedness aspects of disaster management apart from its traditional responsibility of relief and rehabilitation and renamed as Department of Revenue and Disaster Management. The Principal Secretary to the government is the State Relief Commissioner. The organizational structure of the department dealing with disaster management is so tailored as to reflect the change in focus from post-disaster relief and rehabilitation to prevention, mitigation and preparedness in addition to relief and rehabilitation. The Department of Home is the nodal department for the management of manmade and human induced disasters including air and rail accidents. The Department of Public Health shall be the nodal department for chemical, biological (health related), radiological and nuclear disasters.

• *Framework for Mainstreaming Disaster Management*

Government of Kerala ensures that State Government, district administration, local authorities and departments take into account disaster risks and provide for suitable preventive, mitigation and preparedness measures in their regular development planning activities. The State Disaster Management Authority has formed a frame work for mainstreaming disaster management integrating performance indicators for key elements for ensuring translation of policy goals into outcome and for enhanced accountability towards critical parameters like integration of disaster management framework into development framework of the State and medium term expenditure framework (MTEF) that indicate budgetary commitment of the State Government to the policy *(SDMA, 2005)*. Disaster management is included as an integral part of development plans of the State and Disaster Risk or Environment Impact Analysis is introduced as a binding requirement for development and infrastructure programmes. As part of mainstreaming, Course Curriculum in disaster management is included in the school curriculum of State Education Department, in the high school syllabus. School disaster management programmes and formation of Safety Clubs is promoted by the State. Universities and self-financing colleges shall be encouraged to conduct postgraduate and diploma courses in disaster management.

• *Stakeholders in State Disaster Management*

The State Government acknowledges the following set of institutional stakeholders that play key roles in disaster management and calls for systematization of a frame work of operation under the leadership of Kerala State Disaster Management Authority *(SDMA, 2005)*.

- State and Central Government Departments
- District Disaster Management Authorities
- Local authorities such as Municipal Corporations/Municipalities, District/Block/Grama Panchayats.
- Voluntary and civil society organisations
- Red Cross, multilateral aid agencies and UN agencies
- Community – village disaster management committees/task forces
- Public/Private sector undertakings

- Army, Navy, Air Force, Coast Guard, Airport Authority, National Disaster Response Force etc.

- ***Roles of Key Stakeholders***

I. The Kerala State Disaster Management Authority

The Kerala State Disaster Management Authority act as the nodal agency for prevention, mitigation and preparedness and facilitate and monitor the same as the capabilities developed in this phase would play a critical role in subsequent phases of disaster management.

II. Departments of State

Under the overall direction of Kerala State Disaster Management Authority, the departments at State and district levels is responsible for preparing 'Departmental Disaster Management Plans' that involve programmes within the routine departmental works for disaster prevention, mitigation and preparedness and strategies for its successful implementation, description of departmental responsibilities during disaster situations and preparation of contingency plans for different types of hazards and formulation of department-level capacity building policy. Further, the State departments formulate 'Disaster Management Cells' within the departments at State and District levels and deploys a senior officer as 'Nodal Officer for Disaster Management'. 'Control Rooms' has been established for effective coordination and speedy decision making. Details of the main departmental officials (name, designation, and contact details), inventory of departmental resources (resource, capacity, location etc.) and departmental standard operating procedures is prepared as part of departmental plans that keep integration with the functioning of Crisis Management Groups and State/district EOCs. Standard Operating Procedures that precisely define how operations are to be carried out, explain what is expected and required of the department personnel and procedures for evacuation, procurement of essentials, deployment of resources and such other activities is prepared and simplified by relevant departments to ensure effective functioning in the event of disasters *(State Disaster Management Authority, 2005).*

III. District Collector / District Disaster Management Authority:

The District Collector who also acts as chairman of the District Disaster Management Authority plays a vital and coordinating role in ensuring that disaster risk management activities in this phase are effectively carried out by the District Disaster Management Authority, district administration, government departments, local bodies and other stakeholders at the district level. The District Collector ensures that there is a plan for disaster management for the district which promotes a culture of prevention, mitigation and preparedness. The District Disaster Management Authority ensure that the 'District Disaster Management Plans' are operational and regularly updated. The District Collector facilitate and coordinate with local bodies to ensure that pre-disaster activities in the district are carried out successfully and ensure appropriate linkage between disaster management activities and regular development activities. The District Collector facilitates training and awareness programmes for communities and ensures that relevant officials in the district are properly trained in handling possible disasters in the district.

IV. Local Authorities

Local self-governments work in close harmony with various government departments under the supervision of District Disaster Management Authority. They are responsible for ensuring compliance to various disaster management specifications and codes stipulated by relevant agencies based on hazard zonation and risk and vulnerability assessments. The local authorities shall coordinate community based disaster preparedness activities of the district.

V. Non-Governmental Organizations and Community Groups

The entire process of disaster risk management will center stage the community and will be provided momentum and sustenance through the collective efforts of government agencies and non-governmental organizations. Civil society organizations, voluntary agencies and local community groups would actively participate in prevention, mitigation and preparedness activities of the district under the overall direction and supervision of District Disaster Management Authority. They would assist the district administration and local bodies in the identification of hazards and assessment of vulnerability and risks and actively participate in the training activities in the pre-disaster stage familiarizing themselves with their role in community based disaster risk management. Non-governmental organizations and community groups under the supervision of District Disaster Management

Authority and local bodies would be encouraged to develop mechanisms to mitigate disasters at the grass root level through participation of communities.

Crisis Management Groups

Crisis Management refers to the organization and management of resources and responsibilities for dealing with response and immediate restoration of essential services. It involves plans, structures and arrangements established to coordinate the response of State Government. A well-coordinated and unified response of various State departments and agencies appropriate to the proportion and demand of the crisis situation is ensured by the State government to improve the process of relief and recovery through rapid dissemination of information, quick response and effective decision making.

An institutional mechanism distinguished as 'Crisis Management Group' under the chairmanship of Chief Secretary with representatives of Department of Home, Department of Revenue and Disaster Management and Department of Health function at the State level as a nerve center to support, coordinate and monitor crisis management activities related to natural disasters, manmade/accident related disasters, industrial/chemical disasters, biological disasters and radiological/nuclear disasters. Accordingly, 'Crisis Management Plans' that clearly define response roles and responsibilities of government agencies, facilitate communication across agencies, specify protocols and procedures, and detail actions to be taken by government departments shall be prepared and made operational by the State Government *(State Disaster Management Authority, 2005)*. 'District Crisis Management Group' headed by District Collector would flash the 'first information' to the 'State Crisis Management Group' and activate crisis management plan under the guidance of State Crisis Management Group, as and when a crisis situation is developed. 'State Crisis Management Group' would be updated by District Collector with subsequent Post Disaster Assessments on Damages and Needs. The unprecedented crises left over by 2004 Tsunami urged the state machineries to robustly plan for disaster management and mitigation activities on a long term basis. Policies and Acts were drafted in lieu with the same.

(6) Conclusion

There is need for professionalization of disaster management to cope with the rapidly changing environment. This could be achieved only slowly over a period of time by inducting professionally-trained disaster managers at all levels in the hierarchy of development administration. Reorientation of the existing staff through short-term training programmes in disaster management in NIDM, ATIs, and other reputed institutes is also necessary. Unfortunately, at present, supply of professional disaster managers and facilities for in-service training are both extremely limited in our country, this should be most important aspect in disaster management.

The HPC has advocated that a Trigger Mechanism is necessary to minimize response time when disaster strikes. Establishment of Civil Defense Warden System involving Panchayat members as wardens and providing communication network through wireless stations and-HAM (Help AII Mankind) radio systems seems to be promising development in this context *(GOI, 2001).* The HPC has also made a strong case for ushering a new culture of disaster management which will stand on the four pillars of culture of preparedness, culture of quick response, culture of strategic thinking, and culture of prevention.

Until recently, in India, disaster management was normally viewed as a post-disaster function. It comprised of such activities as rescue, relief and rehabilitation after the occurrence of a disaster. Such an approach was short-sighted, extravagant, and prone to unnecessary interference of politicians, and others having vested interests. However, in the recent past, there has been a paradigmatic shift in India's approach to disaster management. The new approach is multi-sectoral, multi-disciplinary, holistic and proactive, and disaster management is now sought to be built into the development planning process itself. Currently, India has a well-defined institutional framework at the national and sub-national levels, and a funding mechanism for providing relief assistance to the victims of disasters. As it is not possible to prevent the occurrence of natural disasters and measures altogether, there is need for taking appropriate measures for reducing their impacts.

Disaster management is an important issue that cannot be addressed by any one agency, technology or institution alone. It calls for convergence of technologies and institutions with the goal of fulfilling the various dimensions, timeliness, accuracy, scope and coverage, formats and standards to match the user needs and finally assimilation of information for decision-making. A holistic approach encompassing a suitable mix of policy reforms, institutional changes and technology options. Without this, it will not be possible to achieve longer term immunity against natural and man-made disasters.

It is quite evident that economic development may not be sustainable under conditions of vulnerability to natural disasters. Recognizing the fact that hazard mitigation pays high social and economic dividends, especially in a country like India such measures must be seen as investment and not a luxury that may or may not be affordable. Development and disaster management should go hand in hand. Disaster management must be mainstreamed into the development planning process at all levels and development models must have in-built components of disaster reduction, mitigation and preparedness. As per the HPC's recommendations, at least 10 % of the Plan Funds at the national, state, and district levels be earmarked and apportioned for schemes which specifically address prevention, reduction, preparedness, and mitigation of disasters *(GOI, 2004).*

There is a pressing need for a focused, professional approach at all levels of government. But at the same time government must realize that disaster management to be effective has to be a community based response system with disaster driven strategic planning. As advocated by the HPC a Trigger Mechanism is necessary to minimize response time when disaster strikes. Establishment of Civil Defense Warden System involving Panchayat members as wardens and providing communication network through wireless stations and-HAM (Help All Mankind) radio systems seems to be a promising development in this context.

Notes

1. Social Work Chronicle, as the name of the journal denotes – this peer reviewed bi-annual will always have a prime focus to explore the emerging issues and challenges in the sphere social work education and practices across the globe with an aim to strengthen the base of Social Work literature and to enrich the scope of social work research and practice. Editor: Anupam Hazra ISSN: 2277-1395, Chapter 1, Volume 1 Issue 1 May 2012, Disaster Management and Role of Academic Institutions written by Meena Galliara and Ananya Prabhawalkar, Page no 1-29.
2. Since 1988, the WHO Collaborating Centre for Research on the Epidemiology of Disasters (CRED) has been maintaining an Emergency Events Database EM-DAT. EM-DAT was created with the initial support of the WHO and the Belgian Government. The main objective of the database is to serve the purposes of humanitarian action at national and international levels. It is an initiative aimed to rationalize decision making for disaster preparedness, as well as providing an objective base for vulnerability assessment and priority setting. EM-DAT contains essential core data on the occurrence and effects of over 18,000 mass disasters in the world from 1900 to present. The database is compiled from various sources, including UN agencies, non-governmental organisations, insurance companies, research institutes and press agencies.
3. Orissa State Disaster Mitigation Authority (OSDMA) was set up by the Government of Orissa as autonomous organizations vide Finance Department Resolution No. IFC- 74/99-51779/F dated the 28th December 1999 (in the intermediate aftermath of the Super-cyclone in 1999). It was registered under the Societies Registration

Act, 1860 on 29.12.1999 as a non-profit making & charitable institution for the interest of the people of Orissa, with its headquarters at Bhubaneswar and jurisdiction over the whole State. The Department of Revenue is the administrative department of OSDMA vides Revenue Department Resolution No.39373/R dated 26th August 2000. Subsequently, the name of the Authority was changed from Orissa State Disaster Mitigation Authority to Orissa State Disaster Management Authority vide Revenue & Disaster Management Department Resolution No. 42317/R&DM dated 27th September, 2008.

4. The GSDMA has been constituted by the Government of Gujarat by the GAD's Resolution dated 8th February 2001.The Authority has been created as a permanent arrangement to handle the natural calamities. The objectives for constitution of this authority have been clearly spelt out and precisely defined in para (2) of the said Resolution.
5. Vulnerability Atlas of India: An indispensable tool for pre-disaster pro-active approach in disaster management Building Materials & Technology Promotion Council, Ministry of Housing & Urban Poverty Alleviation, Government of India collaborate with national and international agencies/organizations. This Atlas has served as a useful tool for policy planning on natural disaster prevention and preparedness especially for hosing and related infrastructure.
6. UNISDR is part of the United Nations Secretariat and its functions span the development and humanitarian fields. Its core areas of work includes ensuring disaster risk reduction (DRR) is applied to climate change adaptation, increasing investments for DRR, building disaster-resilient cities, schools and hospitals, and strengthening the international system for DRR.UNISDR's vision is based on the three strategic goals of the Hyogo Framework for Action: integrating DRR into sustainable development policies and planning, developing and strengthening institutions, mechanisms and capacities to build resilience to hazards, and incorporating risk reduction approaches into emergency preparedness, response, and recovery programmes.
7. Habitat Global Forum's 'Plan of Action for a Safer World' that emerged from the 1996 City Summit in Istanbul have noted the challenge to reduce urban risks. The Yokohama Strategy emphasized the manner in which high urban densities contributed to vulnerability. 'Disasters contribute to social, economic, cultural and political disruption in urban and rural contexts, each in its specific way. Large-scale urban concentrations are particularly fragile because of their complexity and the accumulation of population and infrastructures in limited areas.' The Habitat Plan of Action spoke of the basic un-naturalness of urban disasters.
8. A Status Report on Disaster Management in India was prepared in February, 2004 for presentation and circulation in the World Congress on Natural Disaster Mitigation. The Report summarizes various initiatives taken by the Ministry.
9. The Disaster Management Act, 2005: (As Passed By The Houses Of Parliament), Bill No. LV-F of 2005, NO. 53 passed on 23rd December, 2005. An Act to provide for the effective management of disasters and for matters connected therewith or incidental thereto. BE it enacted by Parliament in the Fifty-sixth Year of the Republic of India as follows Short title, extent and commencement.

It clearly indicates the establishment of National Disaster Management Authority and its allied activities.

10. The National Disaster Management Authority (NDMA), headed by the Prime Minister of India, is the Apex Body for Disaster Management in India. The setting up of the NDMA and the creation of an enabling environment for institutional mechanisms at the State and District levels is mandated by the Disaster Management Act, 2005.
11. The National Institute of Disaster Management constituted under the Disaster Management Act 2005 has been entrusted with the nodal national responsibility for human resource development, capacity building, training, research, documentation and policy advocacy in the field of disaster management. Upgraded from the National Centre for Disaster Management of the Indian Institute of Public Administration on 16th October, 2003, NIDM is steadily marching forward to fulfill its mission to make a disaster resilient India by developing and promoting a culture of prevention and preparedness at all levels.
12. Action Aid International works with poor people in over 40 countries across the world. The major goal of the agency is to end poverty. Action Aid India is an anti-poverty agency, working in India since 1972 with the poor people to end poverty and injustice together. Action Aid working in partnership with formations of excluded people, mass movements, knowledge institutions and civil society organisations, Action Aid Standing with people in their struggle towards a world free of poverty, exclusion, patriarchy and injustice. The agency greatly involved in disaster management activities including disaster preparedness to disaster response.
13. The Kerala State Disaster Management Authority was formed as stipulated in the National Disaster Management Authority Act of 2005 with the Chief Minister as Chairman and the Revenue Minister as Vice-Chairman. It has a State Executive Committee. Formulation of a state policy, identification of disaster -prone areas and planning of disaster management programmes incorporating the services of various departments comes under the purview of the State Executive Committee. District Disaster Management Authority was constituted with the District Collector as Chairman in each district.

Chapter - 4

Disaster Management at the Local Level-Role of Local Self Government

"Natural hazards continuously occur and shape the environment on which our societies depend, but there is much appropriate and scientific knowledge that public can use to prevent human disasters resulting from them".
— International Decade for Natural Disaster Reduction (United Nations, 2005).

Introduction

Disasters like Floods, Cyclones, Droughts and Earthquakes are increasing in India and almost all parts of the earth, due to environmental degradation, deforestation, increasing population, global warming, nuclear explosions, and air pollution. There is also worldwide concern to mitigate the growing incidence of disaster and their toll on human life, property, and environment. The role of Panchayats (local self-governing institutions) is important in view of their proximity to the local community, universal coverage and enlisting people's participation on an institutionalized basis. It is possible to ensure accountability and transparency through the institution of Gramsabha. It is inevitable to involve Panchayats in Disaster Management and sensitize the local communities through them to develop coping mechanism in preparedness and mitigation measures to minimize its destructive effect on life and property at the local level. This chapter highlights the various areas of involvement of Panchayat Raj Institutions (PRIs)[1] in the disaster management programmes, some case studies that illustrate the effective role of PRIs in disaster management, and certain issues and challenges that development professionals face to effectively involve PRIs in all phases of disaster preparedness, response, and recovery.

Significance of Local Self Government

Local self-government institutions have always existed in India in one form or the other since ancient times. The present form of urban local government owes its genesis to the British rule. The initiation began with Samuel Laing, member of the Viceroy's Council, in the Budget Speech (1861-62) proposing that local services should be based on local resources. Lord Mayo's Resolution of 1870 introduced the concept of elected representatives in the municipalities. Lord Ripon is considered to be the founding father of urban local government as he implanted the concept of municipal authorities as units of self-government. His Resolution of 18 May 1882 on local self-government dealt with the constitution of local bodies, their functions, finances and powers and laid the foundation of local self-government in modern India. Local self-government played an important role in the Independence Movement. After Independence, the Constitution of India was framed on federal principles. Indian Constitution makers divided the government functions in three lists: Federal, State and Concurrent. Local government bodies are covered in the State List and are governed by the State Statutes or in the case of Union Territories by the Union Parliament *(Golandaz, H. M. and B. Mohanty, 1993).*

Local government is an integral part of the national government structure, the level of government closest to the citizens and in the best position both to involve them in the decision making process of improving their living conditions and to make use of their knowledge and capabilities in the promotion of all round development. There are two types of local government: urban local government and rural local government. Until recently, urban local government was manifested in Municipal Corporations, Municipal Councils, Town Area Committees and Notified Area Committees. However, the Seventy-Fourth Constitution Amendment Act adopted in 1992 proposes to form a uniform structure of Municipal Corporations, Municipal Councils and Nagar Panchayats in transitional areas. Rural local government operates through Zilla Panchayats (Parishads), Taluka Panchayats and Village Panchayats *(UN ESCAP, 1993)*[2]

Rural Local Self Government of India is a three tier system which looks after the necessities of the villages and encourages the development of activity in the villages. In rural areas there are certain local problems which can be solved efficiently only by the local people. More than eighty percent of the Indian people live in villages and the welfare of the people implies an all-round improvement of the Indian villages. With this end in view three types of self-governing institutions were created to look after the affairs of rural areas *(Rural Local Self Government- Informative Article, 2010).* With the decentralization of powers to Local self-government Institutions, Local administration department has an important role to play in the formulation of policy and implementation of developmental works at the grass roots level. Director of Panchayat and Director of Municipal Administration form the two field departments.

The Kerala State has been divided into 14 Districts spreading over 21 Revenue divisions, 63 Taluks and 1453 Revenue Villages. There are 14 District Panchayats, 152 Block Panchayats, 978 Grama Panchayats, 60 Municipalities, 5 Corporations and 1 Township. Consequent to the 74th Amendment to the Constitution of India, the Local self-government Institutions (LSGIs) are to function as the third tier of Government. In Kerala, LSGIs have been meaningfully empowered through massive transfer

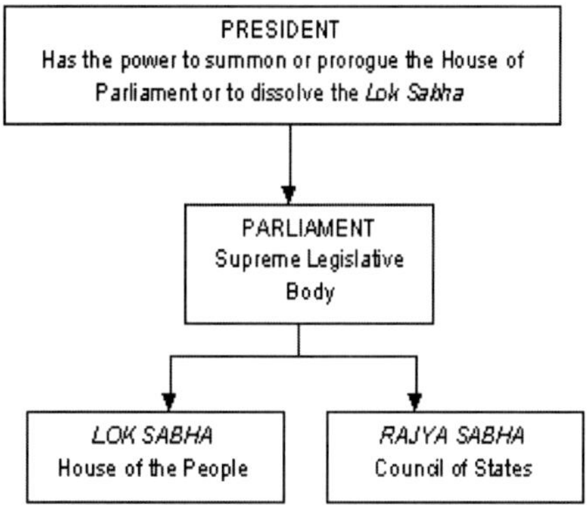

Figure 4.1. Political Structure at the National Level.

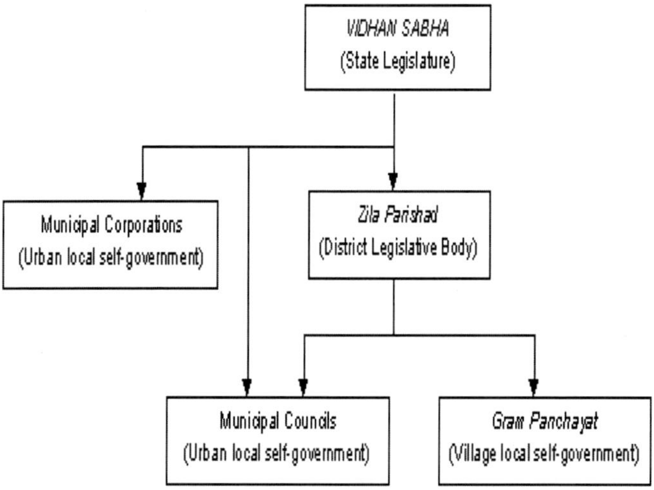

Figure 4.2: Political Structure at the State Level.

of resources as well as administrative powers. Coupled with a grassroots level approach of Participatory Planning whereby the developmental programmes are identified and implemented through Gramsabhas, the LSGIs have emerged as effective agencies for the implementation of developmental programmes (www.kerala.gov.in).

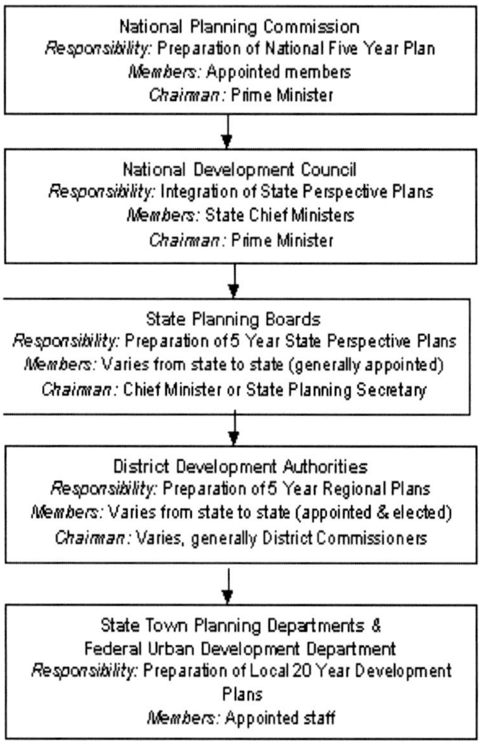

Figure 4.3: National, State and Local Planning.

Local Government Bodies

Rural local bodies are supposed to be formed as democratic institutions based on the principle of self-government and should represent people's desires and strengths. The rural quality of life was fast deteriorating and this created an urgent necessity for having vibrant and efficient rural local government bodies that could deliver adequate services and improve the living conditions in the rural areas.

Panchayati Raj System

Panchayat Act of 1920 was conceived as local courts and was completely judicial in character. As there was hardly any devolution of finances and responsibilities, its role as the local unit of administration, development and rural upliftment remained non-functional. Among the Indian leaders, Mahatma Gandhi made a very strong plea for village republics *(Golandaz, H. M. and B. Mohanty, 1993).* Articles 40 under the Directive Principles of State Policy included in the part IV of the Constitution advised the government to take steps to organise village Panchayats and endow them with such powers and authority which would enable them to function as units of self-government. State governments were supposed to enact appropriate legislation for this purpose *(UN ESCAP, 1993)*

The Indian planners and policy makers launched a multipurpose Community Development Programme (CDPs) with the objective of improving the conditions of the rural masses. This programme aimed at training and sending development personnel Block Development Officers (BDO), Extension Officers and Village Level Workers (VLWs) into villages. These groups of officers were supposed to act as agents of change. They were expected to galvanise rural masses by encouragement, demonstration and offer of material assistance. The CDPs failed to achieve the desired objectives. The Planning Commission requested a committee under the chairmanship of Balvant Rai Mehta to develop the ideas for a system of democratic decentralisation which would anchor the rural developmental efforts. The Balvant Rai Mehta Committee Report came up with a number of recommendations that were incorporated in the Panchayat legislation of the various states in the following years. This committee recommended democratic decentralisation with a provision of a three- tier structure [village-block- district]. It also recommended for transfer of resources and responsibilities and channelization of funds for various developmental programmes through the three- tier system. This report generated opportunity for launching block planning in states like Andhra Pradesh and Tamil Nadu and district planning in others like Maharashtra and Gujarat *(United Nations Economic and Social Commission for Asia and the Pacific, 1993).*

In the 1960's Panchayati Raj Institutions were portrayed as a God that failed. One of the main reasons for the failure was the sabotage by state politicians who were not enthusiastic about devolving powers to the district level or below. They were apprehensive that Panchayati Raj Institutions with real powers may pose a threat to their power and influence. Towards the end of the 1960s when Indira Gandhi was donning a progressive garb and wished to implement land reforms, it was argued that Panchayati Raj Institutions could not be involved as they were dominated by the upper caste and landed elements. The 1960s also witnessed the advent of the

Green Revolution that necessitated centralised planning and came in conflict with the ideals of decentralisation on which PRIs were based. Since rural areas in many parts of the country were still under the hands of feudal landed interest, government sponsored inputs for ushering the Green Revolution could have been monopolised by them. Both central and state government had started bypassing and thus undermining the authority and significance of the PRIs during this period. Central government created its own administrative machinery for implementing many of Indira Government programmes such as Small Farmers' Development Agency, Drought Prone Area Programme, Integrated Rural Development Programme and National Rural Employment Programme, aiming at economic justice. The lack of resources, absence of coordination, dependence on district development staff, lack of delegation of effective authority, domination by the higher castes and better off sections of society had rendered the PRIs ineffective and purposeless as institutions of decentralisation and development. By the middle of the 1970s governments both at the center and in the states had become indifferent to the PRIs. They had become defunct; elections to these institutions were not being held and at most of the places the sitting councils were either dissolved or suspended *(Jha, Gangadhar and B. Mohanty, 1993).*

Reconstitution of Panchayat System

The process of rejuvenation started with the reconstitution of the Panchayats in West Bengal and by the appointment of the Ashok Mehta committee by the Janta Party government in the late 1970s. The mid-seventies also marked a discernible shift of opinion in favour of conceding larger political space to local communities in the governing process. Local self-governing institutions were supposed to play an important role in reordering societal power equations. As the Janata Party Government had pledged its commitment to the Gandhian philosophy, the overall atmosphere seemed to be conducive for the resurgence of the Panchayati Raj Institutions. Another plausible reason seems to be the fact that by the late 1970s the Green Revolution had become a decade old and it had given birth to rich peasant class that had benefited from the Green Revolution. The rich and middle class peasants were fully aware of the importance of the direct access to decentralised government machinery more particularly its delivery system. Capturing village councils was very much in tune with the newly acquired economic power of this class and their motivation to count politically. The central place of the Panchayati Raj Institutions was restored *(Jha, Gangadhar and B. Mohanty, 1993).*

The Ashok Mehta Committee Report mentioned rooting of developmental programme through official bureaucracy, inelastic finance, and dominance of local institutions by economically and socially privileged sections of society as reasons for the failure of the Panchayati Raj Institutions. Ashok Mehta Committee report refused to accept the view that Panchayati Raj was a failed God. In fact he credited these institutions for starting the process of democratic seed drilling in the Indian soil and making the citizens more conscious of their rights than before. Among other positive fallouts was the bridging of gap between bureaucratic elite and the people. It also gave birth to a young dynamic leadership with a modernistic vision and social change oriented outlook. Mehta also averred that it helped rural people to develop a development psyche *(Local Government in Asia and the Pacific, Reports, 1997).*

Devolution is a form of decentralization which seeks to create independent level of authority of government with functions and responsibilities. It is an arrangement for central or state governments to relinquish some of its functions to the new units of government that are outside its control. This can be achieved by providing for it in the Constitution itself or by ordinary law of the land. One of the major reasons for the failure of the local self-government institutions in India has been half-hearted devolution of powers to them. The 73rd and 74th amendments also contained provisions for the devolution of powers and responsibilities to rural (Panchayati Raj Institutions) and urban (Nagarpalikas) local self-government institutions. These amendments respectively provided that the Panchayats at village, block and district levels would have 29 subjects of rural importance as listed in the 11th schedule and municipalities would have 18 subjects of urban importance as listed in the 12th schedule. These amendments bestowed upon the local self- government bodies - both rural and urban - the responsibility to prepare and implement a number of development plans based on the needs of local people. They operationalise the concepts of spatial planning and micro level planning to facilitate decentralized socio economic development in India. With the help of these powers the local self-government institutions are supposed to promote agricultural, industrial, infrastructural and ecological development, poverty alleviation and development of women, children, scheduled and backward castes. These development functions are in addition to the obligatory functions such as ensuring the supply of drinking water, street lighting, maintenance of schools and hospitals etc *(Local Government in Asia and the Pacific, Reports, 1997).*

According to Lieten and Srivastava, the Village Panchayats were established as units of local self- government and focal points of development in the country at large more often than not captured by autocratic and invariably corrupt leaders from among the male elite. Rajani Kothari argued that village councils were nothing but catchy slogans and false promises had enabled the rulers to contain the forces of revolt and resistance and prevent public discontent from getting organised. Ashok Mehta who headed the second Committee on Panchayati Raj refused to be pessimistic about the PRIs. He thought that the process of democratic seed drilling in the Indian soil made people conscious of their rights and also cultivated in them a developmental psyche. He was of the opinion that these institutions had failed because development programmes were channelized through official state bureaucracy, finance had been inelastic and these institutions were dominated by privileged sections of society. Noorjahan Baba argues that centralised planning and administration were considered necessary to guide and control the economy and to integrate and unify new nations emerging from long periods of colonial rules. This might have been possible because as Lieten and Srivastava had thought, the Indian state was reputed to have an enlightened vision and a developmental mission. According to Baba in the 1960s there was great disillusionment with centralised planning because it failed to achieve equitable distribution of the benefits of economic growth among regions and groups within developing countries. Henry Maddic is of the view that there exists a triangular relationship between democracy, decentralisation and development *(Golandaz, H. M. and B. Mohanty, 1993).*

The experience of the PRIs in different states of the country has not been the same. The formal beginning was made when Jawaharlal Nehru inaugurated PRIs at Nagaur in Rajasthan in October 1959. The Rajasthan model of PRIs revolved around the three tier, village Panchayat, Panchayat Samiti and Zilla Parishad. The Panchayat Samiti at the block level was the kingpin of the Rajasthan model. In contrast to the executive role of the Panchayat Samiti the Zilla Parishads were advisory bodies. Maharashtra and Gujarat followed a model in which Zilla Parishads were nodal points of action as main units of planning, development and administration. In Maharashtra, the Zilla Parishad executed not only the schemes under Community Development Programme but also a large portion of programmes of various government departments. In Karnataka, after the introduction of Panchayat reform act of 1985, all functions and functionaries of development departments were transferred to Panchayati raj institutions. The District Rural Development Agencies were merged with the Panchayati

Raj Institutions. To give substance to the idea of decentralisation, the state budget of Karnataka was split into two providing a separate budget for PRIs. The plans and budgets prepared by Mandal Panchayats could not be altered by Zilla Parishad or state government in Karnataka. Similarly district plans of the Zilla Parishad could not be touched by the state government. In Andhra Pradesh, the Zilla Parishads endowed with limited functions have shown encouraging results in the field of education. Even in Tamil Nadu PRIs have done a commendable job in the fields of education, water supply, roads and nutrition *(Golandaz, H. M. and B. Mohant, 1993).*

The PRIs had been functioning in West Bengal, Karnataka, Kerala, Maharashtra, Gujarat and Andhra Pradesh with varying degrees of success. But the experience in the field of local self-governing institutions is qualitatively different after the 73rd and 74th amendments became acts because they made parliamentary democracy in our country participatory in the real sense. These amendments gave substance and meaning to the local self- governing institutions. These amendments removed the bottlenecks from the paths of empowerment of the weaker sections of society like the dalits, tribals and women. Consequent upon the enactment of the act almost all the states and union territories have enacted their legislation. Election to the PRIs has been held all over the country. The elections to PRIs in different parts of the country have brought out some encouraging facts. Karnataka sends maximum number of women to the PRIs followed by Kerala and Manipur. Uttar Pradesh ranks the lowest in this regard *(Golandaz, H. M. and B. Mohant, 1993).*

73rd & 74th Constitutional Amendments

The 74th Amendments Act provides for the constitution of three types of local self- governing institutions in the urban areas. It provides for Municipal Corporations for major cities like Delhi, Mumbai, Chennai, Kolkata, Allahabad, Lucknow, Patna etc. Middle rung cities have Municipal Councils and smaller towns have Nagar Panchayats. Every Municipal Corporation has a General Council. It has members elected by the adult citizens of the city. These members are called Councillors. Apart from the elected members, the Council also has elder men elected by the elected Councillors. The MPs and MLAs are also the members. The Mayor is elected by the members from among themselves. Some of the states provide for direct election of the Mayor. He is known as the first citizen of the city. The Municipal Commissioner is the chief executive officer of the Corporation. The Mayor may ask the Municipal commissioner to prepare and present a report on any matter. The compulsory functions of a Municipal Corporation includes maintenance of hospitals, supplying safe drinking water and electricity, running of schools and keeping an account of births and deaths. The developmental functions of the Municipal Corporations include launching of poverty alleviation programmes for the weaker sections. A Municipality is composed of Councillors elected by the local population. Seats have been reserved for SCs and STs according to their proportion in the population of the town and one third of the seats have been reserved for women. The Presiding officer of a Municipal Board is called the Chairman who is elected by the voters of the town. In some states the Chairman of the Municipal Board has powers to appoint teachers of primary schools and even lower level staffs. An executive officer looks after the day to day administration of the Municipality. Among the compulsory functions are supplying electricity, drinking water, health facilities, schools and maintaining roads and keeping records of weaker sections of the society. The small towns have Nagar Panchayats. Its members are elected by adult citizens of the town. As in the case of other local self-governing institutions, seats are reserved for SC/ST and women. Their functions include provision of drinking water, maintenance of primary schools and registration of births and deaths *(Reports, Govt of Kerala, 1992).*

In spite of the revolutionary changes brought about by the 73rd Amendment it suffers from some serious limitations. Ambiguity about the functional jurisdiction of Panchayats is one of its serious limitations. In the absence of properly defined jurisdiction, it is dependent upon the discretion of state legislatures for being assigned the functions. This act does not mention the powers and functions of the Gram Sabha. This amendment mentions that the Gram Sabha will perform the functions which may be assigned to it by the State legislature. The provision relating to Gram Sabha in the laws enacted by most of the states reduces the Gram Sabha to a powerless body which routinely rubber stamp the decisions taken up by the Gram Panchayat. The Chief Ministers' Conference held in August 1997 at New Delhi ruled that it would be necessary to vest in Gramsabha the powers to sanction and disburse benefits in open meetings, to decide location of drinking water hand pumps etc without having to refer the matter to officials or other authorities. It is necessary to vest the ownership of natural resources in Gram Panchayats and also the decision - making powers concerning the management of and income from such resources in the Gramsabha. Another important limitation of the PRI's is after the amendment is that they still function in the grip of the state bureaucracy. The village Pradhan has to contact the block office several times in a month for technical and financial sanctions *(India Report, Govt of Kerala, 1992).* Yet another omission of the act is that there is no mention of the employees of the Panchayat and their administrative autonomy. Panchayats in the past failed to deliver because they had inadequate control over people working to implement the programmes. Even when responsibilities in the field of health and primary education have been transferred, PRIs have no control over the staff and budget of these departments. The power of the dissolution of the PRIs in the hands of the state government is also seen as a limitation of the post Amendment PRIs. It is argued that the power of their dissolution should rest with the electorate and not with any other authority. Even the provision for MP's/MLA's optional membership of the Zilla Parishad and Panchayat Samiti respectively with or without voting rights is seen as a limitation because it may restrain the powers of the PRIs. In the past, a major stumbling block in the path of the PRIs has been the resource crunch faced by them. This was due to meager resources at the disposal of the PRIs. Even the new amendment does not evolve any source of revenue for the PRIs. It has left these to be considered by the state finance commission. The urban local governing institutions are also faced with paucity due to increase in population and with people from rural areas coming to the cities in search of jobs and better life *(India Report, Govt of Kerala).*

Local democracy is sometimes treated as synonymous with 'decentralisation', but the two are in fact quite distinct. In particular, decentralisation is not necessarily conducive to local democracy. In fact, in situations of sharp local inequalities, decentralisation sometimes heightens the concentration of power, and discourages rather than fosters participation among the underprivileged. To illustrate, in some tribal areas where upper caste landlords and traders dominate village affairs, the devolution of power associated with the Panchayati Raj amendments has consolidated their hold and reinforced existing biases in the local power structure *(Second Administrative Reforms Commission, 2004).*

The Tenth Five-Year Plan highlighted the importance of governance for tackling the problems of poverty, backwardness and low human development and pointed out the importance of embarking on comprehensive governance-related reforms agenda. A multi- faceted approach was adopted, with particular emphasis being laid on the implementation of the 73rd and 74th Constitutional Amendment Acts, 1992, which gave Constitutional status to Panchayati raj institutions (PRIs) and urban local bodies (ULBs) respectively, in both letter and spirit in order to bring about greater decentralisation and increase the involvement of the community in planning and implementing schemes and, thus, increase accountability. The agenda also included institutional reforms, including those related to the civil service, judicial system, policing and the criminal justice administration system. It also emphasized the role of e-Governance, which can improve the delivery of a wide range of services to citizens and businesses *(Ministry of Rural Development, Govt. of India, 2004).*

Functional Demarcation between the Three Tiers

Although 29 subjects have been allocated to the PRIs, there is lack of clarity about the distinct roles of the three different tiers of the PRI system in relation to these subjects. The Eleventh Schedule does not specify the principles of functional demarcation between the Zilla Panchayats, the Panchayat Samiti and the Gram Panchayat. The S.B. Sen Committee on Decentralisation of Powers set up by the Government of Kerala had recommended that the principle of subsidiarity functions which could be performed best by the lowest tier, should be entrusted only to that tier and not to a higher tier could be followed while demarcating the functional domain of the three tiers. This is even more necessary as the three tiers are not hierarchical *(Reports, Planning Commission, 2004).*

All India Institute of Local Self Government, established in 1926 has been actively working in the field of urban development management and is an active partner in promoting the cause of local government in India and overseas. The Institute also recognizes the efforts put in by Urban Local Bodies, fighting all the odds. Kerala Institute of Local Administration (KILA) is an autonomous body constituted under the Ministry of Local Self Government, Government of Kerala, registered as per Travancore – Cochin Literacy, Scientific and Charitable Societies Act-1995. KILA was established in 1990, in the pattern of a national institute, with the main objective of strengthening local governance through training, research and consultancy.

The role of the local self-government is so significant when it comes to disaster management. In the following chapters the researcher tries to analyze the various roles and responsibilities of local self-government in the management of natural catastrophe.

(3) Role of Local Self Government in Disaster Management

The Role of Local Self Government in managing natural disasters and thereby implementing relief, rehabilitation and reconstruction activities are considered one of the major tasks entitled to the local self-governments. Panchayati Raj institutions have already been recognized as capable and competent to shoulder the constitutional responsibilities. Without proper examining and facilitating atmosphere, there has been an emphasis on degrading and downgrading their potential *(Taori, 2005)*[3].

Disaster Management, in its true perspective, includes policies, administrative decisions and operational activities pertaining to disaster prevention, mitigation, preparedness, response, recovery and rehabilitation. Capacity for disaster management intervention calls for perspective building through training and awareness programmes for staff, community organisations and the community at large, as well as the creation of an organizational set up for intervention. Capacity means that a disaster management plan is in place, along with a contingency plan. Resources need to be set apart, facilities need to be created and equipments have to be purchased. Roles are to be defined and responsibilities are to be allocated among officials, elected members, government departments, community based organizations and NGOs *(Kamal, 2005).* Viewed in this perspective, the Panchayat at present has little capacity for disaster management. The very concept of 'disaster management' is alien to the Panchayati Raj Institutions. The lessons from Bihar and Latur clearly brought out the need for "technical guidance and capacity building" of the Panchayats in reconstruction and rehabilitation work. The increasing potential of Panchayats to manage and implement post disaster reconstruction and rehabilitation programs is not a need but a real urgent requirement *(Kamal, 2005)*[4].

The 73rd Constitutional Amendment of India entrusts the Village Panchayats to be the sole responsible bodies for the development of villages and function as local self-governance institutions. Their primary duties are: (a) Effective habitat development including zoning for safe locations and sites for the site less; (b) Providing basic infrastructure such as roads, electricity, drainage, waste management, safe drinking water and sanitation facilities; (c) Providing adequate employment to provide food security and to prevent the starvation and deaths; and (d) Disaster preparedness and management. *(Report of the Task Force on Panchayati Raj Institutions (PRIs) Planning Commission, New Delhi, December 2001).* Apart from these mandatory responsibilities, there are "29 other areas such as, but not limited to, land and water management, vulnerability reduction, social security, and child development " earmarked as the duties of Village Panchayats under section 243G of the Constitution of India.

Role of Panchayati Raj bodies in Disaster Management: General Perspectives

While the government has the duty to help people in distress, the latter have a greater responsibility to help the government help them to cope with disasters. Panchayati Raj bodies are the most appropriate local institutions for involving people in natural disaster preparedness. Panchayati Raj bodies have a role to play in all phases of disaster management. The ensuing analysis discusses the major roles of PRIs during a crisis situation *(Jain & Polman, 2003)*.

Panchayats Role during the First Phase of Disaster Management:

The following are the major roles and responsibilities of the three - tier systems of local self-government before, during and post- disaster management period.

Gram Panchayat or Village level

- Convene meetings to ensure timely warning
- Update information on civic amenities/population, etc.
- Select safe locations for people and livestock
- Arrangements to evacuate the elderly, the disabled, children and women
- Medical and sanitation facilities at relief camps
- Disconnecting power lines during high winds/gales; storing food grain, drinking water, etc.

Block/Mandal Panchayat

- Supervise preparedness of Gram Panchayats (GP)
- Consolidate village-level information on items listed under GP
- Assessing preparedness of: primary health centres/evacuation arrangements, etc.
- Engineering staff at the Block/Mandal level should repair drainage/ canal/roads, etc.
- Contact ex-army/security forces personal/volunteers to organize task force for assistance
- Procure and keep ready rescue material, including boats
- Function as link between district and village-level counter-disaster activities.

Zilla Panchayat or District level

- The District Collector/CEO should convene a meeting of all District Heads of sectoral departments and ZP members before the start of likely cyclone periods (May to June & Oct. to Nov.)

- Initiate all concerned departments to take up necessary repair and maintenance and related works for preparedness
- Organize 'Task Forces' at district, block and village levels
- Identify NGOs useful in providing assistance during disasters
- Check inventories of items required at short notice for rescue and relief operations
- At first warning, call meeting of Crisis Management Group (CMG) and alert blocks/villages
- All CMG members should be asked to keep their personnel in full preparedness
- District Collector should be made the CMG Leader and establish a control room managed by senior officers round the clock during the crisis *(Jain & Polman, 2003).*

Panchayat Role in Rescue and Relief before and during Natural Disaster impact:

Gram Panchayat or Village level

- Set up temporary shelters/relief camps after initial warning/store food and water for people/livestock
- Evacuation of people and livestock should start immediately after final warning
- Keep rescue volunteers and task forces ready
- District/block medical/relief teams may be asked to take position at strategic points and coordinate with village volunteers/task forces
- Organize veterinary aid teams for taking care of livestock and removal of carcasses
- Disposal of dead bodies and prevention of the spread of epidemics
- Assessing loss of life, livestock and damage to farming, property, etc.

Block/Mandal Panchayat

- Identify vulnerable areas and send task forces/volunteers to supervise safety measures
- Evacuate people from these areas and help GPs in organizing relief camps
- Arrange for emergency communication through police wireless/ ham radio, etc.

- Arrange supply of food and other items to relief camps in adequate quantities
- Supervise rescue and relief activities with district-level officers
- Inform CMG if help is needed from police and defense forces
- Assist armed forces in rescue and relief operations
- Supervise rescue and relief and coordinate with various agencies including NGOs.

Zilla Panchayat or District level

- Monitor situation, identify blocks and villages most likely to be affected and issue warnings
- Activate control room and keep a full watch on the situation
- Arrange emergency communication with the help of police wireless/ham radio, etc.
- Put CMG on the job of assisting block and village Panchayats with counter-disaster steps
- Arrange transport for evacuation of people and livestock
- Arrange for temporary shelters/relief camps
- Seek assistance of the armed forces if necessary
- Monitor rescue and relief operations at village and block levels
- Assist lower Panchayats in mobilizing task forces/volunteers/ NGOs for rescue and relief *(Reports, The Panchayati Raj model in India, 2003).*

Role of Panchayat in Reconstruction and Long-term Mitigation Planning:

Gram Panchayat or Village level

- Assist in identifying victims for compensation, and then in its distribution
- Formulate reconstruction plans for houses, community buildings, roads, etc. within GP jurisdiction with the assistance of technical departments at block and district levels.
- Enforce minimum specifications for safe construction.
- Help district and block level organizations in arranging awareness camps for management and mitigation of disasters and ensure participation of the villagers.
- Organize village-level task force/volunteers and train them in counter-disaster measures.

- Assist in supervising and monitoring reconstruction and development projects.
- Encourage local people to insure assets/livestock, which should be mandatory for those who can afford. Seek government help for those who are too poor to afford insurance *(Reports, the Panchayati Raj model in India, 2003).*

Block/Mandal Panchayat

- Assist in rehabilitation, repair and reconstruction
- Assist gram Panchayats in identifying victims for payment of compensation and in its distribution
- Prepare village and block-level mitigation plans; consolidate/ integrate these with the block plan
- Enforce minimum safety specifications for construction
- Assist in long-term mitigation planning and its integration with block/district development plans
- Supervise and monitor reconstruction and long-term mitigation projects implemented by GPs and Block Panchayats.

Zilla Panchayat or District level

- Planning and implementation of rehabilitation, repair and reconstruction
- Compensation for loss of life, property, etc.
- Hazard and vulnerability mapping
- Anti-disaster measures to be integrated in all development projects
- Special funding to use disaster-resistant construction technologies in vulnerable areas *(Reports, The Panchayati Raj model in India, 2003).*

Opportunities to engage with Panchayati Raj Institutions:

Local self-governance has existed in India in the name of village council, caste Panchayats, and village Panchayats. Since independence, there have been many half-hearted attempts to revive this local self-governance as the Village Panchayats. The 73rd and 74th amendment of the Indian Constitution has been the latest and perhaps the most significant step in this direction. Yet, in practice, the Panchayats are sidelined in decision making with regard to village development. As a result, Panchayat leaders have become merely agents of district / state governments to implement state and central schemes. The Panchayats, however, are the only "sustainable local institution" to carry out the process of development. The opportunities to engage with and engage the Panchayats in the reconstruction processes are manifold.

The Panchayati Raj Institutions have a significant place in the process of disaster preparedness and management. The functionaries of the Panchayati Raj Institution involved in disaster management can train the people to face disasters through the community initiatives; keep people in safer places and maintain proper administration of relief in emergencies; mobilize the people and sensitize them to have enough courage and preparedness to face the situation; reduce the extent of loss and damages caused by the disaster; take initiative to develop micro plan for reconstruction; and initiate long-term measures to prevent or minimize the intensity of disasters *(Jain & Polman, 2003)*[5].

Role of Panchayati Raj Institutions in Post Tsunami Rehabilitation and Reconstruction in Kerala- An Analysis

The Alappad Gram Panchayat, Kerala has been reduced to a mute spectator to the tsunami death and destruction as well as to the relief and rehabilitation activities. As seen everywhere in the state, disaster preparedness, disaster management or mitigation does not find a place in the Panchayat plan, and there is no budget allocation for the purpose *(SAHAYI, 2005)*[6].

Many NGO's had come together and involved themselves in the relief and rehabilitation activities carried out. In spite of the strenuous efforts, concerns of different grades and proportions erupted. But there were notable serious concerns that came up in the post disaster context. One of the major errors was that the local democracies were not much involved in the relief, rescue, and rehabilitation efforts *(Placid, 2005)*. The major reason for this lack of involvement could be the strict administrative restrictions from the government. The state government handed over all the responsibilities to the District Collector to carry out the disaster relief, rescue, and rehabilitation operations. All the meetings were held at the collector's office which is very far from the disaster affected area. Local Panchayat leaders were not adequately represented in the meetings, and their voice wasn't strong enough to influence the decision making processes. It was the revenue officers who prepared the list of the disaster affected population without consulting with the local people and their elected local representatives (*Reports, SAHAYI & Malteser International, 2006)*[7].

In the initial relief and rehabilitation phase itself, the local self-governance institutions had very less role or intervention in the tsunami relief and rehabilitation efforts. They had practically no stake in the disaster management – no administrative decisions or operational activities pertaining to prevention, mitigation, preparedness, response, recovery or rehabilitation. No wonder, eleven of the thirteen elected representatives of the last Panchayat committee lost their seats in the recent elections at Alappad Gram Panchayat, which saw the maximum tsunami death toll in the state *(DEEDS, 2006).*

The serious limitation is the lack of a legislative framework. Current legislations do not entrust disaster management functions with the PRI institutions. Disaster relief operations of the state government are governed by certain regulatory restrictions. The Chief Minister's Relief Fund provides the resource for disaster relief and the use of these funds is governed by the provisions relating to the Discretionary Grant of the Financial Code of the state government. According to the relevant legal provisions, the use of the relief fund should be entrusted to the officials of the Revenue Department. These legal provisions restrict the involvement of Panchayat Raj institutions (PRIs) in disaster relief and rehabilitation operations *(Reports, SAHAYI, 2005).*

The strict regulatory regime that has characterized the tsunami relief operations in Kerala has not sufficiently encouraged or motivated the NGOs and other civil society organizations to fully commit themselves to the tsunami relief, rehabilitation and reconstruction. The administrative restrictions have constrained the involvement of the local self-governance institutions such as the Panchayat. Even the elected representatives of the people in the local self-governance institutions have not been involved in the need assessment or beneficiary selection. Community participation in the state sponsored relief programmes has been absent. The tsunami affected families, the real stakeholders, are not involved in the need assessment, programme formulation or selection of beneficiaries. This has led to problems in planning and implementation of the relief and rehabilitation programmes. The benevolent state administration has been facing criticism, opposition and sometimes violent revolts from the tsunami affected people. This has led to delay in the delivery of the state sponsored relief and reconstruction programmes. The state government is aware of the limitation and has promised that a new legislation for disaster relief would be brought in *(G.Placid, 2005).*

The Panchayats can develop disaster management plans and strategies in accordance with their communities' vulnerabilities and their own capacities and needs. It is important that the community as a whole -

business, neighbourhood associations, local and international NGOs, and the media- are involved in this effort. Where communities and the local self-governments are not directly involved and are passive recipients of relief, the result will be the aggravation of a "dependency" syndrome. Disaster management, therefore, needs to be a coordinated effort between national government, state government and local self-government. They should also involve different government departments, non-governmental organizations, private sector and community-based organizations such as NGOs and other civil society organizations *(World Disasters Report, 2004)*[8].

Role of Panchayats in Disaster Management

The potential of the Panchayat in managing the implementation of disaster management plan at the grassroots can be understood in the following ways. The Panchayat:

- has the wherewithal to compile and provide the correct data regarding, loss of life and livelihoods, availability of resources, family details and other such local information that is required to assess damage and develop rehabilitation plans.
- is in a unique position to provide contact with all local families and connect them with relief and reconstruction benefits ensuring fairness and avoiding duplication
- has the administrative authority to provide land to the landless from the village common lands thus supporting relocation needs that have emerged post tsunami in South India.
- has the administrative authority to manage physical and institutional assets of the village.
- Constitutionally, it is expected to make and implement development plans for the village which include habitat development, livelihood supports and also vulnerability reduction – disaster mitigation measures. The Panchayat can provide critical support and direct the reconstruction and rehabilitation in many ways: These are:
- Planning and design: Based on correct and actual data of damage and needs of the various village communities, provide a village level plan for reconstruction and rehabilitation. Moreover they would be able to help develop designs of houses and community structure in line with the local cultural and lifestyles thus ensuring that these are acceptable to the village community (*Role of Panchayati Raj Institutions in Post Tsunami Reconstruction and Rehabilitation, 2005).*

- Educating the village community regarding safety of new construction: The Village Panchayat has to "educate and convince" the village families about safe construction practices and safety of new structures being constructed. Thus, to a large measure the acceptability of reconstructed houses can be addressed.
- Quality control: With adequate technical guidance, the Panchayat can provide the necessary manpower to manage the quality of the physical reconstruction work. They also have the necessary authority for ensuring that quality measures for construction works are implemented.
- Ensuring community participation: Panchayat members, being the elected representatives of the families are best placed to motivate families to participate in the process of reconstruction and provide inputs– both time and labor towards the reconstruction.
- Facilitation and implementation of reconstruction plans: As critical members of reconstruction committees in the village, the Panchayats can provide facilitation of work, land use planning and zoning, decision on location of community assets, conversion of land, allotment of land for the landless and also validating and verifying claims of various families for compensation and new constructions.
- Implementing community based disaster mitigation measures: The Panchayats are best placed to motivate and include the Gram Sabha in order to set in place localized measures to prevent large scale damage in case of natural climatic extremities. These included plantation at the coast line, creation of sand barriers, training of local youth to take immediate evacuation and relief measures, maintaining records of vulnerable families and village resources that need immediate attention in case of a natural calamity. Interestingly, on 17th December, 9 days prior to the Tsunami all village Panchayats in Tamil Nadu conducted special Gramsabha to constitute Village Level Disaster Management Committees. Basic functions of the Panchayat for preparedness and response were defined. These Local Panchayat committees are best placed to implement disaster response and future disaster preparedness and mitigation measures *(Role of Panchayati Raj Institutions in Post Tsunami Reconstruction and Rehabilitation, 2005).*

Disaster Preparedness and Management: Panchayats' Participation

As mentioned before, Panchayats and Municipalities as local governing institutions have a constitutional mandate under the 73rd and

74th Constitutional Amendment Act. Subsequent to the 73rd Constitutional Amendment Act, all four states have passed the confirmative act. For the first time women, Dalits and Adivasis were elected as leaders of local body institutions. Past studies show that if the capacities of the local bodies' institutions developed through training, they can work more efficiently and in a participatory way with accountability and transparency. Good governance could be an instrumental feature in poverty reduction. The Articles 243G of the Constitution visualizes Panchayats as institutions of self-governance. A comprehensive list of 29 subjects has been provided to the Panchayats through 11th schedule. The success of the Panchayats depends upon the devolution of powers, functions and functionaries. This particular study conducted a few intensive case studies with select Panchayat Presidents to find out the role played by them in the recent disasters in the four states *(Jena, 2009).*

Some past experiences clearly show that the Panchayats have proved the capability to carry out disaster preparedness and disaster management. In Tamil Nadu, many Panchayat leaders exhibited their capacity during and after tsunami disaster. In Andra Pradesh, a few leaders had the capacity to carry out the relief activities; they were regularly attending the district level meetings. In Gujarat, few NGO's trained the Panchayat leaders on disaster management. Now, they have taken up rehabilitation activities in their respective Panchayats. In Orissa, Panchayats are part of the Cyclone shelter Management Committee, DMT. House benefits to needy survivors are distributed through Panchayat. In addition, if there is hunger in any Panchayat, it is the responsibility of the Panchayat to provide food. Need of the hour is to strengthen the Panchayat in the disaster management aspects. It should be a part of their regular activities along with development activities. Trained, sensitized leaders will be able to manage disasters effectively.

Every Gram Panchayat should have a committee exclusively for disaster management. They have to be fully trained and they have to be involved in all disaster management activities. In Tamil Nadu, training was given to PRIs even before the tsunami struck the coastal areas and those Panchayats had their own advantages of the training programme in the preparedness and were able to save the lives of many and was instrumental in reducing the material loss as well.

Role of Panchayats in Disaster Mitigation

Involvement of Panchayats in disaster mitigation and preparedness is beneficial in view of their proximity, universal coverage and enlisting people's participation on an institutionalized basis in hastening the process of rural transformation. In general, local bodies like Panchayats have not been consulted for planning in disaster preparedness, the relief and rehabilitation work *(Jena, 2009)*. This leads to absence of transparency, accountability and social audit in the mitigation efforts. The whole approach of rehabilitation work even now continues to be 'top down' in nature. As the relief and restoration efforts involve investment of hundreds and thousands of crores of rupees, there should be satisfaction of having utilized them properly and efficiently.

There should be introspection as to how the local communities and local institutions like Panchayats face such disasters and how best they handle crises. There is a view that local bodies like Panchayats should be encouraged and empowered to manage the local affairs with the available local resources. The elected leaders and officials of Panchayats are to be trained to develop capacities to handle crisis situation in preparedness, warning, rescue, relief, medical assistance, damage assessment, counseling, water and sanitation and rehabilitation operations. It is felt that even during the biggest disasters the role assigned to Panchayats was meager in handling the problems of various types at the grassroots level *(R.K.Sharma and Gagandeep Sharma, 2009)*.

In Orissa Super Cyclone (1999), the total number of severely affected Gram Panchayats was 2399 covering 17993 villages. Had those bodies have been given sufficient powers; the situation would have been different during the relief and rescue operations. No doubt that Central and State Governments, NGO's and International Agencies have their role to play in disaster mitigation. Various government agencies rush with their disorganized relief and rehabilitation efforts whenever large scale devastation takes place. Similarly in Gujarat, 10 districts consisting of 95 taluks, 7904 villages and several towns were severely affected by the earthquake. It was reported that comprehensive rehabilitation package was prepared based on conventional bureaucratic understanding. It gave priority to physical rehabilitation but the economic rehabilitation of the affected was completely ignored. Even for physical rehabilitation, there was no mention of delivery mechanism of inputs like finance, material and technology and skill. While NGOs figure as significant stake holders in the rehabilitation programme, local self-governing bodies like Panchayats and municipalities do not appear as partners in the process of recovery. In a responsive administrative system, when power is in the hands of democratically elected institutions, relief and rescue operations and day- to-day managing of civil services, providing medical assistance, etc, can be attended to by local institutions like Panchayats *(A.C.Jena, 2009).*

The Karnataka Panchayati Raj Act (1993) as part of powers and duties of Adhaksha of Taluka Panchayat under Section 152, "have the power to accord sanction up to a total sum of Rs.25000 in a year for the purpose of providing immediate relief to those who are affected by natural calamities in the Taluka." Similarly, under Section 193 (E) as part of powers and duties of Adhayaksha of Zilla Panchayat, they "have power to accord, sanction up to a sum of Rs. 1 lakh in a year for the purpose of providing immediate relief to those who are affected by natural calamities in the district." Under Section 58-Schedule 1, Village Panchayats is supposed to provide relief in natural calamities, under Section 145, Schedule II, The Taluka Panchayat is supposed to provide relief in natural calamities, similarly under Section 184, Schedule III empowers Zilla Panchayat to provide relief in natural calamities. In West Bengal Panchayat System there are Standing Committees at Zilla Parishad and Panchayati Samithi Level namely "cottage and small industries, relief and social welfare" (standing committee No. 7) as provided by the West Bengal Panchayati Raj Act *(A.C. Jena, 2009).*

There is a view that the activities like distributing immediate relief in the form of money, food grains, Medicare, medicines, clothes, tents, vessels, drinking water and other necessities, efforts of restoration, rehabilitation, reconstruction, efforts of damaged villages and towns can be implemented better with the involvement of local bodies. It must be conceded that wherever it struck strong roots, PR has played a crucial role in mobilizing people in various crises situations. For example, the lead taken by the PRIs in the wake of calamities such as 1993 flash floods in Jalpaiguri district of West Bengal is a positive step towards counter-disaster preparedness operations. However, it is germane to add that it is difficult to preempt disasters as also predict their magnitude. But the debilitating effects of disasters on people living in vulnerable area/zones and losses to the property can be minimized by involving various institutions like PRI's at the grassroots level, to the extent possible *(Jena, 2009).*

Government, Civil Society Organizations and Panchayats

In the absence of relief code and disaster management policy; the state government had created a framework for relief and rehabilitation under which the state took its dominant, regulatory, supervisory role and civil society organizations undertook the activities as implementing agencies. Moreover the lessons learnt in the past have not been used. India also has got rich experience in disaster mitigation but they are not being properly used. Mahatma Gandhi himself had undertaken relief and rehabilitation works which is known as the Gandhian perspective of disaster management. In Tamil Nadu after tsunami, district Administration was fully empowered to take decisions and hence the confusions seen in Gujarat, Orissa and Maharashtra were avoided. The whole relief activities were managed in decentralized way under the leadership of many ministers and rural development officials. The approach was totally decentralized but not integrated with local bodies *(G.Palanithuurai, 2009)*[9]

Panchayats and Civil Society Organizations in Community Based Disaster Preparedness

Following are the activities of the Panchayats in association with civil society organizations:

(a) Upgradation of contingency plans regularly,
(b) Proving capacity building to task force regularly by the Panchayat,
(c) Providing resource to task forces,
(d) Keeping rescue equipment's and survival kits ready,
(e) Safe storage of essential commodities and material construction of temporary shelters should be ready,
(f) Feeding cattle's medicine and water,
(g) Providing food to the task force in time,
(h) Restoration of infrastructure,
(i) They have to link CCP programmes with existing development programmes. They have to provide basic services. Coordination and networking is most important. They have to conduct awareness camps regularly (G.Palanithuurai, 2009).

Role of Panchayat in Cyclone Shelter Maintenance: A Case study

Government of Orissa has constructed 99 multi-purpose cyclone shelters. Sarpanches were the integral part of the cyclone center from the construction to maintenance of the cyclone shelters. Government of Orissa is following decentralized disaster management system. The Sarpanches have financial devolution power also. Sarpanches not only distributed relief materials but also acted as facilitators. The house building assistance to the beneficiaries should be distributed through the Sarpanches. Relief should be distributed within 10 days. Destitute families should be given special assistance *(G.Palanithuurai, 2009).*

Ways and Means to Strengthen Communities and Panchayats in Disaster Management

The past experience shows that Government, INGO's and NGO's have taken number of measures for relief, rehabilitation and reconstruction activities regarding disaster. Based on experience an array of reports have prepared for dissemination. Very useful recommendations have been made. But there is no proper initiative to make use of all those suggestions. Government structure in Orissa is very weak but bureaucrats in Tamil Nadu are efficient and they are delivering goods. When tsunami struck, decision making powers were decentralized and District Collectors were given power to take decisions based on the ground realities. Apart from the District Collectors many officials efficiently worked. In that situation, the local body institutions were sidelined both by Government and NGOs. The situations not only prevailed in Tamil Nadu but also in Andhra Pradesh and Gujarat also *(G.Palanithuurai, 2009).*

People and their assets were damaged due to flood, cyclone, tsunami and earth quake and they are still in the process of rehabilitation and reconstruction. We have already discussed in the previous chapters about the roles played by the Government, NGOs, INGOs and Gram Panchayats. It is to be noted that assistance could be extended to the affected at any amount. And people must be made to work for their development. The external agencies can work with people in the system created for them. If any institution or organization or group works for them, communities' pride and self-respect will be eroded. People should have a feeling that they can manage on their own with support from others. Despite huge loss of life and livelihoods in the recent disaster, generous support from the donor agencies and Government enabled the communities to overcome the shock and they started rebuilding. They spent huge amount on relief, rehabilitation and reconstruction process. But the study found that it had not produced the results to the level of investment. The study found that the relief activities were not gender sensitivity and equity oriented. It was supply driven and not demand driven. In this situation, the 73rd and 74th Constitutional Amendments envisage the Panchayats should strive for the welfare, safety and the prosperity of the villagers *(Panchayats in Disaster Preparedness and Management, 2009)*[10].

According to the 74th Constitutional Amendment Act, the Panchayats should prepare the plan for the socio-economic development of the people. While preparing the socio-economic development plans the Panchayat could include disaster management as one of its components. As there was no system, structure and procedure at the grassroots level, the resources dumped at that level had not met the felt needs of the community. In this situation, reconstruction could be done by preparing micro plan at the Panchayat level. While preparing micro plan, Panchayat could make reliable assessments on the nature and the extent of the damage caused by the disaster. The environmental norms such as distance from the sea, identification of safe locations, designs, technologies and materials for construction of safe disaster resistant buildings should be considered. It could ensure that the entire vulnerable are identified and included so that they get what is due to them from the reconstruction activities. Panchayats could make use of this opportunity to meet long felt needs. For instance, they could develop new connecting roads that didn't exist earlier *(Palanithurai, G, 2009).*

With regard to damage assessment, the Panchayat could identify number of houses damaged and its magnitude. Public buildings (Anganwadi, schools, health centers, community halls, Panchayat building, PDS shop, vocational training centers or any other governmental structures can be used very effectively). Panchayats should be aware of the damages caused to the basic services including drinking water supply, access roads, sewage disposal, drainage, electricity and communication apart from the physical damages. Panchayats should take responsibility to assess the damages and relief has to be given accordingly *(Palanithurai.G, 2009).*

To ensure the rehabilitation for a long-term development, the Panchayats must be made to concentrate on the following activities:

(a) Rebuilding livelihoods,
(b) Opportunity for adopting innovative approaches,
(c) Build their sustainable network of village-based economies, and
(d) Use the opportunity to strengthen and improve livelihood among the people of the village.

Through proactive and well-planned rehabilitation work, we can reduce gender based, caste based, religion-based, class-based divisions in relief and rehabilitation activities. A few well trained, well oriented Gram Panchayat presidents took efforts in relief, rehabilitation and reconstruction activities in certain Panchayats. This yielded good results. Based on the field experience, this study suggested that in every gram Panchayat, Disaster Management Committee headed by gram Panchayat presidents is to be formed. Government should form disaster management committees as statutory committees. In such disaster management committees, Self Help

Groups, youth, and elders should be integrated and they have to be oriented. In every ward, a sub-committee at village level headed by a ward member has to be constituted. Integrated Disaster Management Training should be provided to the Panchayat members and other stakeholders regularly. In every committee women and Dalit representatives should be included *(Palanithurai.G, 2009).*

Allocation of separate Contingency fund for Disaster Management for every gram Panchayat is an imperative. Government should allocate Rs. 1 lakh as united fund every year to each gram Panchayat for disaster preparedness and management activities. There should be synergy between the constitutional Panchayats and traditional Panchayats. For all relief activities, the government departments have to rely on the community constituted at the grassroots. A new culture has to be created to involve people. It requires a special training at all levels from Gram Sabha members to higher officials at the district and state level. At every Gram Panchayat a contingency plan has to be developed. At every block and every district, plan has to be prepared and implemented with the active participation of the stakeholders *(Palanithurai, G, 2009).* Panchayats have to take responsibility from the stage of assessment of the losses to reconstruction. Panchayats should have contingency fund. In the same way, every Grama Panchayat should have food stock through every ration shop. The entire physical infrastructure created through various government departments have to be handed over to the Panchayats during the period of disaster.

Every state should have a Disaster Management Act, policy and clear-cut guidelines of carry out relief, rehabilitation and reconstruction works. Role clarity has to be ensured. Clear-cut guidelines have to be prepared for disaster management at the Grama Panchayat level. As drought, flood and other disasters do not occur frequently, each state should have a department meant for disaster relief with sufficient authority. In the regular department activities, preparedness component has to be incorporated consciously. A well-maintained communication system has to be developed. With regard to data on the loss and compensation, the Panchayat should be held responsible. Gram Panchayat should be made responsible for collecting vital statistics. It has to update the data regularly. This data should be validated by the Gramsabha. The data have to be confirmed in the Gramsabha meeting. All relief and rehabilitation activities will be carried out only based on the data already confirmed.

Currently, we need people-centered approach. It should be community-based intervention. Involvement of constitutional local bodies is more important. All reconstruction activities should be carried out with the support of village micro plan. Building confidence among people to organize and respond to disaster is also essential.

The Promise of Decentralization

Much has been written about decentralization and the local civil society institutions-local government interface, although the political character of the process, particularly in developing countries, has often been underestimated. "Decentralization and Participation are means of bringing a broader section of a given population in to public decision-making processes – in a role of information and/or controlling those processes" *(Ribot, 1999).* The assumption is that greater participation in public decision making is a positive good in itself, and / or that it can improve efficiency, equity, and, especially important in the context of local institutions involved in Disaster Risk Management, Development and Resource management. By bringing government decision making closer to the citizenry, decentralization is widely believed to increase public sector accountability and therefore effectiveness, whilst contributing to the strength of a genuinely people-centered type of democratic culture *(Prasad. S, 2009).*

Unwittingly, local population group themselves often do their part to further increase their risk exposure, for example, through unsafe settlement on steep slopes, unsustainable deforestation leading to soil degradation, etc. This has been the unintended outcome of a lot of spontaneous house hold relocation and formal resettlement programmes promoted by government, in which newcomers lack the necessary local agro-ecological and farming system knowledge to devise risk coping strategies suited to their novel surroundings. This constitute all the more reason to inform local population groups about the risks they are exposed to, involving them as responsible actors in disaster prevention activities – usually, everyone has something to contribute to the reduction of disaster risk hazards and should be provided with the opportunity of doing so. It's a way of increasing the self-reliance of the population at risk and sustainability of disaster prevention measures, all of which is more easily achieved by the decentralized, local government level, and below *(Prasad.S, 2009).*

As Crook and Manor (1998) argue, bringing government closer to people increases efficiency by helping "…tap the creativity and resources of local community…" Decentralization is believed to increase coordination, vertical linkages (discussed in the section 8 below) and flexibility among administrative agencies and effectiveness in development and conservation planning and implementation. Where it is real, local government bureaucrats and technocrats are in a position to invest in DRM as they have been devolved the power and provided with sufficient funds to do so. It is however often difficult to use scarce public funds for environmental conservation – which contains elements useful to natural disaster prevention – given the unattractiveness of such activities in political terms; on the other hand, it is the aftermath of catastrophic events that provides opportunities to accumulate political through (donor-funded) infrastructure reconstruction (*Prasad.S, 2009).*

If participatory, decentralization can increase managerial efficiency by allowing local population groups, who bear the cost of resource, make those decisions, rather than leaving them in the hands of outsiders or unaccountable locals can increase efficiency by internalizing economic, social and ecological costs and benefits; reducing administrative and management transaction costs via the proximity of local participants, accessing local skill and local information; and using local knowledge and aspirations in project design, implementation, management and evaluation for better matching of actions to needs *(Ribot, 1999*). Given that natural disasters rarely hit whole countries, but, rather hazard risk often varies even from one micro-region to another, it becomes essential to use local knowledge for effective prevention measures and to adapt these to local threats and vulnerabilities. Whereas this trends to happen within the confines of DRM project frameworks, (as we will see further below) this is far from being institutionalized in the public sector *(Prasad. S, 2009).*

National disaster plans may mention mitigation and preparedness, but often lack detail and dedicated resources. Social, political and macroeconomic pressures can undermine the capacity of state authorities to reduce risks. Cash-strapped central governments may simply abdicate their responsibilities, leaving disaster management to local governments and NGO's, even though they (know they) lack the skills and recourses to do so. In many parts of the world, fiscal and financial decentralization have not kept up the pace of politico-administrative decentralization. Local government can thus often only count on a narrow tax base and are not usually given sufficient central funds to be able to afford "luxurious" expense such as those committed to NRM, let alone ex-ante investments in DRM, which remain difficult to justify vis-à-vis local constituencies often angry at continuing budgetary cuts in the health and education [8] sectors, for example.

Notwithstanding these state of affairs, initiatives have been taken in many regions, although it appears to have happened mostly through externally-financed projects and programmes. Where these keep on occurring repeatedly, contributing to the creation of a "handout syndrome", government post-disaster relief compensation programmes international assistance may also act as 'incentives' for people to locate disaster prone areas *(Charveriat, 2000).* Certain more recently instituted local government arrangements serve, amongst other objectives, to contribute to alleviate the plight befalling the coffer of the local administration: beyond their role in cross-cultural exchange, twinning programmes between municipalities in the south and north, for example, seek to also bring together all types of resources and experiences to that effect. They are often among the first channels to be appealed to in order to mobilize supplementary external funds to deal with emergencies such as natural disaster, and, often more importantly, play an important advocacy role vis-à-vis regional and national governments as well as, sometimes, the international community *(Prasad. S, 2009).*

As intermediaries with more affluent urban or industrialized rural environments, often in Europe and in the USA, migrant associations have sometimes also been carrying out comparable functions. The impact of their activities tends to be localised, at the intra-community level, not least because of the influence of clan-based and other kinship related social networks within them. Although this is yet another area in which research data is scarce, it appears that the commitment of such associations to play a prominent role in DRM depends partly on their degree of politicization, both vis-à-vis their host countries and those of their origin. With Diasporas acting as financiers and fund-raisers for the immediate rehabilitation needs of households to whom they are connected through familial ties, the bulk of such assistance however tends to take place at the individual level, a phenomenon facilitated by the increasing international out reach of commercial money transfer services and the concomitant diversification of transfer options.

Local Emergency Committees

In Costa Rica there exist more than 60 local emergency committees, at the local administration level of the 'canton', composed of the delegates of various institutions, with each member being assigned a role in case of an emergency; these bodies are integrated in to regional committees. The local committees aspire to be facilitators of community mobilization and organization. Only some few institutions are however represented permanently on the committee, which limits their possibilities of pacification and action. In certain instances, activities are carried out such as the laying out the inventory of resources available to face emergencies and the establishment of several brigades (rescue, first aid, food distribution, transport, etc.). These activities lead to the drafting of Local or Regional Emergency Plans. The latter provides the population with information on where to go in case of an evacuation alarm, who will assist and be assisted, and which other activities are to be joined.

Unsurprisingly, the extent to which DRM measures are institutionalized and streamlined with in local governmental systems and depends largely on the regularity and intensity with which their constituencies keep being affected by extreme natural events. In many parts of the world, during period of heavy rainfall for example, clogged up drains can have a dam effect preventing water from flowing freely, thus creating overflows and ultimately giving rise to flooding. In most of Latin American and the Caribbean, like in Jamaica, drains maintenance is carried out by government and local parish councils, which include the parish disaster committees. These are local government bodies providing residents with evacuation procedures and are responsible for organizing and directing local disaster preparedness and emergency relief operations in collaboration with other voluntary agencies and the government's emergency services *(Prasad. S, 2009).*

In coastal Asia where flood risk is severe, for example in Bangladesh and Cambodia, several projects have been built specifically focusing on people's perception of flood risk; the purpose and tools of community flood risk assessment; the strategies for community organization; and resource mobilization and capacity building. In these cases, the rationale for doing so can be traced back to the sequencing of DRM activities, with an emphasis on local scoping studies and capacity building that are to precede community interventions. North-west china, extension mediation groups were to be used in a similar fashion. With the exception of flood-prone Mozambique, most of the relatively few examples of local government involvement in DRM in sub-Sahara Africa, on the other hand, are not related to rapid onset phenomena such as floods; rather, they can be found in the Sahel, were the recurrent droughts and a strong associational culture coupled with advanced decentralization have led to some degree of success in coping with these slow onset disasters.

In Mozambique, clients of the 'Fondo de Credito Communitario' (FCC), which applies a village or community banking methodology were facing unprecedented floods when a cyclone hit on February 22 in the year of 2000. The flooding, considered the waste in fifty years, caused more destruction to infrastructure than the whole the civil war experienced by the country until the early 1990's. Most FCC clients were displaced for about two months and the emergency response phase took two more months after they returned to their homes as a pilot test during the emergency, cash grants were offered directly to these households by another organization; FCC clients had the option of using this grant to pay off their outstanding debt or restructure their loan in order to keep the grant. Of a total of 89 community banks targeted, only 3 chose to restructure. The community banks that choose to repay, paid the loans before the anticipated repayment date. Evaluations suggest that the cash grants did not have any negative impact on the credit culture of FCC clients since, first, the grants were offered by a different organization, and second, most used the grant to repay their loans in order to obtain a new order.*(Planning For Human settlements In Disaster prone Areas (Prasad.S, 2009).*

Horizontal and vertical institutional interaction local-, meso-, and macro levels:

> Disaster risk mitigation is a cyclical, dynamic process that requires continuous adjustments, decision making and interaction at different yet interrelated levels and among verity of institution and actors, including individuals, householders, communities, non-governmental organizations, market institutions, and government (*World Bank, 2001).*

Local institutions may thus appear on the scene at various stages; regrettably, not many case studies exist on the role they play or may during the different phases or thought out the DRM cycle. Following the latest earth quake in Gujarat (India), the decentralized and well-coordinated nature of its relief distribution network enabled SEWA to provide adequate and timely post-disaster assistance. A three tier mechanism, with team working from the village through the district to the state level, was adopted by the institution to carry out its earth quake response and assistance programme. At the community and district level, teams ensured that the distribution of relief materials was adequate and timely and the state level corresponding to the national level-mechanisms. They were established to ensure coordination with concerned actors such as officials from the government control room and external aid cell, donors, United Nations Agencies, NGOs, and the private sector. SEWA, an already much respected and inspiring institution, thus gave further proof of its logistical capacity and technical competence.

Demand-driven (and often project-confined) processes of participation don't always meet the supply-driven (and often top-down) process of decentralization, and in some cases both are mostly externally driven. Even in historically relatively more inward-looking countries such as china *(Yongong et al. 1999)* find for the North West that 'since the establishment of the household responsibility system, herders' groups are even playing important roles in risk management activity meditating between household and production team level. Village leaders and production team leaders play important roles in risk management, poverty alleviation and extension as agents of the administrative line agencies at the community level. They hold both coordinating and management functions during disaster emergencies as well as during disaster prevention and recovering periods. Yet although the Chinese institutional reform was launched in 1998, the community organizations have not been reached by the reform taking place at the higher institutional level (*Prasad.S, 2009).*

Helping to provide better access to information and its flow between different levels of the administrative system, in Orissa (India), some NGO's ran legal aid centre's with the aim of sensitizing cyclone-affected people about their legal right to compensation by government. The authors of the report describe constraints experienced by responding to disaster through local government in Orissa, India as follows: "Within most governments there are real difficulties in achieving integration between sectors at the policy making level. In India integrated planning does occur to a certain degree at the district level where district and block level planning brings the line ministries together in a more coordinated and harmonized way. DFID India did encourage a more geographical basis for planning but this did not emerge. Had this been taken forward with support to develop proposals on a district-by-district basis it may have created the conditions required for the desired level of sectoral integration? This in turn would have been a significant opportunity to build experience and awareness with in government of a more integrated and holistic approach which would have provided longer- term benefits in the implementation of the western Orissa Livelihoods Project *(S Prasad, 2009).*

Comparison between the 73rd, 74th Constitutional Amendment Act, 1992 and Disaster Management Bill, 2005

The comparison between disaster management bill of 2005, and 73rd & 74th Constitutional Amendment requires the attention of the policy makers and other field experts to make sure the provisions being incorporated are put into the practice.

73rd and 74th Constitutional Amendments Acts, 1992	Disaster Management Bill, 2005 in Parliament
Panchayats and Municipalities are institutions of local self-governance	Panchayats and Municipalities are at par with any other local authorities/ bodies
Local Governments will lead local economic developments and social justice	Collector and his/her advisors will coordinate and implement Disaster Management Plan
District Planning Committee will prepare Draft District Plan	District Authority will prepare plan (after consultation with Zila Parishad and Municipalities)
These Amendment Acts will prevail over all other past Acts	The provisions of this Act, shall prevail

Recommendations Regarding Disaster Management Bill, 2005

On the basis of above discussions in the workshop following Urgent Changes Required in Disaster Management Bill, 2005:

1. Part IX and IX-A of the Constitution define Panchayati Raj Institutions and Municipalities as institutions of local self-governance. However, the Disaster Management Bill describes them as one of the local authorities as described in (clause 2-h, page 2) Chapter- I of the bill. These institutions of local self-governance should be provided due respect in the said Bill. (The primacy of roles of Panchayats and Municipalities was reinforced by experience sharing from different states that in any disaster situation, Panchayats and Municipalities are the first institutions to respond).
2. District Disaster Management Authority (Chapter- IV, clause 25-2, page 10 of the Bill) should not consist of district officials only. It should also include proportionally the representatives of Panchayats, Municipalities and NGOs.
3. National and State level Disaster Management Authorities are headed by Prime Minister and Chief Minister respectively. Following the same principles, District Disaster Management Authority (clause 25 –2- a, page 11) should be headed by the elected chairperson of District Panchayat (not the collectors, as bill proposes now).
4. District Disaster Management Plan (clause 31-2, page 13, chapter-IV) should be prepared on the basis of participatory Disaster Management (DM) - plans prepared by Panchayats and

Municipalities. These DM planning process should be integrated to regular planning process at Panchayat and Municipal levels (Art 243-G and 243-W). The DDMA in turn should assist District Planning Committee (Art.243ZD) in finalization of District Disaster Management Plan.

5. Panchayats and Municipalities must be provided (Chapter VI, page 19) unambiguous and genuinely effective roles in
   (a) Planning for prevention and mitigation of Disasters
   (b) Vulnerability assessment in terms of people and area
   (c) Damage Assessment
   (d) Development of rehabilitation packages and Identification of Beneficiaries
   (e) Information dissemination and Knowledge Building
   (f) Monitoring and Ensuring Implementation of Rehabilitation and Reconstruction.
6. The Bill should delineate the means and modes of Capacity Building for prevention, mitigation and management of disasters. It should specify resources (human and financial) available for Capacity Building of Panchayats and Municipalities by encouraging collaborative efforts of SIRDs, ATIs and other governmental institutions as well as NGOs who can provide training.
7. It was also observed that the Bill does not specify specific measures required as per need of women and children who are most vulnerable during such calamities *(Taori, 2005).*

Issues in Engagement of Local Governments in Disaster Management

Obviously there are some issues pertaining to the Disaster Management. ACT needs to be reviewed and it will be helpful in making amendments to the better coordination of disaster preparedness and response plan with the involvement to all the stakeholders. The following are the key points put forward by the different experts in the field *(Palanithurai, 2009).*

- Current legislations do not entrust disaster management functions with the Local Government.
- The provision in the Kerala Panchayat Raj Act and the subsequent government order on role related to natural calamities is ambiguous.
- The Chief Minister's Relief Fund provides the resource for disaster relief and the use of these funds is governed by the

provisions relating to the Discretionary Grant of the Financial Code of the state government.

- According to the relevant legal provisions, the use of the relief fund should be entrusted to the officials of the Revenue Department.
- These legal provisions restrict the involvement of Local Self Governance Institutions in disaster relief and rehabilitation operations.
- The delivery of relief and rehabilitation would have been far better, if Local Government had at least a nominal role.
- The Panchayat could have assisted many of the NGOs to plan their programmes effectively with information and data support from the Panchayat.
- In fact if the Panchayat were the nodal agency for relief and rehabilitation, the relief and rehabilitation intervention would have been much better with better programme planning, coordination and monitoring.
- The strict regulatory regime that has characterized the tsunami relief operations in Kerala has not sufficiently encouraged or motivated the NGOs and other civil society organizations to fully commit themselves to the tsunami relief, rehabilitation and reconstruction.
- Even the elected representatives and the people in the local self-governance institutions have not been involved in the need assessment or beneficiary selection.
- Community participation in the state sponsored relief programmes has been absent.
- The tsunami-affected families, the real stakeholders, are not involved in the need assessment, programme formulation or selection of beneficiaries.
- Local governments can be quick in response, have local knowledge and can also act as important channels for awareness raising and education.
- However capacity building at local level is imperative among, elected representatives, Panchayat officials and staff of departments and citizens.
- They need to be aware of the rationale and implications of different aspects of disaster management such as disaster prevention, mitigation, preparedness, response, recovery and rehabilitation.

- The Panchayats can develop disaster management plans and strategies in accordance with their communities' vulnerabilities and their own capacities and needs.
- Where communities and the local self-governments are not directly involved and are passive recipients of relief, the result will be the aggravation of a "dependency" syndrome.
- Disaster management, therefore, needs to be a coordinated effort between national government, state government and local self-government.
- They should also involve different government departments, non-governmental organizations, private sector and community-based organizations *(G.Palanithurai, 2009).*

The Role of Panchayats - *Experience from Disasters*

We had earthquake, super cyclone, tsunami, floods, drought and fire in different states in different magnitude and for which center and state governments responded through their resource allocation for relief and rehabilitation activities. At the micro level, a large number of institutions and organizations were involved in the activities with the support of government, NGOs and INGO's. After the enactment of the 73rd amendment, constitutional Panchayats were in position. From the experience of the states in responding to the natural disaster, a perspective could be developed for further action. It will strengthen the local organizations, communities, and institutions and reduce their risks through their preparedness.

The international organizations and the non-governmental organizations were working with the following principles with regard to the disaster:

1. People Centered: Most of the organizations worked with pro-poor disadvantaged and marginalized approach.
2. Participation: Organizations were committed to ensure the local people's participation and stake holder's involvement in all their projects. They were also committed for the strengthening of the local institutions and action on the basis of help for self-help.
3. Development Oriented: Many of them declared that the activities should have focus with development.
4. Gender Sensitivity: Organization made it very clear that all the relief and rehabilitation activities should be carried out with a gender perspective. A gender sensitive approach should be infused in every action.
5. Sustainability: Sustainability is seen as a core principle.

Another striking point related to tsunami is that most of the non-government agencies and other relief organizations working in the state of Tamil Nadu lacked faith in the local body institutions. Many of the organizations lacked disaster perspectives and as a result October to December 2005 saw persistent heavy rains caused severe flooding in fifteen districts of Tamil Nadu. The loss of life was minimal when compared to tsunami and the media coverage was poor. But the flooding affected twenty times more than the population affected by the tsunami the previous year and the community suffered huge losses but all international organizations and non-government organizations did not realize this impact. Finally when people were contacted, the unanimous response was that neither communities nor the Panchayats were consulted in taking major decisions. As a result people suffered during the floods *(Palanithurai, 2009).*

There is a great need to develop the capacities of the local self-government officials in dealing with disasters such as earthquakes, landslides, floods, cyclones and tsunamis which are conquering their own localities. So, providing knowledge building exercises and skill oriented activities play a vital role in empowering the concerned people. The local knowledge and the experiences of the particular community leaders should be incorporated to the disaster policy development activities *(Palanithurai, 2009).*

Tsunami Rehabilitation of Fisheries Livelihoods in India - Integrated Coastal Management, India- *A Situational Report: The Role of Panchayats*

The Institutional Context

This session briefly discusses the role of different institutions in the rehabilitation of fisheries related livelihoods. Apart from the usual quibbles that are part of government rehabilitation efforts anywhere, the state government in Tamil Nadu was widely seen to have handled the disaster admirably, particularly because dealing with a disaster like tsunami was a totally new experience for everyone. The Government went about the rehabilitation programmes in a transparent manner by feeding all relevant information in the Internet and updating frequently. It also actively solicited public-private partnerships and allowed the NGOs and other civil society organizations to take a lead role in the rehabilitation efforts, contenting itself with coordinating their activities and providing the backstopping support when necessary. This might have to do with the fact that the NGOs had more money for rehabilitation than the Government, but its own rehabilitation programmes were also markedly farsighted and holistic, taking into account the long term needs of the people and addressing them by measures that went beyond the tsunami (for instance, see the Policy Note of the Department of Fisheries for 2005). Decentralization of decision-making powers and delegating powers to the district administrations also ensured rapid responses to the crisis *(G.Palanithurai, 2009).*

Another important feature of the Government's efforts was the coming together of different departments to work under a central command (i.e., the district administration), which helped in responding to the multiple needs of the affected people simultaneously, which was in contrast to the more restricted approaches of the other players in the rehabilitation work. A notable difference from the other disaster situations in the country in the recent past was the very low profile maintained by the political class in the rehabilitation effort. The near complete absence of the political class in the rehabilitation programmes in Tamil Nadu was remarked upon by many people as having helped with the smooth execution of the rehabilitation activities. However, one cannot but feel a little concerned about the lack of a role for people's representatives (particularly the Panchayats) in the decision-making processes at a momentous time like this and wonder about its deeper implications in the long term. But in Kerala, the tsunami was much politicized, to an extent that some organizations kept off working in Kerala on tsunami The Tamil Nadu Government's insistence on taking advantage of surplus funds to build better houses at a higher unit cost proved to be a very productive idea and may have partly stemmed the flow of funds into providing boats. Its shelter guidelines, though contested and finally ignored, acted as a benchmark and helped everyone to focus on the practical aspects of the shelter business. It was true that the Government could have come up with similar guidelines in other areas, particularly for fisheries sector rehabilitation to highlight issues related to problems with excess supply and quality control issues in boat building *(G.Palanithurai, 2009).*

The Tamil Nadu Government's firm stance against the plea of the boat owners to be allowed to take the compensation money and move out was highly debatable and highlighted the need for a comprehensive long-term fisheries policy for the state. On the other hand, the Government's decision to extend assistance to the affected the fishing community in cash rather than in kind turned out to be – perhaps unintentionally – a wise choice, in so far as it allowed a few people to move away. Also, it was the compensation money for boats (which were seldom built, thanks to the NGO) that kept the communities afloat in the face of poor fishing, right from the time the relief assistance had been stopped *(G.Palanithurai, 2009).*

Lack of clarity was a complaint that was frequently leveled against the Government's directives. This led to confusion and also giving different interpretations to the orders in different districts. One such issue related to the registration of boats in Nagapattinam and elsewhere, group-ownership was allowed by the Department of Fisheries, but in Cuddalore, it was reported that boats would not be registered as group-owned, because of the potential for trouble such an arrangement would have for the administration. Similarly, while some district officers demanded compulsory registration of all new boats in the post-tsunami period, others were not so insistent. Even in districts where this was made mandatory, there was no apparent mechanism to ensure the strict implementation of such measures and several boats thus avoided being registered. The result was that no one still knew how many boats were in existence in Tamil Nadu now and it would take an elaborate census to obtain a reliable figure *(G.Palanithurai, 2009).*

The implications for fisheries' management as well as for dealing with future disasters are quite clear. There were also differences in the mode of payment of compensation to the tsunami victims. In Nagapattinam, the compensation for boats was paid in full, but in Kanyakumari, only a part of the money – about Rs. 10,000 per – was provided. The remaining amount was deposited in a joint bank account with the Assistant Director of Fisheries as co-signatory, on the understanding that it would be released to the fisherman as and when he produced the new boat. Seeing that many fishermen had already received boats from the NGOs, it was clear that the fisherman would not get a new boat built, so the money might be a saving for the Government in Kanyakumari. The fishermen tried to pass off the NGO-given boats as new, but this was not possible where the NGOs took care to register the boats. In Andhra Pradesh, the biggest constraint had been the choice of a nodal agency for rehabilitation efforts. The choice of 'Velugu', an ongoing state government rural poverty elimination programme focusing on the poorest of the poor with a specific mandate and a clearly defined framework to implement it (see www.velugu.org) to act as the nodal agency for the tsunami rehabilitation programme, which involved short-term, one-off measures and addressed the needs of a much wider constituency of people than are covered under Velugu, was problematic. For instance, Velugu's programme implementation strategies (group-based; women-oriented) did not jell with the objectives of a rehabilitation programme (particularly where a predominantly male-oriented support package – boats and nets – was sought to be implemented) and caused much heartburn among those not covered. Another very troublesome aspect of tsunami rehabilitation in Andhra Pradesh was that information on the progress of activities was not easily accessible to the public, which was in stark contrast to the situation in Tamil Nadu *(G.Palanithurai, 2009).*

Challenges and Obstacles faced by Panchayats in Disaster Response Programs

The remaining section in this chapter specifically addresses the challenges, concerns and problems which was highly visible and experienced during the disaster response programme of South India in the context of 2004 Tsunami.

(a) *Capacity needs and limitations faced by Panchayats today*:

For the village level disaster management plan to be activated, it is important that Panchayats are strengthened in the enforcement and implementation of the plan. They need to be equipped with information skills and technologies to manage disaster situations more effectively within the framework of overall governance and the longer-term development agenda of the village. The first critical need of the Panchayats is to access information about their constitutional portfolios. Most Panchayats are unaware of their jurisdiction and areas of operation. Beyond this, they suffer from: Poor information about technical possibilities and solutions. It was discussed that simple and local solutions can be found for most seemingly complex problems and Panchayats can easily implement the solutions provided they have basic orientation and technical guidance. Many examples were quoted at the workshop relating to tree cover, to address the needs for water harvesting, and also provide economic benefits to village communities in Tamil Nadu, safe construction methods in Latur and simple protection mechanisms for the village during floods in Bihar *(TVSG Trust for Village Self Governance, Tamilnadu, 2007)*[11]

(b) Inadequate Management Capacities and Orientation for Technical Decision Making:

The Panchayats need to build up capacities in management and also technical decision making to be able to manage the reconstruction. Lessons from Latur again revealed that given the supports, Panchayats were able to make appropriate decisions regarding selection of technologies, training of artisans, and orientation of families towards safe construction practices.

Decisions on technologies and systems of construction, house design and location were all taken by the Village Panchayat based on technical guidance and consensus in the Gram Sabha. Lack of trust of the Gram Sabhas, many Panchayats, although constitutionally elected do not carry the trust of the entire Gram Sabhas with them. Many constituents in the village feel they are not adequately represented. The Panchayats need to examine this issue and need to carry their constituents with them rather than their politicians. It is sad but true that many of the Panchayats have become politicized to a point that party politics and not village development is the basis of local election agendas. The lessons from Latur clearly brought out that Panchayats need to be the voice of the village first and must gain confidence of the Gram Sabha as a whole. The Panchayat operations are not transparent to the Gram Sabha and hence corruption and unfair practices are rampant. Lessons from Latur revealed that conflicts must be sorted out in a transparent manner. In village Jawali, Latur, 131 village meetings were held over the course of 2 years during the reconstruction after the 1994 earthquake and every conflict was resolved through an open forum and a meeting could not be adjourned till an acceptable solution was found for the conflict *(Role of Panchayati Raj Institutions in Post Tsunami Reconstruction and Rehabilitation, 2005).*

(c) *Lack of a platform to advocate for common issues:*

Panchayats across the country face similar problems of planning for local development, management control of local natural resources – such as water bodies, sand, stone, forests etc., availing funds for implementing their plans, accessing training to build up their capacities etc. However, each Panchayat operates in isolation. A common forum to share experiences, learning from each other and advocating their common cause is absent. The Panchayats need to be regionally united so that they can advocate for their administrative authority and enhance their capacities to design and implement development programs on a united front.

(d) Lack of focus on core issues and motivation:

The Panchayat leaders felt that they should exercise their constitutional right to administer the village and not wait for the district and state departments to invite them to do so. In order to do so, they felt the need to focus on village based development issues and not caste or petty politics *(Role of Panchayati Raj Institutions in Post Tsunami Reconstruction and Rehabilitation, 2005).*

The Panchayat leaders in a post disaster workshop defined three core needs of a village today;

- Employment – alternative non-farm opportunities,
- Housing, and
- Habitat infrastructure

They however felt inadequately equipped to design solutions and implement action plans for fulfilling these needs in a cost effective and sustainable manner. The Panchayats therefore emphasized on their own need for intensive training and links with technical support agencies. Further, they felt that in most cases, Panchayat members themselves need to be motivated to take on their responsibilities.

The Panchayat leaders expressed a need to identify the pressing issues and unite to find solutions for these and to seek technical assistance and financial access to convert their plans into actions. The Panchayat leaders at the workshop felt that they needed to have greater financial control on the Panchayat funds. There is currently a restriction on them for expenditure. They also need funds to train and equip themselves to manage disaster mitigation and reconstruction programs *(Role of Panchayati Raj Institutions in Post Tsunami Reconstruction and Rehabilitation, 2005).*

(e) Problems faced by the Panchayat in and during disasters:

1. Problems in distributing relief materials and preparing lists of participants,
2. Construction of storage rooms for the storage of stock.
3. Lack of training on the PRI representatives' roles and responsibilities with regard to Disaster Management.
4. Multipurpose cyclone centers-they are under construction through SSA funds, but most of the godowns are constructed in low lying areas and while constructing godowns officials failed to consult with the PRIs and people.
5. Non-availability of cyclone centers in many Panchayats.
6. Non-availability of health facilities.
7. District collectors do not invite the gram Panchayat leaders for disaster committee meetings.
8. Availability of limited funds for disaster management.

9. Lack of awareness on environmental issues among the Panchayati Raj institution members. Creation of awareness among Panchayati Raj institution members on raising the embankment level and improving infrastructural facilities are very much difficult and so the disaster mitigation programmes suffer *(Palanithurai, 2009).*

Obstacles faced by the Panchayat

Many Panchayat presidents faced obstacles and problems in establishing temporary shelter. The officials who were deputed to oversee the relief and rehabilitation did not pay heed to the word of the Panchayat Presidents. In Prathabaramapuram Panchayat, the president requested the officials to establish temporary shelters in one place. But the officials constructed them in different places and tin sheets were used for the purpose. Within a few months after the tsunami, there was heavy rain. Rain water logging created a huge problem. The tsunami occurred in the month of December and three months later dawned the summer season. The tin sheets absorbed too much heat and became a source for worry of the fishing community. Many suffered from heat related diseases. This created problems for the people and the Panchayat President. Some people amputated the fingers of the dead bodies and took away the gold rings and some even stole the mangal sutra and gold chains from the dead bodies. People who lost their relatives suffered a lot. But some just wanted to collect freebies. The NGOs and government officials distributed more relief materials than was required. During the relief operations an NGO distributed water packets to the victims who later discarded them as they were given water bottles an hour later *(G. Palanithurai, 2009).*

In the beginning, affected people accepted old dresses. Once they started getting new ones, they started throwing the old ones away. The Panchayat President found it very difficult to clear the old dresses from many places; he did not know how to dispose these old ones. Regarding the food packets, each person got 10 to 12 food packets at a time which were thrown away the very next day as they were more than what was they needed. In this regard, Prathabaramapuram Panchayat wasted nearly 10 tons of rice. Many officials were biased towards the Panchayats. They concentrated only on the fishing community because the officials misjudged them to be the worst affected; but, in reality, the non-fishermen like the landholders and the Scheduled Castes were also affected. The lands of the farmers were damaged and their life stocks lost. Further, the houses of the non-fishing community were also damaged; with regards to permanent shelters, the buildings were not strong as per international standards. The ratio of cement and sand was not correct. Most of the houses lacked toilets. The houses with toilets did not have septic tanks in the Kameshwaram Panchayat. In many places, there were conflicts between the traditional and constitutional Panchayats.

In Samiyarpettai Panchayat the constitutional Panchayat leader and self-help group members underwent training in Disaster Management in the State Institute of Rural Development. A self-help group member named Meera did commendable work during the tsunami. The chief minister appreciated her and honored her by giving Rs. 5 lakhs. But the traditional Panchayat harassed her and they claimed that it was not an individual's work and it was a group work. So, they argued that either she has to share the award money with other self-help group members or with the traditional Panchayat. But she refused to share it either with SHGs or with traditional Panchayat and left her Panchayat. Even on this small issue, the constitutional Panchayat was unable to solve the problem *(G.Palanithurai, 2009)*.

The government gave Rs.30,000 to the damaged houses, but the traditional leaders shared this money with all the village people. So, it came down to 10,000 per family. In many Panchayats, there was no disaster management committee. The NGOs gave training only to SHGs in Disaster Management. In Chinoor Pudhupetti of Kadalur District, a big conflict arose within the traditional Panchayat and they were divided among themselves into three groups. The constitutional Panchayat was unable to keep them together at least for their children who lost their parents and got compensation of Rs.50, 000. But not all children who lost their parents got compensation which mushroomed conflicts of varied proportions. The Panchayat President tried to solve the problem by writing letters to the officials but did not have a proper record in this matter. The leader dominated the traditional Panchayat meetings. The women representatives were not allowed to speak out their concerns neither allowed them to attend the public meetings but were allowed to participate in self-help group activities to get government benefits. Constitutional Panchayat could not sensitize the Panchayat leaders on gender sensitivity.

In Kanyakumari District, in some Panchayats, the parish priest worked in collaboration with the constitutional Panchayats where the President belonged to the same community and in some villages, they usually worked with the traditional Panchayats. Only with the consent of the parish priest, the government or any other organization could carry out relief and rehabilitation work in the Panchayats. Another important problem faced by the Panchayats was in getting the exact figures of the affected and the

Panchayats are still struggling to get facts of the real losses. During the tsunami, officials were not sensitized on rehabilitation. As there was no relief code and disaster management policy in our state, it was utter confusion for several days *(G.Palanithurai, 2009).*

To sum up, Panchayats have the capability to carry out disaster preparedness and disaster management. In Tamil Nadu, many Panchayat leaders had exhibited their capacity during tsunami disaster. In Andhra Pradesh, a few leaders had the capacity to carry out the relief activities. They were regularly attending the district level meetings. In Gujarat, a few NGOs, trained Panchayat leaders on disaster management. Now they take in rehabilitation activities. In Orissa, Panchayats are part of the Cyclone Shelter Management Committee, DMT. House benefits should be distributed through Panchayat. If there is hunger in any Panchayat, it is the responsibility of the Panchayat to provide food. The need of the hour is to strengthen Panchayats in the disaster management aspects. It should be part of their regular activities along with development activities. Trained, sensitized leaders will manage disasters effectively *(G.Palanithurai, 2009).*

Conclusion

As a result of all these highly publicized disasters today, more than ever before, there is a growing consensus at all levels that 'something' should be done to prepare and respond to disasters as and when they occur. Given the frightening trends of 2005 tsunami, everyone is convinced now that the future is going to be full of nasty surprises, for no amount of preparedness is usually enough when a disaster ultimately strikes. But in all these responses from governments, international agencies and NGO's, run a common thread- the assumption that disasters are sudden and unforeseen events that we need special institutions, policies and even gadgets to cope up with the ability to reduce social and economic risks from natural and man-made hazards requires adoption of a "culture of prevention". It can only be accomplished through global commitment of nations for development of effective disaster reduction polices through partnership for 'safer world 'and preparation of societies at the local level who, had to face the consequence of a disaster. The crucial role of local self government institutions is awfully significant in pre and post disaster initiatives to act as a leading force to deliver the best to the sake of the community.

Notes

1. The 73rd Constitutional Amendment Act has created three tier PRIs in the rural areas with allocation of specific subjects to them. In pursuance of this, States

have initiated action to devolve administrative and financial powers and resources to PRIs to enable them to discharge their Constitutional role. It is expected that once the process of devolution is effectively operationalised, resources from the Central and State Governments meant for programmes falling within the jurisdiction of the PRIs would directly get allocated to them.

2. The United Nations Economic and Social Commission for Asia and the Pacific (ESCAP) is the regional development arm of the United Nations for the Asia-Pacific region. With a membership of 62 Governments, 58 of which are in the region, and a geographical scope that stretches from Turkey in the west to the Pacific island nation of Kiribati in the east, and from the Russian Federation in the north to New Zealand in the south, ESCAP is the most comprehensive of the United Nations five regional commissions. It is also the largest United Nations body serving the Asia-Pacific region with over 600 staff. Established in 1947 with its headquarters in Bangkok, Thailand.

3. Dr. Kamal Taori belongs to the UP cadre of the 1968 batch of the I.A.S. He had a short stint in the Army and has doctorate in Rural entrepreneurship. He has been with the Khadi and Village Industries Sector for nearly 12 years. This was his opportunity for a deeper understanding of Gandhiji's, Vinoba, Lohia and Kumarappa and to sublimate his ambition in to a mission with holistic action. A short assignment with the UNDP, and subsequent study of the United Nations system were helpful in the convergence of his lifelong studies, experience and understanding into a world-view and a global vision. He is always concerned about what could have been done, as against what has been done. A Social Science Scientific researcher and author of a number of books and research papers, he has organized and led many a seminar and workshop on a whole range of socio-economic issues and topics.

4. This book attempts to examine the role of Panchayati Raj in disaster management, with special reference to India. Based on a study, conducted by the author, under the aegis of Indian Institute of Public Administration (IIPA), New Delhi, it discusses at length the challenges of disaster management and Gandhian alternatives for sustainable human development. Tracing the missing links, the book further addresses the key issues for action and presents operational guidelines. Also, it explores the role of community based organisations, NGOs, World Association of Small and Medium Enterprises, Information Technology, the convergence of delivery system and the Inter-State Council Secretariat in the mitigation of disasters. The means and ways for empowering Panchayats have been highlighted as well.

5. The Panchayati Raj model in India, S.P. Jain & Wim Polman: A handbook for trainers on participatory local development: The Panchayati Raj model in India" supports the world's biggest endeavour in grassroots governance taking place in India. The 73rd Constitutional Amendment, adopted in 1992, established a solid legal base for participation of the rural poor in local (district, sub-district and village level) government institutions. Some 238 000 Panchayats (village councils) representing about 600 000 villages have been constituted and about three million rural people, a third of whom, by law have to be women, elected to Panchayat bodies. The handbook is focused on the training needs of these three million newly elected Panchayat members, the majority of them semi- or even

non-literate and unprepared for the responsibility of local governance. The Government of India has recognized the need for training of these Panchayat members for capacity-building on participatory local development. August 2003, FAO Regional Office for Asia and the Pacific, Bangkok, Thailand.

6. SAHAYI- a Center for Learning and Collective Action based at Trivandrum initiated Tsunami Relief and Rehabilitation Project in the Tsunami affected places of Kollam with the support of some international key players. The psychosocial programme jointly initiated by the DEEDS, Sahayi and Malteser International with the technical inputs of NIMHANS Bangalore completed its second phase at Alappad. Families who have under distress were reduced and improved their mental strength clearly indicates the quality of the services provided by the entire team on psychosocial care. This was effectively shared by the affected people in the One day Sharing programme organized by DEEDS with the support of partners and technical agency. Yet some of the families need the support to maintain their mental health and face up the future so the CLW's were need to provide such services to them. The new establishment- drop- in center need to concentrate the current and the future psychosocial needs of the community by utilsing the trained hands of the CLW's and thereby mark their value of the services in their own community. The developments of CBO's, the effective utilization of the skills of Community Level Workers and an attainment of a Caring community on psychosocial care are the major challenges raised towards the concern to the sustainability.

7. "Psychosocial Rehabilitation programme for the tsunami survivors of Alappad, Kerala with special emphasis on building psychosocial competence among disaster affected population was carried out in the second phase of the project. Feedback from various reviews and reflection conducted by the psychosocial team during the intervention period not only helped but also highly supported to get improve the whole activities. The learning and findings has been absorbed into the program delivery system which helped remarkably in improving the quality of the psychosocial care programme. The psychosocial care team was able to improve the standard of life of the targeted families who have been receiving psychosocial support from the initial period onwards. The psychosocial care team had a meeting by the end of the first phase of the project and discussed the current activities, outcome, and about the possibility of extending support to the same community based on their needs. The major observations and lessons learned clearly contributed in developing the new proposal aimed at to implement the psychosocial rehabilitation programme jointly initiated by DEEDS and Sahayi with the technical support from NIMHANS Bangalore. A variety of activities were implemented in the current project year in Alappad, the worst affected area, to fulfill the psychosocial needs of the community with their active participation and partnership.

8. World Disasters Report 2010-Focus on urban risk: This year's World Disasters Report takes an in-depth look at the consequences for humanitarian action of the dramatic surge in the numbers of people living in cities and towns which will be the hallmark of the 21st century. It examines the issues around this irreversible trend as the world comes to terms with the fact that more people now live in cities and towns than in the countryside for the first time in human

history. Has development aid kept pace with this dramatic shift? Why are almost a billion people worldwide still living in slums? How can vulnerable cities protect themselves from climate change? What are the emerging health issues of rapid urbanization? Can anything be done to turn back the tide of violence sweeping many inner cities and ghettos? The World Disasters Report 2010 features: Avoiding the urbanization of disaster, Urban disaster trends, Starting over: Community rights and post-disaster response, Urban violence, Urban risk to health, Urbanization and climate change risk, Urban governance and disaster risk reduction.

9. Prof. Ganapathi Palanithurai, Coordinator in Rajiv Gandhi Chair, Gandhigram Rural Institute, presently heads the Department of Political Science and Development Administration, Gandhigram Rural University, Tamil Nadu. He is also associated with Centre Planning Commission, State Planning Commission of Tamil Nadu, Population Foundation of India, Ford Foundation, UNICEF, Rajiv Gandhi Foundation, CAPART, Ministry of Rural Areas and Employment and DANIDA (Danish-Indo Development Agency) in specific areas of activities in connection with empowerment of people. Prof. Palanithurai has to his credit twenty-nine books and seventy-five articles on three major areas, namely, legislative behaviour, ethnicity and Panchayati Raj system. He was recipient of Fellowship from Sastri Indo-Canadian Institute, New Delhi and World Academy of Art and Science, USA. He is the Chairman of the Tamil Nadu Council for Sustainable Livelihoods. He was a visiting fellow in the MiGill University, Canada in 1989. He is a member of the expert committee constituted by the Government of Tamil Nadu to monitor the training programme for local body leaders.

10. This book examines the role of Panchayats in disaster management in India. Based on an action research carried out in four states? Gujarat, Orissa, Andhra Pradesh and Tamil Nadu, it analyses the response of the communities and Panchayats towards tsunami and other natural disasters, with specific reference to the issues of gender and exclusion in relief as well as rehabilitation work. Also, it deals with the communication system in the entire coastal area for early warning messages to the communities, the interface between traditional and constitutional Panchayats, the disaster management policy, and relief codes from the perspective of local grassroots governance. The relief, rehabilitation and reconstruction activities undertaken by government institutions and NGOs have been evaluated as well. The book is useful for researchers, policy makers and development workers.

11. TVSG Trust for Village Self Governance, Tamilnadu, 2007, Managing Disasters: An Introductory Guide for Panchayats from a Panchayat, Published by Trust For Village Self Governance (TVSG), Prepared as part of the project on Strengthening of Panchayats in Self Governance, Disaster Management and livelihood Creation, Supported by Swiss Agency for Development and Cooperation (SDC), Embassy of Switzerland, Chandragupta Marg Chanakyapuri, New Delhi 110 023 2007.

Chapter - 5

Community Participation and Disaster Management

"Empowering families and communities to take preventive action on their own behalf, without being dependent on external support, is one of the clear, unalterable lessons learned from the tsunami experience. The aim is always to leave people better off, to reinforce their existing coping mechanisms and to build their resilience to whatever the future holds. This is the true legacy of the tsunami operation"

- (International Federation of Red Cross and Red Crescent Societies, 2009).

Introduction

Much of the literature on participation in emergencies focuses on the role of community engagement in disaster preparedness. However, the literature that does address participatory approaches in disaster-affected contexts highlights the advantages, which include better analysis, effective programming and implementation, and increased accountability. In addition, such participation creates linkages between relief, rehabilitation and development work, and allows members of affected populations to emerge as social actors in their own right, with valuable knowledge and insights on their situation, as well as competencies and ideas of their own *(ADRRN, 2007)*[1].

Thus, there is general agreement that while it may be unrealistic to aim for community participation in the initial relief phase, it is important that communities are included in the design and implementation of assistance programmes, to ensure greater ownership over the recovery process. However, there is no standard participation model. Any approach must remain flexible, and sensitive to the local context. Aid agencies should take local coping strategies into account and build upon them instead of imposing their own "ready-made" interventions. Important ways of ensuring community engagement include providing timely and regular access to information, and recognizing the capacity of local community organizations. Much of the literature shows that while there is widespread theoretical recognition of the importance of community participation, this has rarely translated into reconstruction practice, and grassroots participation in recent crises has remained insignificant *(Asian Disaster Reduction & Response Network, 2007).*

Supporting meaningful participation by 'vulnerable groups', in disaster response is another challenge. Past experience has shown that local participation can often be captured by local elites, and the vulnerable left out of the process. Some commentators argue *(ADRRN, 2007)* that the long-term strengthening of local communities that is needed in this respect requires a lengthier commitment from aid agencies than their funding and staffing cycles currently allow. In the short-term, however, the literature below highlights that aid agencies should learn to see these groups less in terms of their vulnerability and more in terms of their resilience and potential to contribute. Agencies should recognize and build upon the ways in which local and vulnerable groups are independently responding to the crisis. This query includes materials from both academic and operational perspectives. Literature on sectoral issues has been included as it illustrates the more general recommendations and may provide more widely applicable lessons learned. Some materials offering practical guidelines, toolkits and approaches to facilitating community participation have also been included. Nevertheless to say that a true community-based approach requires a different programming flow, one that begins not with assessment, but with mobilization of social groups and communities, which is then followed by a community-based assessment. This mobilization may be done by the community on its own initiative or as a response to signals from government about how reconstruction will be undertaken.

Community Participation in Disasters: *The General Perspective*

The first people to respond to a disaster are those living in the local community. They are the first to start rescue and relief operations. Many of the international agencies were keen in working with the affected community to a certain extent. The Red Cross and Red Crescent National Societies, focus on Community-Based Disaster Preparedness which assists communities to reduce disasters and strengthen their capacities to resist them. When the capacity of a community or country to respond and recover from a disaster is overwhelmed, and upon request from the National Society, the International Federation uses its regional and international networks, assets and resources to bring assistance to the communities to extend support to the relief programmes *(IFRC, 2009).*

National Red Cross Red Crescent Society is considered as one among them which is assisting their own international association during emergencies and similar kind of events. At an international level, the International Federation advocates with Governments, international organizations and humanitarian donors for better practice and accountability in disaster management and greater respect of the dignity of the vulnerable people *(IFRC, 2009).*

There is a fact that community input and participation are crucial to the success of disaster response and development programmes. Consulting with community members is intended to ensure that programs are aligned to their needs, but does it go far enough? In the year of 2007, Oxfam collaborated with the Institute for Participatory Interaction in Development (IPID)[2] in Sri Lanka to carry out a review of post-tsunami capacity building programs for disaster preparedness. The research served a joint impact assessment of community capacity building efforts in disaster preparedness by participating governmental and non-governmental organizations (NGOs); it also provided an opportunity for community members to articulate their observations and needs and to develop their confidence as analysts. Both the findings and the participatory process of the IPID study point the way to a fuller and more equal partnership between aid providers and affected communities *(Oxfam International, 2008)*[3]. As disaster experts suggest: "There is difference between consulting with communities about a program, which most aid providers already do, and really engaging those full partners. Without full and active partnership, there is a risk that the program might not turn out to be suitable or sustainable" *(Mallika Samaranayake/Atul Loke/Panos, 2009).*

In order to get populations back on their feet as quickly as possible and to allow organisations to tailor appropriate responses to the needs of different categories of people, the genuine involvement of local communities is fundamental. Participation and early national and local ownership in the design and implementation of programmes is essential to ensure that aid is distributed fairly and impartially. Local communities have contributed immensely to relief and reconstruction efforts in Tsunami affected areas to date.

Participation empowers communities; however, the outcomes of that participation can be unpredictable. The participatory process may give rise to new actors or interests or may create conflicts between organizations that had previously worked together harmoniously. Guiding the participation process includes making sure that people's expectations are realistic, especially if they believe that large amounts of funding are available. At the same time, an agency may observe a multiplier effect from its support of a participatory project, as the community realizes its capabilities and new ideas for activities and projects. The organization and facilitation of community participation should not be done on a purely ad hoc basis. Trained facilitators and other experts in community participation should be part of the management team for any project that entails participation *(World Bank, 2010).*

Community participation is seen by some as a way for stakeholders to influence development by contributing to project design, influencing public choices, and holding public institutions accountable for the goods and services they provide. Some view participation as the direct engagement of affected populations in the project cycle assessment, design, implementation, monitoring, and evaluation in a variety of forms. Still others consider participation an operating philosophy that puts affected populations at the heart of humanitarian and development activities as social actors with insights, competencies, energy, and ideas of their own.

Community engagement has numerous benefits and is critical in every stage of post-disaster recovery and reconstruction. It encourages agencies involved in reconstruction to offer affected communities a range of options for involvement in reconstruction. It addresses the organization of affected communities and participation by individuals, communities, and community-based organizations (CBOs). Incorporating participation by the community in reconstruction projects funded by local and international non-governmental organizations (NGOs) is largely voluntary, yet the commitment to participation is generally quite high. However, the level of this commitment may vary in projects sponsored by the public sector. In their decentralization framework, planning law, or local government ordinances, some countries require community participation and information disclosure for publicly supported projects. This participation may include anything from public hearings on project budgets to comment periods on procurement documents to "sweat equity" contributions in community infrastructure projects. Compliance with these laws may at times be pro forma; this is even more likely to be the case if government is operating on an emergency footing and fears that projects will be delayed. Under these circumstances, the pressure even from the communities themselves may be to act quickly and to impose top-down, technocratic solutions *(World Bank, 2010)*.

Experience is increasingly demonstrating that an emergency is the time to expand, rather than reduce, participation, even if there is no formal policy framework for participation in place. By including properly structured community participation mechanisms, physical outcomes and the quality of oversight can actually be improved, especially when large sums of money are involved. Local and international NGOs and other agencies involved in reconstruction can help operationalize these mechanisms. Or local government may be able to establish the guidelines and coordinate community participation in reconstruction. The role of local government is especially critical when local land use decisions and infrastructure reconstruction are involved. Thus the vital role of the involvement of the affected community in all aspects of the disaster management is not only a requirement but also gives a positive and right direction in all the efforts of the disaster management activities *(World Bank, 2010)*.

NGOs Lead the Way to Community Participation in Disaster Management *(Voluntary Organisations Response in Community Participation)*

The purpose of NGOs[4] is not to supplant the governmental relief agencies but to act as a coordinating mechanism between the government apparatus and the affected populace. The role of NGOs assumes significance in view of their wider engagement in civic and development initiatives. Factors such as disillusionment with centralised structures; emphasis on pluralism, expanded civic engagement; and collaboration amongst multiple actors explain this change in perception. The growing importance of NGOs can also be attributed to the realization that neither the state nor the market can fully address enormous problems facing the world today. Over the last few decades, NGOs have become important players in the development process across the globe, engaged in wide ranging activities starting with community development to training, policy research, and advocacy. Their organizational flexibility, informal work style, and close engagement with grassroots communities enable them to deliver services to people at lower costs. They supplement government initiatives by acting as a conduit between development programmes and beneficiaries, informing and sensitizing people about their rights and entitlements. Their ability to mobilize people and understand people's concerns enables them to better articulate problems encountered by people *(Aurobindo Behera, 2002)*.

Today, NGOs play an important role in disaster response and mitigation in different regions. Many international NGOs specifically focus on providing humanitarian aid to disaster victims. Local NGOs in South Asia have also played an active role in disaster management in recent years. In India, NGOs played a significant role in emergency response and rehabilitation following recent disasters: the 1993 earthquake at Latur, which killed 7601 people, the 1999 Orissa super cyclone which killed 8931 people and the 2001 Gujarat earthquake which killed over 13,000 people.

Action Aid, an international aid agency, tried to ensure a people centered approach in the assessment and more qualitative and people participation based tools were used to assess the needs of the affected populace. In keeping with their global objectives for work in early recovery, Action Aid Bangladesh focused their interventions on livelihood, psychosocial, gendered impacts of Strategy for International Disaster Risk Reduction impacts on diversified ethnic and occupational minorities, and disaster risk reduction aspects *(UNISDR, 2005).* Action Aid – India in the immediate aftermath of the Tsunami, distributed relief, including food packets to survivors of the Tsunami. Amid reports of "dumping" of unsuitable aid by a proliferation of agencies, Action Aid then began to focus on coordinating efforts among areas through the instigation of the "Tamil Nadu Peoples Forum for Tsunami Relief". In the longer term, ActionAid is working with fishermen in Tamil Nadu, to preserve traditional fishing methods and is engaged with specialists in coastal areas around the Indian Ocean to advice on the lengthy process of desalinating land. As in some areas it could be years before land is again fertile for cultivation, ActionAid has responded with cash for work programmes, in which local people rebuild and reconstruct their local environment in exchange for a daily wage. Participation of women has been encouraged through the provision of crèche facilities. ActionAid is also engaged in advocacy programmes with affected communities to work on allowing them to realize their rights in the reconstruction effort *(CONCORD, 2005).*

In India, Cordaid [5] (Dutch Caritas) had a large network of local partners working in development programs. After the Tsunami struck, many of these partners turned to Cordaid for support in their emergency activities. As local NGOs were familiar with the area and the communities, Cordaid decided to concentrate on working with them and not to look for other partners. Because of existing relationships and mutual trust, Cordaid was able to disburse funds for emergency relief to them very quickly. However, Cordaid realized that many of these NGO's did not have much experience in emergency and rehabilitation work. Cordaid immediately put in place a team of 4 Indian consultants with different expertise that worked side by side with these partners from the start, advising them and building their capacity step by step. In addition, Cordaid agreed with a partner from Gujarat to work with a couple of smaller NGOs in Tamil Nadu to share the experience gained in the Gujarat earth quake. The immediate guidance of a team of Indian consultants has stimulated Cordaid's local partners to be more involved in coordination and has also enhanced both the quality and added value of the rehabilitation projects that followed the emergency work *(CONCORD, 2005).*

Local NGOs in Thailand were indispensable in organizing operations and in calling attention to those who might have otherwise have been neglected (such as Burmese migrant workers or the Moken, one of the last sea minorities leading a traditional existence).Countries around the globe have recognized the impact of collaborative efforts in disaster recovery. For instance, Sri Lanka has very low insurance coverage for disasters. The Sri Lankan Reconstruction and Development Agency has worked with the private sector to launch a micro-insurance program to help the poorest people to recover after natural disasters. For example, companies may work with NGOs or the government to pay insurance premiums on behalf of low-income households. Additionally, the documentation process for claims needs to be simplified, and the industry needs to promote risk reduction awareness. However, the real challenge ahead will be to make micro-insurance more profitable and sustainable.

In another notable experiment, a case study approach was used to accomplish to study the response programmes in the two affected communities in Thailand, namely *Ban Namkem* and *Ban Tungwa*. Experiences of the two communities were presented and analyzed through document review, participant observation, and semi-structured interviews. Interviews were also carried out with key informants from the Thai government and international and national non-government organizations that assisted in the tsunami response and recovery efforts. Results show that there was no consensus on the success of the tsunami disaster response in Thailand. The rapid response of the Thai government was effective for the search and rescue operations, but in terms of aid distribution and relief operations, errors were made that should be examined. The Thai government immediately formed a chain-of-command and distribution of responsibilities to different ministries. The response phase focused mainly on assisting the victims with search and rescue teams and basic necessities. Donations and volunteers came from aid organizations as well as the Thai citizens residing within and out of Thailand.

Community participation during this phase was shown in the establishment of temporary relief camps for the victims of Ban Namkem and Ban Tungwa communities provided by local NGOs. Overall, there was, however little involvement of the impacted public in the response despite the fact that those affected were in fact the first responders *(Wannasorn 2008).* The tight timeframe and overwhelming number of tasks carried out by field staff, as well as the strict criteria for aid, prevented the government from reaching out to all victims. These factors discouraged field staff from implementing programs that would enable the community to participate and voice their concerns during the recovery effort. Failure to involve the affected communities or lack of meaningful public participation led to time consuming and costly delays and development projects which were not popular with the affected community. In fact, a housing project implemented without community input was abandoned due to its low quality and failure to meet the affected community's lifestyle. Findings show that the two communities studied were capable of making their own decisions and organizing themselves to assist each other as early as possible after the disaster struck. It was also clear that community participation in the decision-making process could empower and promote the solidarity of the community, which in turn enables community members to protect themselves from outsiders' exploitation, as shown in the fight for land rights that ensued in Ban Namkem and Ban Tungwa communities *(Wannasorn, 2008).*

Obstacles that either prevented or decreased the capacity of community members to participate arranged from a general lack of opportunity to participate in any of the response or recovery decisions to low expectations within the affected communities regarding government assistance and/or any call for their involvement in the decision-making process. The overwhelming number of responsibilities placed on field staff also impacted their ability to involve people in a timely way *(Wannasorn, 2008).* Though many aid providers involved communities in some respect on shelter construction, their participation was usually limited. Respondents know best what they need to restore their livelihoods, rebuild their lives, maintain their community networks, and stay out of harm's way. They should be brought into genuine partnerships with aid agencies at every step of the way *(Oxfam, 2008).* As aptly noted by a community member in Sri Lanka, "If any aid organization comes to this village, we would like them to realize that even in the village, even in rural area; we have our own traditional knowledge and methods of doing things'. Before, implementing aid agency plans here, we would rather listen and understand the rural villager's traditional knowledge and methods *(L.W.Sunil Edward, 2008).*

In their reliance on community participation for disaster management, the Honduran and Nicaraguan projects are building on experiences pioneered by NGOs. Following Hurricane Mitch, CARE, Catholic Relief Services, The Red Cross, CATIE, and the Cooperative Housing Foundation, to name a few, worked with affected communities to develop strategies for recovery and for facing future disaster events *(Tova Maria Solo, Myriam Godinot,,Osmar Velasco,2010).*

CARE's approach emphasizes risk prevention and mitigation through community participation with the objective of reducing the probability of life and property losses *(CARE International, 2009)*[6]. CARE's methodology was piloted in twenty communities in three Honduran municipalities and adopted by the Nicaraguan Executive Secretariat for Disaster Prevention, Mitigation and Response. In Guatemala, as part of its Mitch Recovery Program, CARE created Local Emergency Committees, which are now in place and ready to respond to any event. The Catholic Relief Services developed a regional program for disaster mitigation which includes building disaster response capacity in local communities through, for example, the identification of emergency shelters and procedures. Participating communities provided labor and a portion of the materials needed to implement mitigation measures. CATIE has promoted risk management capacity building in two groups of Honduran municipalities (man comunidades) six in Copán and ten in Reitoca. In each case, CATIE worked with municipalities to ensure that preventive measures are a part of the municipal development plans. CATIE has also established local environmental funds, financed through tourism, taxes, and by donor grants, to cover costs of mitigation measures.

The Cooperative Housing Foundation (CHF) also worked with communities in two Honduran municipalities to carry out risk assessments and to identify and implement mitigation measures under Proyecto Impacto, a post-Mitch program financed by U.S. donations. In this case, private sector groups provided technical assistance or facilities. CHF reports that prevention is such an economically justified concept that private sector participation was relatively easy to leverage. In one of the municipalities, the project resulted in the creation of a mitigation department at the municipality, showing the awareness raised locally. In both the Honduran and Nicaraguan projects, the door has been opened for more participation from NGOs and the private sector. NGOs are encouraged to offer creative methods to work with communities under the risk assessment and mitigation planning phases. The governments, both national and local, are relying on participation from civil society to develop local capacity *(Tova Maria Solo, Myriam Godinot, ,Osmar Velasco,2010).*

In India, The National Disaster Management Authority in consultation with eminent humanitarian assistance practitioners, civil society representatives and senior administrators in the country is in process of developing Guidelines on 'Role of Non-Governmental Organisations (NGOs) in Disaster Management'. These Guidelines have been formulated by Core Groups of eminent humanitarian assistance practitioners based on the consultation with various stakeholders, national & local level NGOs and UN Agencies in the concerned subject and officials from the Ministries and Departments of Government of India and State Governments. The Guidelines on the Role of NGOs in Disaster Management have been prepared to facilitate greater coordination between NGOs and Government institutions during various phases of the disaster management cycle, within the framework of the Disaster Management Act 2005. These Guidelines have explored the scope, role and opportunities for NGOs to mainstream disaster risk reduction into their developmental activities *(G. Padmanabhan, 2010)*[7].

Community Participation -*Case Studies*

(a) ***2006 Java Earthquake, Indonesia - Organizing Community-Based Resettlement and Reconstruction*:** Somewhat hidden from the world by the ongoing flurry of Aceh tsunami recovery, the 2006 Java earthquake with a magnitude of 6.3 on the Richter scale was nevertheless an enormously destructive event. Over 350,000 residential units were lost and 5,760 persons were killed, most from the collapse of non-engineered masonry structures. Using lessons learned from the tsunami experience and resources from the ongoing Urban Poverty Project (UPP), the Indonesian government was able to respond quickly and efficiently. Facilitators were recruited and villages elected boards of trustees, which later were instrumental in organizing community meetings and supervising implementation. Key activities included (1) identifying beneficiaries and prioritizing the most vulnerable; (2) establishing housing groups of 10-15 families, who chose their leaders and a treasurer; (3) developing detailed plans to use the construction grants for each group; (4) opening group bank accounts; and (5) obtaining approval of plans, disbursement in tranches, and group procurement, construction, and bookkeeping. Training was provided to community members and local workers to ensure earthquake-resistant construction. Later, the community developed plans to rebuild village infrastructure and facilities, with a particular focus on disaster resilience. Communities conducted self-surveys, prepared thematic maps, analyzed needs and disaster risks, agreed on priority programs, and established procedures for operations and maintenance. Grants for infrastructure were also disbursed in tranches through the selected bank as work progressed. An adequate understanding of rules and a sense of ownership by the community were essential to ensuring good targeting and plans, accountability, and social control of implementation. The involvement of women increased accountability and enhanced the appropriateness of technical solutions. The role of facilitators was crucial, as they both ensured effective communication and adaptability of the program to local situations as well as compliance with program principles. In all 6,480 core houses were funded by a World Bank loan under UPP, and another 15,153 units were funded by the multi-donor Java Reconstruction Fund. This approach to reconstruction became the model for the much larger government-financed rehabilitation and reconstruction program, under which about 200,000 houses were rebuilt in Java *(Probo Sudarmo, 2009)*.

(b) **2003 Bam Earthquake, Iran - Community Participation in Developing the Structure Plan (2015) for the City of Bam:** After the 2003 earthquake in Bam, Iran, a national strategy for housing reconstruction was published. For urban areas, the strategy featured (1) provision of interim or transitional shelters on existing vacant lots, including the distribution of prefabricated units to address housing needs for a 2-year period; and (2) provision of permanent shelter after preparation of a detailed city master plan and the approval of technologies and legal and procedural mechanisms for reconstruction. The provision of interim shelter in the city of Bam gave government time to revise the existing city plan before beginning reconstruction. The most recent Bam City Master Plan had been developed by a consulting firm and approved by the High Council of Architecture and Urban Development of the Ministry of Housing and Urban Development in the year prior to the earthquake. However, the disaster raised significant new issues, so the same consulting firm was brought back to update the plan. A comprehensive survey sought inputs from local authorities, implementing agencies, community leaders, NGOs, women, youth, and children *(Victoria Kianpour, 2009)*.

In April 2004, the Housing Foundation of the Islamic Revolution-United Nations Development Programme (UNDP) joint housing project organized a technical consultation in which UNDP; the United Nations Children's Fund (UNICEF); the United Nations Educational, Scientific and Cultural Organization (UNESCO); the World Health Organization (WHO); the United Nations Industrial Development Organization (UNIDO); and other UN agencies provided technical assistance and capacity building for the participatory city micro-planning process, to explain such concepts as child-friendly and healthy cities and to discuss the socioeconomic aspects of city planning. The final Structure Plan specifically addressed the need to respect the traditional architecture and urban design of the city and villages, to protect buffer zones, to minimize relocation, and to minimize expropriation through reuse of land. This plan formed the basis for subsequent detailed planning of 11 priority reconstruction areas in the city of Bam. To reduce the chance of excessive uniformity, each area had a different planning team. The modified plan and detailed plans were ratified by the High Council in October 2004, 10 months after the earthquake. Subsequently, the Ministry of Housing and Urban Development, with support from UNDP, published the results of the consultative process and the Bam Housing Typology *(UNDP Iran, 2009).*

(c) 1993 Latur Earthquake, Maharashtra, India - Community Participation in the Maharashtra Emergency Earthquake Rehabilitation Program:

With the help of the World Bank, the government of Maharashtra, India, developed the Maharashtra Emergency Earthquake Rehabilitation Program (MEERP), which institutionalized community participation and ensured that beneficiaries were formally consulted at all stages of the post-earthquake program. Every village created a local committee headed by the sarpanch (the head of the village council), and its subcommittees included women and disadvantaged groups. Consultative committees were also proposed at the level of the taluka (an administrative unit that includes several villages) and the district. To ensure the village-level committees interacted with the project management unit at all levels; government took an innovative step and appointed two respected community organizations to carry out the process, the Tata Institute of Social Sciences and the Society for Promotion of Resource Area Centre (*Rohit Jigyasu, 2002).*

(d) 1992 Floods, Pakistan - Grassroots NGO Introduces Measures to Engage Women in Housing Reconstruction:

Northern Pakistan's catastrophic floods in 1992 were attributed to large-scale deforestation in mountainous watersheds, and led eventually to government imposing a ban on commercial harvesting of forests. After the floods, PATTAN, a local NGO, introduced a number of measures that specifically addressed women's issues in the disaster recovery process. Female relief workers were engaged to assess the needs of women after the floods and to involve them in the planning, implementation, and rehabilitation activities. Local women were registered as heads of their households to help ensure efficient distribution of relief food. Village women's organizations were established (in parallel with men's groups) to articulate women's needs and to take responsibility for community development. These groups also provided a forum for discussing women's views regarding the design and layout of new houses. As a result, women became actively involved in reconstruction activities. Later, women were made responsible for collecting money to repay loan installments on the houses. Some women also participated in construction, traditionally a male activity. Perhaps most important, PATTAN introduced the concept that married couples should own houses jointly *(World Bank, Food and Agriculture Organization, and International Fund for Agricultural Development, 2008).*

***(e) Examples of Community's Role in and after Hurricane Katrina*:** Community responses to Hurricane Katrina demonstrate the importance of local knowledge, resources, and cooperative strategies in determining their survival and recovery, that is, their resilience. These responses can also greatly inform theories and practice of disaster preparedness and risk perception planning, and help us see better how communities' strengths and capabilities can be integrated into these processes. In this section, we present some examples of the social learning that is taking place in various communities in the aftermath of Hurricane Katrina, in the areas of preparedness, response and relief, and recovery *(Olivia Patterson, Frederick Weil & Kavita Patel).*

Civil Society and Private Sector Approaches to Disaster Management- *Building Local Capacities for Disaster Response and Risk Reduction*

This section presents examples of civil society and private sector activities in disaster management from the community involvement standpoint.

"Without innovative local partnerships between civil society, local and central government and other stakeholders, instruments such as public investment planning or conditional cash transfers are unlikely to be effective. Also without such partnerships, land use management policies and building regulations may actually construct risk rather than reduce it" *(UNISDR, 2011)*. Yet, the role of community organizations and the private sector in risk reduction is often not well described in disaster management legislation and opportunities are lost to integrate their efforts into a coherent plan.

Civil Society has a vital role to play in disaster management. In connection with the pre- disaster programme, disaster preparedness, the role of Early Warning is a very important method. CTEC is a community-based volunteer organization working for emergency preparedness in the village of Peraliya, Sri Lanka. CTEC seeks to create a disaster preparedness culture through community participation and empowerment, with special emphasis on the protection of vulnerable groups and the use of information technology. CTEC is trying to create a network among community, district, and national government organizations to formulate and implement a disaster emergency plan. They attend district meetings and participate in policy discussions. Additionally, CTEC has identified village representatives and provided them with communication equipment to use during disasters. CTEC also takes responsibility for identifying and assisting vulnerable populations during disasters. Finally, CTEC conducts awareness raising programs in communities and schools to help people identify evacuation areas and routes *(Oxfam America, 2006)*. With constant access to the Internet, CTEC receives messages from the U.S. Geological Survey. If the center learns of an earthquake in the Indonesian region, it contacts the Meteorological Department and GSMB for confirmation. Once it receives confirmation, the center immediately relays a warning to neighboring villages *(Oxfam America, 2006)*.

An evaluation of this program revealed that CTEC appears to collaborate with the community, and people benefit by having an information center in their area. However, the Meteorology Department claims that CTEC caused a false alarm when it needlessly warned the public of an earthquake. In addition, the department logbook has no record of any calls from the center seeking confirmation of a tsunami warning, indicating that CTEC may be acting independently of the government in issuing warnings. Conversely, CTEC staff members report that the local government officers do not collaborate with them, and they are critical of the government's top-down approach. The government and CTEC came to an agreement to remove the words "Early Warning" from the center's name, as this role should be limited to the government; the NGO sector should only disseminate the government's warnings *(Disaster Management Policy & Practice, Oxfam 2006).*

Role of Civil Society in Disaster Relief

Many critics argued that following the Indian Ocean tsunami both the Indian government and NGOs focused solely on providing infrastructure, such as boats, nets, and engines to the fishermen, rather than seeking to provide new skills or repair social connections *(Aldrich, 2008).* But if ndings from this study and anecdotes from recent disasters like Hurricane Katrina are accurate, simply rebuilding bridges, schools, and power lines will not be sufficient. Local communities and neighborhoods need shared trust, communication, and commitment to return and stay. As the example of the Vietnamese community in Village de L'est showed, communities with deeper connections which stay in touch during and after the disaster are more likely to work together to rebuild their neighborhoods.

Policy-planners should think carefully about the ways that they can facilitate the construction and maintenance of social networks. For example, providing communities and community groups with communication devices such as cell phones and e-mail connections can help them stay in contact during the post disaster context. Further, NGOs and the government can focus on setting up not just temporary homes for people to live in, but meeting places for local community groups. Officials can also sponsor information sessions specically for established faith-based or neighborhood-based groups and do everything possible to house relocated communities together, as opposed to separate locations. These are simple and relatively low-cost solutions, but they may have far-reaching positive consequences for communities struck by disaster *(Aldrich, 2008).*

Sarvodaya disaster management programs

Sarvodaya Community Disaster Risk Management Center is based in Rawatawatta, Moratuwa. Sarvodaya, the country's largest charity, develops comprehensive medium- and long-term preparedness plans for each district in which it works. The organization creates volunteer groups to identify and rank probable hazards in the area. Sarvodaya has conducted community-based risk management trainings in 34 districts for volunteers and for officers from NGOs and international organizations. The Sarvodaya officers establish committees that network with government disaster management officers and other regional disaster management centers *(Oxfam America, 2006).* These relationships enable Sarvodaya to share resources and build its capacity. To maximize its resources, Sarvodaya has incorporated disaster management activities into ongoing programs. Often Sarvodaya is able to work jointly with other local and international groups on projects that reduce risk for coastal communities, such as through identifying hazards and designing evacuation routes and small-scale village alert systems.

Private sector: LIRNE Asia and Last Mile Hazard Information Project

Although many people have televisions and mobile phones, the problem with using such technology as part of an early-warning system is that not everyone is continuously connected. The Last-Mile Hazard Information Project is being implemented by LIRNE Asia in partnership with Sarvodaya and other media and technology companies to determine how to connect people at all hours. Five kinds of radio, satellite, and mobile phone equipment are being tested to determine the best use of these technologies in early warning *(Oxfam 2006).*

The system will use pre-fabricated Common Alerting Protocol (CAP) messages to disseminate information in local languages. The alert system being set up is a closed user network rather than a public alert system. Sarvodaya is the first responder in the system. When Sarvodaya receives an earthquake report, it passes it on for authentication and once authenticated, the message is converted into a CAP message and disseminated among Sarvodaya personnel in villages *(Oxfam Humanitarian Field Studies, 2006)*[50] The DRM Center has a help desk to respond to inquiries from villagers. The warning messages do not order people to evacuate, but rather convey information about the occurrence and location of an earthquake, its magnitude, and the likelihood of a tsunami. It is left to the villagers to decide whether or not to take action, depending on the emergency plan developed for each village.

Affected Peoples View of Disaster Management

Local communities are normally first responders and have coping strategies to mitigate and respond to disasters, such as by moving to safer locations and issuing warnings. Their input into disaster planning is critical. Housing design and construction are key to mitigating damage from future tsunamis or storms. Most informants felt that materials used to build post-tsunami houses were better than what they had used before, although others reported that the materials were worse. Approximately one-third of new houses have been designed to make them more resistant to a future tsunami *(Oxfam International, 2006).*

Preparedness for future disasters

Only 14 percent of the households report knowing how to react in case of a future tsunami, while 61 percent say they have some knowledge and 21 percent have no knowledge about what to do. More than 50 percent of households surveyed have identified safe places to which to evacuate, but only six percent have practiced evacuation drills; four percent have purchased insurance to protect them in the event of future disasters. However, the DMC reports that it has conducted awareness programs and evacuation drills for many households in some tsunami-affected districts, which appears to contradict the survey findings. One explanation could be that information does not filter down to all members of a household. The most important information sources are radio and television.

False alarms and distress

False alarms are a major concern: 69 percent of informants indicated that they had run out of their houses at least once after false tsunami alarms over the previous six months, and 11 percent had reacted to false alarms many times. The proportion of households that responded to false alarms is higher in Ampara, Galle, and Trincomalee where the tsunami had the most devastating impact. In addition, female headed households seem slightly more prone to react to false tsunami warnings. In some cases, false tsunami alerts were issued so burglars could steal from the vacated houses. Feelings of distress and fear are a lingering symptom of the psychological impact of the tsunami. Among the 599 households surveyed, 14 percent of families have found it significantly more difficult to sleep at night, while 45 percent have found it a little more difficult to sleep at night. The percentage is higher for female-headed households (24 percent) than for male-headed households (11 percent). This has been a particular problem for a majority of people living in Ampara District, where 33 percent of families have faced considerable difficulties in sleeping during the night, while 51 percent have experienced slight difficulties. Children have been especially vulnerable, with 14 percent of them reportedly having more nightmares than before the tsunami. This rate was even higher in Ampara and Matara, where 23 percent and 20 percent of children, respectively, had more nightmares *(Reports, Oxfam, 2006).*

Women and Vulnerable Groups

Because of their unequal social, political, and economic status, women are more vulnerable in conflicts and natural disasters. Men, women, boys, and girls experience disasters differently due to asymmetrical power relations based on gender. In the South Asian context, men's greater access to information and decision-making structures give them more opportunities to learn about and prepare for disasters than women. After the tsunami, gender roles influenced how men and women experienced the relief and reconstruction phases of the disaster. Although assessment of the separate needs of women and men is essential to the overall success of the relief and reconstruction effort, there is little gender-specific, quantitative data to inform policy in Sri Lanka. Programs must address gender issues so that women can get the assistance they need *(Oxfam Field Studies, 2006).*

Gender and the tsunami: How women fared

This section highlights the ways in which women were more acutely affected by the tsunami and were neglected during the relief and reconstruction process.

High death toll of women

Available disaggregated data from districts like Ampara show that more women died than men, and in this study, people reported similarly skewed patterns of survival. Analysts have attributed this disparity to socio-cultural and economic factors. For example, women might have had difficulty fleeing the waves because they carried children or were hampered by their clothing *(Reports, Oxfam, 2006).*

Inequality in access to relief grants and property

In most cases, the relief grants that were paid to all households were given to the husband, unless a woman headed the household. However, women are more likely to use the money for household expenses, while men are reportedly more likely to spend it on alcohol or other personal consumption. Additionally, houses reconstructed by the government and NGOs are typically given to the husband. However, as much as 75 percent of the property in the North and East was owned by women before the tsunami.

Low participation in post-tsunami decision-making

Women's involvement in policy planning and implementation is critical. In Sri Lanka, few women typically participate in decision-making processes in their communities and in elected government, although there is significant variation among districts *(Oxfam, International, 2006).*

Domestic violence and sexual harassment

Participants in this study reported that the close living conditions of camps and the mental stress and financial and physical insecurity after the tsunami have led to an increase in domestic violence and sexual harassment of women and girls, although little data on these issues are available. Alcohol consumption by men and some women seems to have increased, as well.

Livelihoods

Women face many barriers to restoring livelihoods after disasters. They often bear the burden of ensuring that the household gets water and other supplies each day. Additionally, women often engage in low-wage, repetitive income-generating activities such as coir production, weaving, and sewing. This work is flexible, which enables women to also carry out child care and household labor. Other barriers to business activities that they face after disasters include disrupted markets, loss of assets, and lack of credit, limited access to raw materials, increased competition, and reduced profits.

Other vulnerable groups

While everyone living in disaster-prone areas is vulnerable, some groups such as children, the elderly, and people with disabilities are more vulnerable than others. Therefore, the needs of vulnerable groups should be addressed specifically in preparedness and relief operations. In Sri Lanka, district committees and NGOs have prepared lists of the elderly and disabled people in their areas, and some NGOs have formed groups of volunteers who are responsible for caring for the elderly during emergencies. The Department of Meteorology is conducting several programs to improve disaster preparedness in coastal schools from Panadura to Hambantota *(BEDROC, 2006)*[7]. These programs teach children how to identify evacuation routes and prepare for disasters. Children then share this information with their families *(Oxfam Field Studies, 2006)*.Building Local capacities for disaster response and risk reduction. A study jointly conducted by Oxfam International and bedrock, on communities perceptions of disasters, aid and their own response capacity. Bhagat Singh, Additional Secretary, Ministry of Agriculture had suggested various ways to reduce disaster impacts. While occurrence of these natural disasters cannot be prevented altogether, their adverse impact can be reduced substantially by undertaking various preparedness and mitigation measures by community involvement. Minimizing the loss of precious human life is the first priority in disaster management. Significant achievement has been made in designing of disaster resistant houses and inventing quality building materials to withstand the fury of natural disasters *(Kumar, 2010)*.

Awareness and Peoples Participation

"Prepare disaster and community action plans, involve community for the purposes of planning to development action plans", says Kobe Town Mayor. What is needed for construction are three things; money, technical skills and the understanding of people in the community, the most important is the latter. Therefore it is required that we must train and educate the community on pre and post disaster situations. Community is required to be better informed through awareness and education programmes. At the same time, the community volunteers can play an important role as they are flexible and that official authorities are not.

Community Participation in Post-disaster Reconstruction

Community participation in the rehabilitation received greater acceptance. While project management unit officials were initially skeptical of the community participation process, they later came to recognize it as an effective tool for dealing with difficulties that arose during implementation. Participation also had a positive psychological effect on communities. Involving local people in the reconstruction process helped them to overcome their trauma. Recognizing the psychological importance of the reconstruction program the government began reconstruction in small villages even before the rehabilitation program began, appealing to donors, corporate bodies, NGOs, and religious organizations to "adopt" villages for reconstruction. Some of these organizations also worked on social issues, such as schooling for children and campaigns against alcohol consumption. Over time the MEERP became a people's project. The participatory process opened many informal channels of communication and accessibility between the people and the government, helping to narrow the gap between the two. Beneficiaries became extremely conscious of their entitlements and worked hard within the process to secure them. Individuals who felt their grievances were not addressed appropriately at the village and taluka level could approach the district authorities and the government in Mumbai. Information on the program, its processes, and mechanisms for redress was accessible, and the level of awareness was high (*Thangaraj Mano, 2011*).

Community Participation in Planning and Implementation – Post-disaster Reconstruction

The active participation of community in planning and implementation will enable them to understand problems and capacities in a reliable and qualitative manner. Also the local communities can easily understand the realities and contexts better than outsiders. Disaster preparedness covers activities to enhance the ability to predict, to issue warnings, take precautions and facilitate a rapid response and cope with the effect of a disaster. It includes pre-cautionary activities by households, communities and organizations to react appropriately during and following the event. Commonly they are used to categorize the main methods of protecting communities against hazards and disasters. Disaster mitigation and preparedness have tended to fall into the gap between development, cooperation and humanitarian assistance. Disaster preparedness is closely linked to emergency response, whereas mitigation approaches tend to have much in common with developmental processes (*Thangaraj Mano, 2011).*

Sustainability and stakeholder's participation in Post-disaster Reconstruction

Government Agencies, NGOs, and international organizations implement various programmes both before and after disasters. Most of these are very successful during the project period, but gradually diminish as the years pass. There are many reasons for the gradual decrease of people's involvement in a particular project. The most common elements are lack of partnership, participation, empowerment, and ownership of the local communities *(Thangaraj Mano, 2011).* All projects should have very broad stakeholders' participation in order to have sustainability. Stakeholders of a CBDM program can be broadly defined as anyone, individuals or institutions, who may have contributed to the configuration of the disaster management or those who are normally affected by impacts of disasters in a locality, and thus have interest in participating in CBDM.

Under this section, it is important to establish the extent of social support systems including their roles and contribution by respective persons. The inter linkages of GOs, NGOs, academic and international organizations should be reflected in terms of concrete projects and initiatives, and a model of cooperation should be devised. This also includes, individuals at risks, women's groups; informal and formal leaders at the village level; volunteers with specific roles, such as in warning and evacuation; villagers with specializations like those who are mobilized to protect dikes and masons who can build earthquake-resistant structures; local business sectors, schoolteachers and administrators, district and local government authorities, research groups, people's organization, NGOs, civil societies, technical resource groups, central government, national universities, UN agencies, and international donors. This exhaustive list indicates that for a CBDM to be successful, implementers should be adept in identifying and mobilizing as many stakeholders as necessary. In some countries relationships among stakeholders are formal and legislated, but some cases also show that informal relationships do not hinder partnership arrangements at the community level. It would seem that the choice is dependent on the political structure in a particular country and the perceived level of governance in the area. Experience, however, shows that formal institutional arrangements among stakeholders improve accountability and transparency, which is important for sustainability of CBDM. Likewise, based on the experiences, role allocation among stakeholders is highly necessary *(Thangaraj Mano, 2011)*.

The methods for participation and empowerment that seek to sustain and institutionalize the process are, use of participatory approaches (PRA/PLA) involving communities in hazard; vulnerability, capacity and resource assessment as a basis for community planning; formation of informal organizations which would represent the community in coordination activities with formal local authorities; institutionalizing mechanisms such as a formal committees or councils with legal tie-ups with local government authorities; sustained public awareness involving all major stakeholders; and the community's active involvement in almost all phases of development from planning, monitoring, and evaluation *(Oxfam Australia, 2008)*.

Most of the projects under study promote tangible accumulation of physical and economic assets to reduce vulnerability. These are in the form of village contingency funds, and availability of credit for income generating activities, micro-solutions, small and medium-scale infrastructure projects that reduce impact of hazards; equipment and materials such as for latrines, water supply, early warning systems, rescue and evacuation facilities. Some focus on providing intangible "assets" such as technology in disaster resistant construction and access to information centers. Successful CBDM ventures have resulted in, increased willingness of individuals to work for a common purpose; use of collective action to solve community problems and decreased dependence on external assistance; increased awareness of possible individual and community disaster preparedness measures; and inculcation of positive attitudes among villagers in terms of their abilities to initiate changes towards the improvement of their communities *(Thangaraj Mano, 2011)*.

Post Tsunami Recovery and Reconstruction in A & N Islands

Community Perspective

The post-tsunami period in the Andaman and Nicobar Islands offered an opportunity to restore affected housing and living conditions of the large number of people whose homes were destroyed or badly damaged. Such a process of restoration of people's lives needed to take place, keeping in mind basic human rights principles of gender equality, non-discrimination and participation. It was clear, however, that even one year after the Tsunami, many shortcomings remained in the process of resettlement and rehabilitation. One important lesson learnt was that all actors involved in relief and rehabilitation work must undertake efforts to make sure that the grave mistakes made in post-disaster experiences of the past are not repeated. Failure to comply with human rights standards immediately will deepen the human-induced tragedy already afflicted on the survivors of the Tsunami. The resolve shown by states and the international community in the immediate aftermath of the tsunami must not be allowed to dissipate. In the process of rebuilding the lives, livelihoods and homes of those affected, it is vital that immediate humanitarian needs be complemented with long-term rehabilitation and reconstruction based on international human rights standards which uphold survivors' rights to dignity, equality, livelihood, and adequate conditions of living.

The feedback which the author collected from various stakeholders especially disaster survivors from Bamboo flat, Tushnabad, Vandoor and other parts of the South Andaman points out in detail that the inadequacy of response from the authorities, evident during the initial relief efforts period to the reconstruction phase, keep promising without utilizing resources and efforts, continues to mark the landscape. *(Amrita SREE, 2010)* Clearly, the opportunities that the post-tsunami phase offered have been squandered by the authorities. One distinct human right, essential in any rebuilding process, is the right to adequate housing. A key element of this human right is 'cultural adequacy'. As stated by the UN Committee on Economic, Social and Cultural Rights: 'The way housing is constructed, the building materials used and the policies supporting this must appropriately enable the expression of cultural identity and diversity of housing. Also vital to the success of any rebuilding process, and related to the element of cultural adequacy, is that authorities grasp the opportunity to train local masons and utilize local building materials and respect local traditions of space usage and layout. Another crucial point which came from the survivors is the implementation of the right to adequate housing, including the standards of cultural adequacy, have been ignored in the reconstruction phase *(DRVC, 2010)*[8].

The A& N Islands government reconstruction programme to replace nearly 10,000 homes that were destroyed has thrown up many important issues. Major concerns voiced by communities include the design, location and cost of proposed housing and the lack of scope for them to be involved in the process. The livelihood and medical concerns of the affected ones are not met and often neglected. From the southern-most and the hardest hit island of Campbell Bay which is home to people from the Nicobarese tribes, to Little and South Andaman, the number of deaths was fewer but damage to homes and livelihoods extensive. Interviews were also conducted with officials and contractors *(Dharam, 2007).*

Relief Phase – Community Responses- A& N Islands

Housing: Related to the housing design and plan, though the traditional houses have withstood earthquakes very well and communities say they prefer them, the Government has decided to construct houses using pre-fabricated materials. These would be imported from mainland India through contractors at an apparently exorbitant average cost of approx. Rs.10 lakh per unit. People have rejected this type of houses. The anger of the marginalized communities of A & N Islands recently was manifested in a protest against the Government in Little Andaman which left more than 100 people injured in police action. Similar sentiments continue amongst inhabitants of other islands as well *(Vivek R, Rajendra D, & Dharmesh J. 2006,)*

Despite the diverse backgrounds and wide range of lifestyles of communities in A & N Islands, government plans propose a single type of house for all 9714 families. The only variation is that the same houses will be on stilts in Car Nicobar. The reconstruction programme guided by the Indian Planning Commission and Empowered Group of Ministers has been entrusted to central and local government agencies (CPWD and APWD) and NGOs. All the houses are to be built as per the design, specifications and technology finalized by CPWD whether being constructed by CPWD (7889 units), by APWD (1066) or NGOs (759).

The houses have been planned as twin units like government quarters– two homes together with a dividing wall rather than free standing. The communities however, say that such houses do not meet their needs. Traditional houses vary for tribal families and non-tribal families, for agriculturist families and fisher families, from one island to the other island, depending on their lifestyle, occupation, customs, local resources and skills. The ecological significance of Andaman and Nicobar Islands need not be reiterated here. In such fragile eco-system, houses are being built with reinforced cement concrete (RCC) isolated footings, steel structures, corrugated galvanized iron sheets (CGI), bamboo boards and aero-con blocks, all imported from mainland India. These are projected to be alternative eco-friendly materials. But, the prototypes based on these materials were rejected by the community. The only significant change the Government made was that aero-con panels on the external face were replaced with timber planks. However, final specifications are not reflected in any model on the islands and are shown only in a model erected at the Chennai office of CPWD. Communities on the islands have been using timber structure houses which they know how to maintain, repair and extend as per their needs. Extensions that are securely connected to the new house would be difficult due to incompatibility between proposed structures and the traditional way of building.

The learning in all past disasters has been to involve the communities in reconstruction work to achieve any satisfactory level of recovery. This has been disregarded in favour of construction through large contractor companies. A & N communities feel that reconstruction could have provided them opportunities for local employment, particularly for the carpenters and other highly skilled builders amongst them, but all this work has been awarded to contractors. Information is the first pre-requisite for any effective participation but communities have little information about their inclusion in the programme, location of the settlements, their own plots, house designs, materials that are being used or the roles and responsibilities of contractors and implementing agencies. Effective community participation needs to be planned through the whole process of design, procurement, implementation, monitoring and supervision *(Kumar & Shikha, 2007).*

Participation of the Affected Community: Despondently, community involvement was limited to only a few consultations at the design stage. The ineffectiveness and inadequacy of these consultations is reflected in the fact that only one type of design is being built for 9714 families across eleven different islands. Clearly, the prefabricated steel structure houses with RCC footings have been conceived more on the basis of capacities of delivery agencies rather than community needs and priorities *(Amrita SREE, 2009)*[9]. Another crucial point was that the affected communities have no information about the proposed site, location or specific plots for their new homes. Though few people have seen the prototype houses built by the government, they have rejected it. The final design, materials and specifications is not known to them. Non-tribal communities have rejected the house because it does not suit the location for their agriculture or fishing activities. Tribal communities in locations like Harminder Bay have also made it clear that any location other than where they presently stay is not acceptable. All families are being relocated on the land identified by the government officials.

Relocation: Many families will be relocated on some different islands now. After the discussions with communities across the islands, it was noticed that a large number of houses are going to remain vacant and unoccupied. At Loknath Pahar and Namunaghar in South Andaman and Machhidera, Netajinagar and Harminder Bay at Little Andaman, agriculturists, fishers and tribal community were not keen to move to any of the proposed relocation sites. The place of residence has always very critical linkages with their livelihoods. It is very likely that the tribal community will build its own traditional houses using their own traditional materials procured from the forests at a later stage though they will wait to ensure their entitlement from the Government.

***Land rights*:** Use of land around the home is crucial to securing the housing rights of tsunami Survivors but it is not clear whether the affected families will be provided any ownership to the homestead plot. Though some local government officials claimed that it could not be allowed, the higher level A & N officials in Port Blair said the policy in this regard is still being worked out. The future growth of the house is critical in the local context as the house being provided is only basic essential space and not sufficient for the families, particularly when the family size grows with time. In a nutshell, the communities we spoke with are not in favour of the declared reconstruction programme but feel vulnerable due to dependence on the government and many feel unable to voice their concerns. People prefer the traditional house design and materials and would have preferred if cash or material support was provided. They would have built a larger-sized house of their own choice in a lesser amount. But the present construction plan does not allow that *(Vivek, Rajendra, & Dharmesh, 2006).*

However, the extent and quality of participation and acceptance of the housing designs by the local communities is questionable. One of the most important things that has emerged in discussions with the communities is that of livelihood. The complexities of the post-tsunami recommendations regarding reconstruction situation are quite clear. There is no clear policy framework and instead, merely a reconstruction project has been formulated. CPWD is steering the implementation under the patronage of MoUD and has already awarded contracts to two big corporate companies. APWD and NGOs are also implementing small number of houses as per CPWD directives. One type of design is being built for all types of the communities, irrespective of their occupation and lifestyle. The proposed cost of each house is estimated to be Rs 6.5 lakh in South Andaman to Rs10 lakh in Car Nicobar and Rs12.5 lakh in Nancowry. There is a huge gap in information with the community about how, why and what decisions have been taken. Finally, it is very clear that the current framework of the reconstruction programme is not people-friendly and raises serious issues. Following recommendations are made by the different expert review team to ensure adequate and dignified housing to the tsunami affected communities *(Vivek, Rajendra, & Dharmesh, 2006).*

Lessons from Cyclone Nargis for the Environment, Sustainable Livelihoods and Disaster Risk Reduction

The aftermath of Cyclone Nargis and the enormous challenges of rebuilding communities illustrate the linkages between the environment, livelihoods and disaster risks. Pre-existing environmental degradation, as a result of inadequate land use and poor resource management, increases the vulnerability of communities, turning a natural hazard into a major disaster and resulting in additional environmental damage *(UNEP 2009)*. Long-term recovery and development plans must, therefore, recognize the key role of sound natural resource management in attaining sustainable livelihoods as well as in minimizing or avoiding the adverse impacts of natural hazards. Lessons learned from Cyclone Nargis point out the necessary conditions for the sustainability of ecosystems and livelihoods as well as for disaster risk reduction, as elaborated below.

Lesson 1: Promoting an integrated approach towards sustainable livelihood development, environmental management and disaster risk reduction

As discussed in this case study, poverty is the root cause of environmental degradation in Nargis affected areas, which in turn has increased vulnerability to natural hazards. However, protecting the sustainability of ecosystems can only be achieved if local livelihoods and household food security is assured. The poor cannot be expected to have an altruistic attitude towards protecting the environment, without having tangible benefits in return.

Recovery efforts should therefore focus on community-based livelihood initiatives through improved management of natural resources. The government's recovery and reconstruction plans as well as PONREPP emphasize the need to restore livelihoods, which create a window of opportunity for integrating environmental considerations as part of long-term recovery and development interventions. Moreover, as a result of the impacts of Nargis, there is now increased awareness of the need for disaster preparedness and risk reduction. A unique opportunity now exists to integrate DRR into the livelihoods environmental management equation. It is essential; for example, that DRR planning processes such as the Myanmar Action Plan for Disaster Risk Reduction (MAPDRR) recognize that sustainable livelihoods development and risk reduction should be based on improving natural resource management, particularly in communities that are vulnerable to natural hazards such as those in the Delta *(UNEP 2009).*

This integrated approach towards sustainable livelihoods development, natural resource management and DRR should be built into and further enhanced in the government's Post-Nargis recovery and reconstruction plans. These plans should not only focus on the restoration and protection of the environment but also need to ensure sustainable livelihoods and food security for communities in affected areas. More integrated plans will be able to maximize the benefits of allocating government resources in Nargis affected areas in the future. Similarly, it is equally critical to integrate environmental components across different PONREPP sectors, in particular into the "productive lives" component, since PONREPP will guide the allocation of donor resources to support government initiatives *(UNEP 2009).*

Lesson 2: Developing alternative livelihoods

In order to reduce pressures on natural resources, it is necessary to provide communities with alternative but viable sources of household income, food security and fuel. For instance, as shown in the case study, mangrove deforestations mainly due to agricultural expansion as well as servicing household needs and income generating activities (i.e. firewood and charcoal production). Therefore, development initiatives designed to introduce more sustainable natural resource management practices must also provide alternatives for securing food needs, income and household energy, which do not rely on the over exploitation of resources. Small-scale efforts in this direction have been undertaken by NGOs such as FREDA. Both PONREPP and the government should take a more pro-active role in promoting the use of renewable energy sources for household fuel and small-scale income generation. Alternatives for renewable energy currently being explored include biogas, use of fuel-efficient stoves and solar energy. Current government plans to supply natural gas from the Andaman Sea to generate electricity for the Ayeyarwady Delta would, for example, reduce the pressure on mangrove forests.

In addition, other sources of achieving household food security and income also need to be identified to shift dependency away from rice cultivation. This is currently being pursued by NGOs such as FREDA and Mingalar Myanmar on a small-scale, as well as by funding agencies through their development programmes, i.e.JICA's mangrove project, Pyopin (funded by the United Kingdom's Department for International Development) and the FAO project on mangroves and sustainable small-scale fisheries. Proposed pilot projects as part of PONREPP to be managed by the United Nations Development Programme should also help develop workable models for sustainable resource management and livelihoods which can be replicated in other villages. It is equally important that the government develops alternative socio-economic opportunities for communities as part of their long-term plans for forestry and agricultural development in Nargis affected areas *(UNEP 2009).*

Lesson 3: Establishing an enabling policy and legal environment

(i) Formulating and implementing policies and laws that promote environment and livelihoods National government agencies, including the National Commission for Environmental Affairs (NCEA), need to ensure that their policies and programmes support environmentally sustainable development. There is an equal need to enforce policy and legal frameworks as intended by the government and translate these instruments into timely and responsive programme interventions. This will require capacity-building and institutional strengthening of sectoral ministries as well as for the NCEA as the central environmental coordinating body within the government. In particular, it is critical that the government enact the National Environment Law, which would help guide the formulation and implementation of policies to support sustainable development priorities and sound environmental management. In addition, a national land use policy is needed to provide the overall direction for land use planning in the country, which takes into account environmental and livelihood priorities within the context of adapting to climate change and reducing disaster risks. This policy would set national priorities for land use, while devolving decision-making powers to local administrations to develop their own specific land use plans which would articulate local needs and priorities within the national framework *(UNEP 2009).*

(ii) Improving coordination in the implementation of government policies Effective implementation of government policies will require improving cross-sectoral coordination in order to balance development and environmental priorities. Increased collaboration across sectoral ministries and agencies (horizontal coordination) as well as between different levels of government (vertical coordination) is needed to ensure a coordinated approach to policy implementation. This would achieve the coherence necessary for implementing an integrated approach to environmentally sustainable development.

Enhancing community access and control of natural resources

Farmers and fishers must have long-term use rights over their natural resources in order to provide them with incentives to manage these resources in a sustainable manner. This is possible within the spirit of Myanmar's land tenure and fisheries licensing laws. In practice, however, the actual implementation of these laws generally does not provide farmers and fishers long-term access and control of land and fisheries. At the same time, there is a need to strengthen community participation in decision-making over the management of natural resources. Presently, 50 percent of the local population remain landless and require sources of income and food security, especially those that also do not have access to fisheries. Although they earn cash incomes by working as agricultural labourers, it is not sufficient to meet household subsistence needs. Landless farmers need access to alternative livelihood sources, including community forestry schemes and subsistence fisheries, in order to minimize illegal encroachment of reserved or protected forests.

Lesson 4: Raising awareness and building

Capacity for improved environmental management and risk reduction Limited awareness and capacity to apply appropriate and sustainable resource management are another important factor driving environmental degradation. This problem has been recognized by the government as well as the international community in Myanmar in their recovery plans. Any initiative to boost livelihoods and provide alternative employment options, therefore, will need to provide capacity-building support *(UNEP 2009).*

(i) Community training on sustainable resource management and DRR Capacity-building on improved environmental management is especially needed at the community level to reduce pressures on resources and boost livelihoods. Training activities will enable people to manage their natural resources in a sustainable manner through better understanding of the linkages between the environment, livelihoods and DRR. Towards this end, government plans in the forestry, fisheries and agricultural sectors include training for communities in resource management. Capacity building activities provided by government, however, should be undertaken through collaboration between different ministries and administrative levels to maximize efficiency and effectiveness of trainings *(UNEP 2009).*

Capacity-building of communities would be best carried out by community-based organizations (CBOs) and NGOs, because they are trusted by local people and have the necessary on-the ground knowledge and experience. However, CBOs and NGOs should work closely with extension services of relevant government agencies such as fisheries, forestry and agriculture. It will be important to ensure that trainings are based on a careful assessment of needs and address environmental, livelihoods and DRR priorities in an integrated manner. Capacity-building programmes should be complemented by the preparation of training materials, such as guidelines and manuals, which would be developed based on the experiences of recovery and development projects (whether implemented by NGOs, the government, the UN system or others) in the Ayeyarwady Delta.

(ii) Strengthening capacities of local authorities' Local authorities play a crucial role in implementing policies, laws and regulations to support sustainable development. They are at a level of governance closest to the people; therefore, their active engagement at the township, district and divisional levels in development initiatives is essential in carrying out coherent and responsive disaster preparedness strategies. Local authorities could also contribute effectively to undertaking local environmental assessments and monitoring as well as raising greater public awareness about the environment. Moreover, they can help address resource access issues. However, local administrations also require training on the implementation of national rules and regulations, particularly those that affect the environment and livelihoods. Trainings would be complemented by the development of guidelines and manuals on how to effectively implement national laws and policies to achieve their intended objectives.

One major area for capacity-building is in developing appropriate, environmentally sustainable local land use plans at both divisional and district levels. To ensure more locally responsive and appropriate land use plans, there is a need to devolve decision-making on the allocation of land based on local contexts and priorities, though working within the framework of national policies. However, allocating greater powers to local authorities must be accompanied by strengthening institutions within local administrations and building capacities of public officials in divisions, townships or districts *(UNEP 2009)*.

(iii) Strengthening civil society organizations NGOs and CBOs serve a critical role in capacity building and support for community-based initiatives. They fulfill an important advocacy role with local authorities and national government, for instance in clarifying land tenure issues and promoting greater community participation in decision-making processes. Increasing in number as a result of Post-Nargis Recovery efforts, national NGOs are often staffed by retired government officials or individuals from the private sector. Civil society engagement is officially recognized in both PONREPP46 and the government's national recovery and reconstruction plans, particularly in the forestry sector. Funding agencies are increasingly working in partnership with civil society organizations to implement community based projects that promote sustainable natural resource management. NGOs as well as CBOs, however, need to develop skills in natural resource management, advocacy, mediation and facilitation in order to provide that essential bridge between government and communities.

Lesson 5: Developing robust information base to guide decision-making

It is essential to recognize the importance of reliable and up-to-date information in helping to formulate and implement policies and programmes for sustainable development and disaster risk reduction. This calls for strengthening systems of assessment and the monitoring of natural resources at village, township, district and divisional levels in Nargis affected areas. Not only would a reliable data base be useful for national policymakers but also would enable communities and local authorities to better manage their natural resources, for instance through appropriate land use planning or development of coastal zone management plans. For Nargis-affected areas, monitoring and surveillance of key environmental features and resources (e.g. water, biodiversity, land and forests) will need to be strengthened, particularly with respect to the potential impacts of climate change including incremental environmental changes as well as increased vulnerability to natural hazards. In addition, a strategic approach to DRR, based on a national vulnerability assessment, should be undertaken to develop effective strategies for climate change adaptation and for reducing future disaster impacts *(UNEP, 2009)*.

Disasters and Communities

Disaster risk is on the rise throughout the world. Over the past two to three decades, the economic losses and the number of people who have been affected by natural disasters have increased more rapidly than both economic and population growth. The physical, social and economic losses caused by these disasters are particularly harsh for developing countries since they have a long-range effect in the development process. The impacts of the disasters are deeply related with the socio economic conditions, tradition, culture, and climate of the communities *(Bishnu Pandey and Kenji Okazaki, 2010)*[10]. To minimize the damages caused by disasters, various efforts have been taken by government, international communities including donor agencies. However, in spite of participation of these sectors during the project period, it has been observed that many of the disaster management programmes have failed to be sustainable at local level after the completion of the project. Without sustainability, disaster management efforts will not preserve. A critical element of sustainable disaster management is communities' participation in these activities.

The most common elements of community involvement are partnership, participation, empowerment and ownership by the local people. The emphasis of disaster management efforts should focus on communities and the people who live in them. Unless the disaster management efforts are sustainable at individual and community level, it is difficult to reduce the losses and scale of the tragedy. There needs to be an opportunity where people can be involved from the initial programming stage of disaster management activities. Through these community–based activities, people should be able to participate alongside government officials and experts group as the direct stakeholders of these activities. While people should own the problems, consequences and challenges of any mitigation and/or preparedness initiative, it is necessary to take people's involvement further, into policy and strategy. This process induces sense of ownership to the people which results in their continuous engagement and long term commitment to these activities. Involvement of communities is important in both pre-disaster mitigation and post disaster response and recovery process *(Pandey and Okazaki, 2010).*

Community Empowerment

While disasters can strike wide region or a nation, that impact is felt at the community level although it may hit one or several communities at once. These communities constitute what is referred to as "disaster fronts". Being at the forefronts, communities need to have capacity to respond to threats themselves. It is for this reason that communities should be involved in managing the risks that may threaten their well-being.

While different community empowerment programmes related to disaster mitigation have achieved their objectives, they are often short term, and issues on sustainability in these efforts are rarely addressed. Government, non-government and international organizations implement various programmes before and after the disasters. Most of them are very successful during the project period, but gradually diminish as the years pass. There are many reasons for this kind of phenomena; however, lack of effective participation and capacity building of the local communities to peruse the program remains a major factor for lack of sustainability. It is accepted that governments have the prime responsibility for managing disasters and for taking into consideration the roles played by different players. In the past, top-down and command-and-control approaches were oftentimes used to manage the consequences of disasters. In this approach, decisions come from higher authorities based on their perception on the needs. The communities serve as mere "victims" or receiver of aid. In practice though, this approach was proven to be ineffective. It fails to meet the appropriate and vital humanitarian needs. Moreover, it increases requirements for unnecessary external resources and creates general dissatisfaction over performance despite exceptional management measures employed. This is due to the fact that the community, as the primary stakeholder and recipient of the direct impact of disasters, was not given the chance to participate in the process of decision-making and implementation of activities. On the other hand, communities if left alone have limited resources to fully cope with disasters. In many developing and underdeveloped countries, those who suffer the most are the poor, who, in the first place have limited survival resources and do not enjoy adequate infrastructure and access to social services. Community empowerment for disaster risk management demands their participation in risk assessment, mitigation planning, capacity building, participation in implementation and development of system for monitoring which ensures their stake (*Bishnu Pandey and Kenji Okazaki, 2010).*

Community Based Disaster Management (CBDM)

Most of disaster response can be characterized as command and control structure one that is top down and with logistic centre approach. Because of this, we observe, lack of community participation that results into failures in meeting the appropriate and vital humanitarian needs, unnecessary increase in requirement for external resources, and general dissatisfaction over performance despite the use of exceptional management measures. Recognizing these limitations, the Community Based Disaster Management (CBDM) approach promotes a bottom-up approach working in harmony with the top - down approach, to address the challenges and difficulties. To be effective, local communities must be supported into analyzing their hazardous conditions, their vulnerabilities and capacities as they see themselves. In case of disasters, the people at the community level have more to lose because they are the ones directly hit by disasters, whether major or minor. They are the first ones to become vulnerable to the effects of such hazardous events. On the other hand, they have the most to gain if they can reduce the impact of disasters on their community. This concept gave rise to the idea of community-based disaster management where communities are put at the forefront. Through the CBDM, the people's capacity to respond to emergencies is increased by providing them with more access and control over resources and basic social services. Using a community-based approach to managing disasters certainly has its advantages. Through CBDM, it is hoped that communities will be strengthened to enable them undertake any programmes of development including disaster preparedness and mitigation *(Bishnu Pandey and Kenji Okazaki, 2010).*

The CBDM helps in building the capacity of local community to cope with emergency faced by disasters. It is well noted that, currently CBDM has gained prominence world over. In India, High Power Committee (HPC) has realized the need for CBDM, and emphasized the role of local government municipalities and Panchayati Raj institutions *(A.C.Jena, 2009).* The CBDM approach provides opportunities for the local community to evaluate their own situation based on their own experiences initially. Under this approach, the local community not only becomes part of creating plans and decisions, but also becomes a major player in its implementation. Although the community is given greater roles in the decision-making and implementation processes, CBDM does not ignore the importance of scientific and objective risk assessment and planning. The CBDM approach acknowledges that as many stakeholders as needed should be involved in the process, with the end goal of achieving capacities and transferring of resources to the community.

Community Based Disaster Management (CBDM) - Some Case Studies

The United Nations Centre for Regional Development (UNCRD) has incorporated CBDM as its approach in disaster management planning under the overall organizational mandate of sustainable regional development and human security. The UNCRD Disaster Management Planning Hyogo Office focused on the community initiatives in the Asian region targeting different stakeholders, from local government decision makers to schoolchildren. In all initiatives, attempts were made to ensure that communities are engaged in disaster risk management phases and are empowered to carry over them in long term run. Some case studies of UNCRD initiatives in this regards are discussed below *(UNCRD, 2002).*Small island communities in the Andaman & Nicobar Islands are vulnerable due to their small size and difficulties in accessibility. Faced with the threat of recurrent disasters viz. earthquakes, Tsunamis and cyclones- the challenge lies in creating disaster resilient communities rather than disaster resistant communities. Peculiarities of the island communities warrant that the risk reduction aims at empowering communities. Increasing population growth, migration from the mainland, unplanned settlements and vulnerable construction practices have increased risks on these islands *(SEEDS India, 2007)*

Hence, it is necessary that the communities are resilient and proactive during the occurrence of such fatal disasters. There is urgency and need to develop a model approach for reducing risks such that it empowers. The community to such an extent is resilient against any future disasters. The Bottom-Up approach in terms of resource allocation and exercising powers in Panchayati Raj Institution will also be the key factor. Community Based Disaster Management and Reduction is the integral part of various programs undertaken by SEEDS and the core sectors identified in order to ensure capacity building and resilience are: Education, Livelihood, Institutional mechanism for Broad Based Disaster Reduction & Development, Safe Construction Practices and Water & Sanitation *(Chavda, 2007).*

Community Involvement in Flood Response and Rehabilitation

Maharashtra was plagued by unprecedented floods causing havoc in Mumbai, Pune and other districts resulting in tremendous loss to human life, public and private property. The development sector responded to the needs of the impact through a process of relief, rehabilitation and livelihood restoration. There is a huge reservoir of knowledge and expertise in the development sector in the world. However, the insights of the local communities and the solutions they find to problems sometimes outweigh this expertise as was experienced by DST in its flood response operations. The needs and opportunities differed at a local level and approaches needed to be adapted to respond to local realities. We, at DST, faced an unprecedented need and an unprecedented opportunity to learn from the disaster response (*Sonia Garcha, 2007).* DST has had the experience of disaster response in the Maharashtra earthquake (1993) and thereafter Gujarat earthquake (2001) where it worked with a number of civil society organizations in planning, funding and executing relief, rehabilitation and livelihood promotion by addressing gender issues and rebuilding communities. This experience proved valuable in responding to the Maharashtra Flood in 2005. The Pune and Pimpri-Chinchwad metropolis's low-lying urban slum areas and districts of Pune, Sangli and Kolhapur where DST has its urban and rural Microfinance programme, were submerged due to heavy rains and water released from dams. DST undertook relief operation in the affected areas *(Community Based Disaster Management, 2007).*

The entire process of damage assessment and distribution of the relief packages was conducted very smoothly with the active involvement of local community leaders and SHG's. It is this background against which a few instances of the best practices of action taken by civil society organization in India could be seen as learnings for all. Our intervention in disaster situation would reveal how civil society can address the issues of disaster management from gender perspectives and help urban and rural women to put the development process back on track evolved through MF programme. This experience in responding to the natural disaster can examine the initiatives of DST and its impact on development and the manner in which this impact has been achieved *(Garcha, 2007).*

During natural calamities, it is a humane tendency to help the affected people in many ways both in relief and rehabilitation on a humanitarian ground and in the process of extending such helps, the organizations, institutions and individuals will tend to forget the role of the communities and the innate capacity, skill and capacity of the local communities in managing their affairs. As a result, the affected people are looked at with pity and they are made to receive the assistance. As a result, the self respect of the community is at question. Further their skill, capacity and capability are not used. One important aspect everyone has to understand that the communities are managing the affairs after disaster till the arrival of the Government Departments and voluntary organizations. It has been witnessed in tsunami affected areas in Nagapattinam that in the first two days only the communities managed the affairs. But in general the affected people are not involved in the relief and rehabilitation activities. As a result, the external agencies work on a supply driven mode not on a demand driven mode. Agencies, organizations, institutions and individuals who gained rich experiences in disaster mitigation in one place, have not utilized the same in other places. In all the times it had been emphasized the role of communities in disaster management *(Palanithurai, 2009).*

Sustainability in Community Based Disaster Management

In the Year 2002, UNCRD launched a three-year project on titled "Sustainability in Community Based Disaster Management", to study the effectiveness of the grass - root projects and to suggest policy input for sustainability, which will be useful for the different communities to take future actions. This was to help understand the gaps in the community initiatives, and to take corrective actions in the future. The study would be an evaluation of what has been done so far in CBDM with specific examples from field experiences, and what should be done in future for the sustainability of these efforts. In this study, the inter-linkages of government, on-government, academics, and international organizations should be reflected in terms of concrete projects and initiatives, and a model of cooperation would be established *(UNCRD, 2002).*

The goal of the current study is to achieve safety and sustainability of livelihoods for effective disaster mitigation, focusing on three key elements: self-help, cooperation, and education. In order to identify the key factors for successful CBDM, six case studies were chosen in the Asian region targeting three specific hazards: Cyclones (India and the Philippines), earthquakes (Indonesia and Nepal) and floods (Bangladesh and Cambodia). At first, field surveys were carried out and the best practices from the case study countries were documented. Based on the analysis of these cases studies, overall framework of action for the sustainability of community based disaster management was prepared. Generic and specific guidelines were developed and field experimentations and testing were made for specific hazards in selected case study countries (*UNCRD, 2003).* From the three-year study, followings were found as key factors for enhancing sustainability:

- The existence of "culture of coping with crisis" and "culture of disaster reduction" exist.
- Risk assessment process involves participation of people and incorporating their perception of vulnerability and capacity.
- Community and supporting agencies share common motivation and ownership for the initiation and sustainability of CBDM.
- Genuine people's participation within capacity building objectives, with specific focus on sectoral groups like women, elderly, children and ethnic minorities.
- Well-delivered training inputs in accordance with the objectives of the project and the needs of the community for training.
- Wider stakeholders' involvement and participation.
- Accumulation of physical, technological and economic assets to reduce hazards and vulnerability.
- Integration of these projects into regular development planning and budgeting to ensure sustainability.

Afgan Training and livelihood Initiative UNCRD Hyogo Office carried out "Afgan Training and Livelihood Initiative (ALTI)" in Afghanistan from October 2002 to June 2003. Under the need of the holistic rehabilitation after more than two decades of conflict and strife, the urgent need was to build houses of people (*R. Shaw, N Britton, M Gupta, 2003).*

Afghanistan is an earthquake prone country, and is located in one of the most active seismic belts of the world; seismic risk needs to be incorporated in its rehabilitation process. The ALTI focused on developments of guidelines for earthquake safe construction practices, training of masons and engineers, and construction of model houses. All these activities aimed to empower the 6 communities with their active participation in this process. In this community based initiative, livelihood recovery was incorporated through revitalization of vineyards using a cooperative system. These efforts altogether develop human resources, provide sustainable livelihood and are linked to the long term recovery of the country *(UNCRD, 2002).*

Patanka New Life (PNY) Plan after the Gujarat earthquake of January 2001, PNY was initiated as joint initiative of diverse organizations including government, non-government, academics and international organizations for community based effective rehabilitation. The aim of the initiative was to train and empower local masons and communities with proper earthquake-safer technologies focusing on local tradition and culture. Emphasis was to ensure confidence building and long-term use of traditional technologies.

There were two major components of the initiative: one construction and rehabilitation of model village, and training and confidence building of communities through stake table demonstration testing. The characteristic feature of the initiative was to focus on the holistic approach of the rehabilitation including livelihood. The initiative was successful, especially in terms of community involvement and ownership. The initiative was considered a successful model for sustainable community recovery. The PNY was conceived as a model program right from its inception stage. It sought to empower the affected community to the extent that they are sufficiently resilient against future disasters *(UNCRD, 2002).*

School Earthquake Safety Initiative

The United Nations Centre for Regional Development (UNCRD) is, currently, promoting School Earthquake Safety Initiative through a project "Reducing Vulnerability of School Children to Earthquakes" jointly with UN Department of Economic and Social Affairs (UNDESA) in Asia-Pacific region. The project aims to make schools safe against earthquakes and build disaster- resilient communities through self-help, cooperation and education. The project includes retrofitting of school building in a participatory way with the involvement of local communities, local governments and resource institutions, trainings on safer construction practices to technicians, disaster education in school and communities. These activities are carried out in *Fiji Islands, India, Indonesia and Uzbekistan as demonstration cases which will be di*sseminated throughout the respective geographical regions. There are three major aspects of the community empowerment in earthquake disaster risk management through this initiative: Seismic safety of school buildings: The project includes seismic vulnerability analysis of some selected schools in a project city of each country and retrofitting of some of them which cover prominent construction typology in the region. This leads to development of country specific guidelines on the earthquake safe construction which incorporates solutions to the practical problems experienced in school retrofitting *(UNCRD, 2002).*

Capacity Building of Communities: Retrofitting of schools in communities serves as a Demonstration of proper earthquake technology to them. Masons in the communities get on-job training during the retrofitting of schools. In addition, technicians in each project cities get trainings on earthquake design and construction of houses. Consideration is given to the local practice, material availability, indigenous knowledge and affordability in trainings on earthquake technology *(UNCRD, 2002).*

Disaster Education and Awareness: The project includes development and wide distribution of educational booklets, posters and guidebook on teachers training and students' drills for earthquake disaster preparedness and response. The guidebooks get verification and updated through trainings and mock drills. The projects also develops an interactive educational tool for awareness raising on earthquake disaster and simple seismic risk assessment of buildings aiming to motivate households for planning seismic upgrading of their houses. It was learned from earlier programs of UNCRD that the process of making safer schools can be used as entry points to the communities at risk to facilitate implementation of a training and capacity -building programme for earthquake disaster mitigation technology besides its prime objective of ensuring the safety of school children against future earthquakes. It is achieved by demonstrating how schools can be used as community centres for earthquake disaster prevention and mitigation. Locally applicable and affordable earthquake-safer construction technology is transferred to these communities *(UNCRD, 2002).*

Lessons learned

In regards to the issue of engaging and empowering communities for sustainable disaster risk management, followings are the major lessons learned:

- Community empowerment and communication help to achieve sustainability in CBDM.
- A holistic secure-livelihood approach enhances sustainability.
- Community based action plans and training improves community's problem solving skills.
- Because disasters are unpredictable, it is important to maintain the projects and people's awareness of disasters.
- Transparency of activities and dissemination of knowledge and information.
- People's participation in activities.
- CBDM efforts need stable financial resources.
- 'What is accepted by the community' is more important than 'what is necessary'?
- Institutionalizing the community and the private sectors can result in more sustainable disaster management programmes *(Pandey & Okazaki, 2005).*

Community Based Emergency Response Teams

A relatively new approach to local involvement in disaster response is emerging across counties and communities in the United States. The Community Emergency Response Team (CERT) program seeks to train and empower local community residents to shoulder the responsibility of being first responders to emergencies. CERTs, which are administered by Citizen Corps and FEMA within the Department of Homeland Security, blend a bottom-up appreciation for the role of local volunteers in emergency response with a top-down institutional framework to facilitate training and coordination.

There is much promise in the CERT program as a strategy for local empowerment and effective disaster response in rural communities. To be effective, however, the CERT program should be adaptable to different levels of local capacity and should broadly represent the citizenry it is intended to protect and serve. It is also possible that by developing local capacity for disaster response, CERT teams may be able to expand their applicability to non-disaster community development activities.

While CERTs have predominantly focused on disaster preparedness and recovery, this does not always need to be the case. CERTs provide a framework for pulling together localities to prepare for times of need. This process of building community and response structures has application beyond the context of disasters. In rural communities with high disaster response capacity, established networks, infrastructures, and alliances are likely to already exist to allow a community to plan for its needs and build on its strengths to achieve desired goals. Such capacity for providing these community services does not always exist, but can be cultivated and should be encouraged and empowered. Extension and other change agents can play a leading role in this process. Where capacity for community involvement in disaster response or broader development is lower, CERT programs provide a potential framework for both.

Including Everyone in Community Responses to Disaster

A critical aspect of CERT effectiveness and potential for expanding into community development or other roles is representation of the entire local population. Drawing together diverse racial, ethnic, religious, and other groups provides a host of resources and experiences, but more importantly provides transparency in the local decision making process. In all communities, a variety of groups exist with diverse skills and abilities combined with personal and professional experiences that are essential to successful preparation and response to disasters (Independent Sector, 2001). Included are residents with needed professional and trade skills for damage control and assessment (engineers, environmental scientists, architects, contractors, and skilled laborers); disaster preparedness and response training (VFW, retired military/national guard/police); medical, psychological and social service delivery experience (health practitioners, counselors, religious/ civic groups); and longtime residents who have witnessed previous responses to natural disasters *(Brennan M.A., 2005).*

Such groups and individuals are also directly suited to local empowerment and community development that serves to enhance rural well-being. Effective community response to disaster and other local needs connects diverse groups within the locality. Successfully linking local organizations, citizens, and leaders provides a network and method for local citizens and groups to become actively involved in local preparedness and response efforts and beyond. Individuals currently involved in CERTs are also likely to provide strong personal and professional connections which can link local interests to state/federal agencies and other outside entities. Such connections and partnerships can facilitate access to information, resources, training, and finances necessary to build local capacities. In this way, CERTs can act as bridges between local and extra-local resources not only to prepare and respond to disaster, but also directly shape rural well-being as part of rural development efforts. Since rural communities are often situated in a unique interface between the physical environment and society, local residents are important to the management of natural resources. CERTs can provide the human resources, initiative, and framework for gathering and disseminating information important to environmental decision making. Such effort is not far removed from disaster preparedness efforts. Linking local land use and natural resource management with risk mitigation and disaster preparedness weaves together an integrated approach to protecting ecological and human well-being. A model of expanding the traditional role of CERTs can be found in Alachua County, Florida where local CERT volunteers were involved in surveying local farmers about drought protection practices and other natural resource management efforts. Building relationships in quiet times creates a valuable network and sense of community to tap into in times of emergency or disaster *(Brennan M.A., 2005).*

Community Participation in Tsunami Disaster Response and Recovery Programs in South India

The impact of the rehabilitation on ongoing grassroots-level institution building – involving the formation of self-help groups and producers' cooperatives – was not very positive. In some cases, for instance in Kanyakumari, the involvement of existing groups may have yielded some all-round benefits, but in others, particularly in Andhra Pradesh, this might have led to negative consequences for the groups and the concept of SHG itself *(Action Aid, 2007).*

There were instances (in Kanyakumari) where members of particular groups were reportedly discriminated against in rehabilitation programmes, while in others, there was an active co-option of members from existing groups into new ones. In areas where the NGOs took a principled stand against providing boats, they came under fire from their groups for not doing enough. This was a real dilemma because, if the NGO stuck to its principles, it stood to lose the groups that it had built by investing much effort and hard work; on the other, if it gave in to the demands, it would lose its ideological strength and that would surely have an impact on its own long term work with the people! A few NGOs did seem to overcome this problem unscathed, but for a majority of NGOs, the costs may have been quite heavy. As one NGO representative told us, "It was sad to see all the work we had done over the decades collapsing like a pack of cards in a matter of months and right before our eyes too." On the other hand, proliferation of village development councils and other SHG-like mechanisms was often done without proper foundation, with the result that these new groups were no more than channels to distribute boats and other support in the villages. Like the fisheries cooperatives of yore, people tended to take a mercenary attitude towards these new groups and this would have long-term implications for the future cooperative-oriented programmes in the villages. The NGOs came forward and acted towards the immediate and long term needs of the affected community *(Action Aid, 2007).*

Coverage of people in the rehabilitation programmes:

- In terms of coverage, the focus was mainly on the primary producers, with boat owners receiving compensation from the Government while the crew received support from NGOs in the form of boats.
- Assistance provided to the post-harvest and ancillary trades was sporadic and patchy, resulting in several categories of people (a majority belonging to poor and marginalized sections, particularly women) being left out or receiving inadequate attention; this lack of support also contributes to a weakening of the production and market chains.

- Avoidance of mechanised sector in the NGO rehabilitation programmes contributed to ignoring the many intermediaries involved in the production and trade chains at fishing harbours.
- People of non-fishing castes (but involved in fishing), those living in the shadow zones, migrant fisher men, and people who were not directly affected by the tsunami but suffered indirectly from its effects or remained vulnerable to future disasters were some other categories who received less attention.

Community Participation and NGO Involvement in Kerala- *Tsunami Context*

The strict regulatory regime that has characterized the tsunami relief operations in Kerala has not sufficiently encouraged or motivated the NGOs and other civil society organizations to fully commit themselves to the tsunami relief, rehabilitation and reconstruction. The administrative restrictions have constrained the involvement of the local self-governance institutions such as the Panchayat. Even the elected representatives of the people in the local self-governance institutions have not been involved in the need assessment or beneficiary selection. Community participation in the state-sponsored relief programmes has been absent. The tsunami-affected families, the real stakeholders, are not involved in the need assessment, programme formulation or selection of beneficiaries. This has led to problems in planning and implementation of the relief and rehabilitation programmes. The benevolent state administration has been facing criticism, opposition and sometimes violent revolts from the tsunami-affected people. This has led to delay in the dispensation of the state-sponsored relief and reconstruction programmes *(Sahayi, 2005)*.The state government has realised the limitation and has announced that a new legislation for disaster relief will be brought in.

NGO Intervention- Tsunami Relief and Rehabilitation Strategy

Sahayi, voluntary organization intensively worked in disaster response in Kerala, defined its role and formulated its programmes, taking into consideration the constraints on NGO intervention in tsunami relief in the state. The scope of intervention was limited. At best the organization could supplement the functions and services of the government; for example, by identifying those needs of the tsunami-affected people that are not met by the programmes *(Placid, 2005)*.

The strategy is to ensure community involvement in relief and reconstruction programmes to a possible extent. This is based on four factors that emerge from our analysis of the community's response to the tsunami relief programmes and activities.

- The self-respect of the tsunami affected people needs to be restored through community participation in relief and rehabilitation. They don't want to be treated as beggars. The people wish that their dignity and self-respect be acknowledged during this time of distress. The tsunami-affected communities need to be actively involved in decision-making and implementation of relief and reconstruction activities, including decisions about rebuilding and relocation of housing, and other services.
- The communities are clear in their desire to have a say in the utilization of resources and to regain control over their own lives. They desire transparency and accountability in the projects undertaken by various agencies, including government.
- Dependency needs to be reduced. While relief and charity are important in the immediate aftermath of a disaster, they should be replaced as soon as possible with assistance to people in regaining their livelihoods and control over their lives.
- There should be an effective role for the local self-governance institutions and grass-root NGOs, other civil society organisations and the media in the programme planning and implementation, and effective linkages among these agencies *(SAHAYI, 2006)*.

Conclusion

The various studies discussed above converged to deliver a key message that disaster affected communities desire to get a chance to guide their own relief and rehabilitation. Too often, the research revealed, the knowledge, capacity and priorities of communities were overlooked, and their members were cast as consultants or passive recipients of aid rather than as equal partners in the process. The study indicates that the true needs and aspirations are looked into and furthermore the community members feel ownership of the programmes aimed at their recovery. Nevertheless to say by reviewing different disasters, the vital role of the community and community based organizations is standing high in planning, executing and continuing the pre and post disaster initiatives. Many of the countries realized the great involvement of the affected community in managing disaster response and recovery programmes. So it is the responsibility of the government and various international and other organizations to understand the significance of involvement of the affected community in all spheres of disaster management activities to make use of the communities' knowledge, skill and experience for helping them to face any kind of calamity.

While going through the different lessons it could reveal that the lack of community participation is visible in almost all the disasters we discussed here. Government and relief officials often failed to consult survivors and their communities about decisions regarding aid distribution, resettlement, and reconstruction aid. In some cases, these officials discredited or ignored the views and opinions of local communities. Donors and aid agencies often prioritized timely outcomes over deliberative processes that allowed for community participation and discussion.

It is evident, as well written in the beginning, "Empowering families and communities to take preventive action on their own behalf, without being dependent on external support, is one of the clear, unalterable lessons learned from the tsunami experience. The aim is always to leave people better off, to reinforce their existing coping mechanisms and to build their resilience to whatever the future holds. This is the true legacy of the tsunami operation" *(International Federation of Red Cross and Red Crescent Societies, 2009).*

Notes

1. The Asian Disaster Reduction & Response Network (ADRRN) is a network consists of 34 national NGOs from 16 countries across the Asia- Pacific region. The mission of the ADRRN is to promote coordination and collaboration among NGOs and other stakeholders for effective and efficient disaster reduction and response in the Asia- Pacific region. With a strong footprint in the region, the network members are constantly engaged with local communities strengthening their ability to combat disasters, providing humanitarian aid like food, water, shelter and health care, protecting critical facilities like schools and hospitals, creating awareness, advocating for policy changes and improving the capacity of the community based organisations. ADRRN membership is open to national NGOs with headquarter in Asia- Pacific region and working in the field of climate change adaptation and disaster reduction and response. The secretariat is based at Kuala lumpur, Malaysia.
2. The Institute for Participatory Interaction in Development (IPID) was incorporated in January 1996 under Section 21 of the Company's Act No.17 of 1982 as a company limited by guarantee (i.e as a Non Profit Company) and is non-sectarian and non- governmental. IPID is committed to community development through participatory approaches. The Vision of the institution is to "The enhancement of the capacities of governmental and non-governmental organizations for supporting a change in the pattern of personal behaviour and attitudes towards a reversal of roles through Participatory Interaction in Development aimed at empowering local communities to manage resources and gain access to available services."

3. Oxfam International is a confederation of 13 organizations working together in more than 120 countries to find lasting solutions to poverty and injustice. Collaboration in Crises: Lessons in Community Participation from the Oxfam International Tsunami Research Program. This report introduces the studies and findings of the Oxfam International. Tsunami Disaster Risk Reduction and Participatory Action Research programme, hereafter referred to as the tsunami research program. For information about the program, including an electronic version of this report, summaries of the research, stories from the field, and details about the research program itself. "Collaboration in Crises" is one of four Oxfam International reports that mark the end of Oxfam's response to the Indian Ocean tsunami. The others are the "Oxfam International Tsunami Fund End-of-Program Report" (December 2008), an overview of the entire tsunami program; the "Oxfam International. Tsunami Fund: An Evaluation of the Tsunami Response" (planned for March 2009), a synthesis of 13 evaluations conducted to extract lessons from the tsunami program; and the "Oxfam International Tsunami Fund Annual Report and Accounts" (planned for May 2009).
4. A non-governmental organization (NGO) is a legally constituted organization created by natural or legal persons that operates independently from any form of government. The term originated from the United Nations (UN), and is normally used to refer to organizations that are not a part of the government and are not conventional for-profit business. In the cases in which NGOs are funded totally or partially by governments, the NGO maintains its non-governmental status by excluding government representatives from membership in the organization. The term is usually applied only to organizations that pursue wider social aims that have political aspects, but are not openly political organizations such as political parties. The number of NGOs operating in the United States is estimated at 40,000. International numbers are even higher: Russia has 277,000 NGOs; India is estimated to have around 3.3 million NGOs in year 2009, which is just over one NGO per 400 Indians, and many times the number of primary schools and primary health centres in India.
5. The Catholic Organisation for Relief and Development Aid (Cordaid) is a Dutch development agency operating worldwide. Codaid fight poverty and exclusion in fragile states and areas of conflict and extreme inequality. In order to stand up for the world's poorest and most marginalized communities, we raise funds in the Netherlands as well as internationally. The Catholic Organisation for Relief and Development Aid (Cordaid) is a Dutch development agency operating worldwide. Fight poverty and exclusion in fragile states and areas of conflict and extreme inequality. In order to stand up for the world's poorest and most marginalized communities, we raise funds in the Netherlands as well as internationally.
6. CARE International (CI) is a global confederation of 12 national member organisations working together to act as a leading relief and development Non-Government Organization (NGO) fighting to end poverty. We worked in 84 countries, supporting 1,051 poverty-fighting projects to reach more than 122 million people in 2011. CARE helps tackle underlying causes of poverty so that people can become self-sufficient. CARE is often one of the first to deliver emergency aid to survivors of natural disasters and war and, once the immediate

crisis is over, we help people rebuild their lives. While CARE is a large international organization with 12,000 employees worldwide, we have a strong local presence: 97% of our staff is nationals of the countries where our programmes are run. CARE India works with the poorest of the poor in more than 200 districts, in a total of 16 states and union territories across India. CARE India is a leading national developmental organization with an extensive global network. Through our pro-poor programmes, we have impacted on extreme poverty and social injustice in India by working with poor women and girls from the most disadvantaged communities. We place a special emphasis on working with poor women because, equipped with the proper resources, women have the power to help whole families and entire communities escape poverty. Women are at the heart of CARE's community-based efforts to improve basic education, boost maternal and child health, prevent the spread of HIV & Tuberculosis (TB) and expand economic opportunity. CARE also delivers emergency aid to survivors of natural disasters, and helps people rebuild their lives.

7. G. Padmanabhan has been handling Disaster Management portfolio of UNDP-India since 1995. He has led the Team involved in implementing the GOI-UNDP Disaster Risk Management Programme in the 17 states. Padmanabhan is also the Moderator of the Disaster Management Community of Practice (electronic network established under the under the Solution Exchange project of the UN system in India with about 2,500 disaster management practitioners as members). He worked for a year in Northern Iraq as a senior manager of a large Electricity Network Rehabilitation Project, executed by UNDP. He has been supporting various UNDP country offices in the Asia region in developing guidelines, conceptualizing and formulating projects. He was also associated with the design and implementation of the state Human Development project of UNDP-India.

8. Disaster, Risk and Vulnerability Conference 2011, School of Environmental Sciences, Mahatma Gandhi University, India in association with the Applied Geoinformatics for Society and Environment, Germany March 12–14, 2011. Critical reflections on post disaster recovery and reconstruction in Andaman & Nicobar Islands: The article examines the post-disaster recovery and reconstruction activities to the major and minor disasters which are frequently disturbing the life of the islanders. The paper is focusing on the various actions taken by the A & N Administration as well as the social and developmental organizations, extracting lessons learned and identifying specific implications towards the episode. The sudden occurrence of the frequent earthquake distracts the normal life of the islanders and it hit in almost all part of the areas of the Andaman's including North, Middle and Southern parts. The paper is at first attempt to review the recovery and reconstruction activities of the various stakeholders in relation with the December 2004 tsunami and earthquakes. Later the author pointed out the frequent incidence of the various disasters especially earthquake, flood and climate related disasters. Lessons that have been learned from the post disaster response are summarized, including: (a) lessons that apply primarily to the relief phase; (b) lessons for rehabilitation and reconstruction; (c) do's and don'ts; (d) island specific observations. (e) Finally the impact and the long-term implications of the intervention on the livelihood of the islanders in the post disaster response period. The author describes his experience and

tries to analyze the role of administration and the various other stakeholders in the areas of disaster recovery and reconstruction. The author finally suggested the unavoidable elements needs to be incorporated in the post disaster response phase. C 2011 Disaster Risk Vulnerability Conference 2003.

9. Amrita SREE programme managed by Mata Amritanadamayi Math is launched in Andaman Islands to promote SHG's, strengthening the existing hundreds of SHG's developed by CARE India through imparting capacity development programmes and initiating Income Generation Programmes among the SHG members. The programme was initiated in Andamans with the support of all Govt departments, organizations and with the cooperation of the community. The project is very closely monitored and guided by CARE India through conducting periodical review meeting, introducing management information system for reporting, and also extending regular hand holding support to strengthen the SHG's in the islands.

10. "Nicobarese fishermen, for example, refused to accept the mainland-manufactured fishing equipment provided in the post-Tsunami period as it was inappropriate for their needs". "As a result of the disaster, fishing communities in the islands are likely to be affected, mangrove forest to be denuded and corals to be damaged". Banerjee et al, 2005: 43.106."

Chapter - 6

Research Methodology

The present study focuses on the nature of local self government and also tries to analyze the nature of community participation in the management of natural disaster in Kerala.

Research Methodology

Statement of the Problem

Kerala has been proud of its decentralized form of governance, with its three-tier Panchayat Raj system. However, the strength of the system was terribly exposed on December 26, 2004 when tsunami waves hit the Kerala coast line. In the current administrative set up for disaster management in the state, there is no space for the Gram Panchayats, Block Panchayats or District Panchayats. No space has been provided for the participation of the tsunami affected people either, in the recovery or rehabilitation programmes. The state government played the lead role, through the revenue department represented by the District Collector (District Magistrate), and the state tolerated to some extent the intervention by the NGO's and other civil society actors. The results are obvious: social infrastructure has been restored to some extent and there has not been any resource constraints; but still some of the affected families are living in temporary shelters, some of the beneficiaries for permanent housing are yet to be identified; uncertainty prevails regarding livelihood support for most of the affected families; many of the men, women, and children who escaped the might of the killer waves are still under trauma, and are scared of the roaring sea without a sea wall. The interventions have been unplanned and haphazard, marked by lack of coordination among government departments as well as NGO's, leading to duplication of programmes particularly by international charity organizations. To top it all, despite high level of vulnerability, a disaster management system at local, district or state level is no where in sight.

Thus this study, concentrates to understand the perception of the people about the role of local self government and the level of community participation in the various aspects of the disaster management programme. This study is conducted at Alappad Panchayat; the worst affected tsunami hit area of Kollam district, Kerala.

Background of the Study

The Alappad Gram Panchayat in Kollam district has been reduced to a mute spectator to the tsunami death and destruction as well as to the relief and rehabilitation activities. As everywhere in the state, disaster preparedness or mitigation does not find a place in the Panchayat plan, and there is no budget allocation for the purpose. The resource constraints of rural Panchayats form a major bottleneck in formulating a disaster management plan, even in disaster prone areas with high vulnerability. Panchayats are not in a position to take at least a reactive approach to disaster management, leave alone a proactive approach.

Absence of space for involvement of local governments and the affected community in the state government's disaster management interventions was a notable factor. The lack of delegation of authority of the Panchayats pertaining to disaster management, absence of clear demarcation of functions related to disaster mitigation, relief and rehabilitation, and the government's reluctance to share relief funds with local Panchayats is major constraints that inhibit the development of local government's capacity for disaster management. Despite these current limitations, the potential role of local self government institutions in disaster management is significant and the required capacity can be created. The delivery of relief and rehabilitation would have been far better, if they had at least a nominal role. Beneficiary selection for housing and livelihood support are examples. The list of beneficiaries for permanent shelters is not yet complete because the revenue officials are not in a position to decide who really lost their houses. People who had left the village several years ago are in the government's list of beneficiaries where as many fishermen families who had their dwellings on the sea shore without 'Patta' are not eligible for any of the benefits including housing as there are no official records of their residence in the village. The case of livelihood support is also similar: government officials are not able to verify false claims relating to the livelihood means and extent of loss of particular claimants. A committee of elected representatives of the Panchayat, with their intimate knowledge about members of the local community, could have done a better job in beneficiary selection. The Panchayat could have assisted many of the NGO's to plan their programmes effectively with information and data support from the Panchayat. In fact if the Panchayat was the nodal agency for relief and rehabilitation, the relief and rehabilitation intervention would have been much better with better programme planning, coordination and monitoring.

We cannot deny the fact that in the relocated places, almost all the families were suffering from a series of issues both internal and external. It can be called as the 'second disaster'. The families who were suffering from problems such as absence of drinking water, electricity, incomplete housing, lack of environmental hygiene, lack of space in and outside their houses and above all non-acceptance from the outside community were innumerable. The neighbours labelled the newly settled families as 'Tsunami people'. It clearly shows the stigma and that some sort of discrimination towards the people has cropped up. Besides this, there is no successful mutual talk or interaction between the 'old' and 'new' Panchayats. These problems took shape due to the absence of proper involvement of local self government and local community especially in the rehabilitation and reconstruction activities. So there is a great need to understand the awareness level of the people about the various roles of local self government and the extent of local community's participation in the total disaster management programme.

Significance of the Study

The need for involvement of the local self government is undeniable. They can be quick in response, have local knowledge and can also act as important channels for awareness raising and education. However capacity building at local level is imperative among elected representatives, Panchayat officials of line departments and citizens. They need to be aware of the rationale and implications of different aspects of disaster management such as disaster prevention, mitigation, preparedness, response, recovery and rehabilitation. They also need to acquire the relevant skills.

The 73rd and 74th constitutional amendments recognize Panchayat Raj Institutions as' Institutions of self- government'. The amendment has also laid down necessary guidelines for the structure of their composition, powers, functions, devolution of finances, regular holding of elections and reservation of seats for weaker sections including women. These local bodies can be effective instruments in tackling disasters through early warning system, relief distribution, providing shelter to the victims, medical assistance etc. It was necessary to train the Panchayats in disaster management in advance. The study attempts to understand the awareness of the public about the various roles enlisted to the local self governments to perform in disaster situations and also the involvement of the local community during the different phases of the disaster subsequent to the Tsunami at Alappad, Kerala. The study intends to understand the various problems or obstacles faced by the local self government while dealing with the disaster situations.

Review of Literature

Disaster is defined as a severe disruption, ecological and psychosocial which greatly exceeds the coping capacity of the individual and the community *(WHO, 1992*). Anything that exceeds one's personal ability to cope with a stressful event becomes a crisis. The Webster's Dictionary defines a disaster as 'a grave occurrence having ruinous results'. In the last two decades over three million people have been killed in natural disasters worldwide. According to statistical evidence there have been three times as many losses resulting from disaster events in the last ten years than was the case in 1960s. As a consequence economic losses have been nine times greater during the last decade, with losses over US $ 90 billion per year. In 1998, natural calamities claimed the lives of over 50000 people worldwide *(CRED, 2000).* Most disaster victims live in developing countries, where poverty and population pressures force growing numbers of people to live in harm's way *(Kofi A Anan, 1999).* Given that the pressures of poverty and population growth continue to increase, the disaster trend is likely to worsen, if we do not take disaster prevention more seriously *(UNEP 2001 GEO 3 Report, UNEP Nairobi, Kenya).* The Centre for Research on the Epidemiology of Disasters (*CRED, 2000)* and Red Cross recently published their report on vulnerability to disasters in 2000. The number of people affected by disasters in 2000 went up to 256 million compared to an average from 1991 to 2000 of 211 million per year (*World Disaster Report, 2001).*

Disaster Management is defined as an applied science which seeks, by the systematic observation and analysis of disasters, to improve measures relating to prevention, mitigation, preparedness, emergency responses and recovery *(Carter, 1991).* When public participation is integrated into disaster management planning and community planning, the result is sustainable hazard mitigation *(Laurie Pearce, 2003).* It is well felt that community participation, local planning, development of self reliance and manpower resource within the community itself can strengthen the efforts of disaster preparedness and response *(Biswas R, et.al, 1997).* The community bears the burden of disaster and is the first responder to the event and so it is imperative to build the capacity of the community to enhance their coping mechanism and resilience to prepare for and face the disaster *(Rabindra, 2004)*.

Over the past decade, the numbers of 'natural' and technological disasters have increased. From 1994 to 1998, reported disasters averaged 428 per year; from 1999 to 2003, this figure shot up by two-thirds to an average of 707 disasters each year. For the first five years of the decade, 213 million people, on an average, were affected. The second half of the decade saw this figure rise by over 40 per cent, to an average of 303 million per year. The loss to assets has been increasing, much more than the number of disasters. The Asian tsunami that devastated the coastal areas of over 12 countries, killing around 200,000 people and seriously affecting over 1.5 million people, has changed drastically human perceptions about the dimensions of natural disaster. Developing countries suffer the greatest costs when a disaster hits – more than 95 percent of all deaths caused by disasters occur in developing countries, and losses due to natural disasters are 20 times greater (as a percentage of GDP) in developing countries than in industrialized countries.

Developing countries suffer the greatest costs when a disaster hits – more than 95 percent of all deaths caused by disasters occur in developing countries, and losses due to natural disasters are 20 times greater (as a percentage of GDP) in developing countries than in industrialized countries *(Luis Flores Ballesteros, 2008).* All disasters are hence the result of human failure to introduce appropriate disaster management measures *(Wisner, P. Blaikie, T & et.al (2004)*[12]. Hazards are routinely divided into natural or human-made, although complex disasters, where there is no single root cause, are more common in developing countries. A specific disaster may spawn a secondary disaster that increases the impact. A classic example is an earthquake that causes a tsunami, resulting in coastal flooding.

Researchers have been studying disasters for more than a century, and for more than forty years disaster research[13]. The studies reflect a common opinion when they argue that all disasters can be seen as being human-made, their reasoning being that human actions before the strike of the hazard can prevent it developing into a disaster.

Disaster management processes depend on administrative as well as civil society actions. The role of the civil society becomes more prominent in states where governments to not have sufficient resources *(SEEDS, 2004)*. At the national level, organizational set-up consists of a cabinet committee on natural disaster management; a crisis management group presided by the cabinet secretary, and a central relief commissioner for disaster relief co-ordination. The State government typically has a relief commissioner and a co-ordination committee. At the district level, the district collector presides over the relief committee, which should consist of people's representatives. Interpretation of "Disaster" under this rule names only small-scale disaster, which occur in specific locations in the Panchayat due to natural calamities like flood, fire etc. This limits the scope for local bodies to get involved in natural disasters like tsunami. Capacity for disaster management intervention calls for perspective building through training and awareness programmes for elected representatives, officials and departmental staff, community organisations and the community at large, as well as the creation of an organizational set up for intervention. Moreover, an inventory of technical and technological manpower, financial and material resources should be kept updated. Apart from responding to a disasters community should also be prepared for disasters. We need to incorporate disaster preparedness in the micro plan. We are good at innovations but who will practice them? The answer is local self-governments. We need to involve them *(Binoy Acharya, 2005)*[14] Section 166 in the third schedule of the Kerala Panchayati Raj Act included Natural Calamities' Relief in the sector wise functions of Gram Panchayat and entrusting the Panchayat to ensure the protection of relief centers and conduct works relating to natural calamities.

The brief literature review reveals that there is the need to explore how best the local self governments and the local people can be actively involved in dealing with natural disasters. The present study will be a pioneering effort in this direction. The following sections will explain the specific study objectives and the research questions.

Research Objectives

The following are the major objectives of the present research.

1. To analyze the formal and informal institutional arrangements that exists towards disaster management in Kerala.
2. To study the nature of local self-governance in disaster management with specific reference to the 2004 Indian Ocean Tsunami.
3. To analyze the nature of community participation in disaster management with specific reference to the 2004 Indian Ocean Tsunami.

Specific Objectives

1. To analyze the policy adopted by the Central and State government

towards disaster management, with specific reference to the 2004 Indian Ocean Tsunami.

2. To analyze the policy adopted by the International Aid Organisations towards disaster management, with specific reference to the 2004 Indian Ocean Tsunami.
3. To review the profile of the organisations established by the Central and State government towards disaster management, with specific reference to the 2004 Indian Ocean Tsunami.
4. To draw a basic understanding on the programmes and projects implemented by the government in disaster management, with specific reference to the 2004 Indian Ocean Tsunami.
5. To analyze the perception of affected communities on the role of local self governance institutions in disaster management.
6. To study the challenges faced by the local self government in disaster management, with specific reference to the 2004 Indian Ocean Tsunami.
7. To analyze the process of community responses to disasters, with specific reference to the 2004 Indian Ocean Tsunami.
8. To identify the level of community participation in disaster management, with specific reference to the 2004 Indian Ocean Tsunami.
9. To identify the challenges faced by local communities in disaster management, with specific reference to the 2004 Indian Ocean Tsunami.
10. To suggest appropriate strategies and measures to improve the role of local self government and community participation in the disaster management.

Hypothesis

1. There is a direct relation between the level of individual participation and effectiveness of the disaster management.
2. There is a significant relationship between the level of local self government's involvement and effectiveness of the disaster management programme.
3. There is a direct relationship between the awareness of the role of local self government among community members and effectiveness of disaster management programme.

Research Questions

The present research, both qualitative and quantitative in nature, is intended to find out the awareness of the people about the role of local self government and the extent of local community participation in the management of natural disaster. In addition to this, the study will also attempt to capture the perceptions of various significant individuals about the role of local self government and the community participation in managing a disaster situation. Case study method will be used to capture the participants' perception about the role of local self government and community participation in managing a disaster situation.

Questions for Quantitative Assessment

1. Is there a significant relationship between the level of community involvement and effectiveness of a disaster management programme?
2. Is there significant association between the level local self government's involvement and the effectiveness of disaster management programme?
3. Is there a direct relationship between people's perception of the role of local self government and their level of participation in disaster management efforts?

Questions for Qualitative Assessment

1. What are the problems and obstacles faced by local self government in effectively managing a disaster?
2. How best the local self government and the local community can be involved in managing a disaster situation?
3. What are some of the problems and challenges encountered by the families in the relocated villages?

Research Design

The study has used a mix method, descriptive design. As explained above, the purpose of this study is to understand the nature of participation of the local self government and the participation of local community in the management of a disaster. The study made use of both qualitative and quantitative research methods to achieve the above objective.

Universe of the Study

The tsunami disaster affected people from the Alappad Panchayat, the members from the Panchayat, taluk and district, policy makers, representatives from non governmental agencies, and experts in the area of disaster constituted the universe of the study.

Sampling Procedures

The researcher used purposive sampling method to recruit the required number of respondents for both the quantitative and qualitative part of the research. The investigator interviewed 306 participants for the quantitative part of the research. Ten respondents were interviewed for the qualitative part of the study. The researcher continued conducting in-depth interviews with participants until data saturation was reached. The qualitative interviews lasted for one to one-and-a-half hours. Secondary sources such as books, articles, journals, internet, and other pertinent documents were also used for conducting this study.

Pilot Study

The researcher administered tools of data collection namely, informed consent form, and interview schedule both for quantitative and qualitative. Researcher made the following observations during the pilot study.

1. A single respondent was taking 45 minutes to 1 hour time to complete the entire process of quantitative data collection. The investigator cleared the doubts of the respondents and obtained their consent to take part in the study. Also the researcher made clarification to all respondents that the study will not fetch any material or monetary benefit and the exercise is purely part of the researchers' academic requirement, and informed them that the necessary permission from their respective authorities have been obtained for the study.
2. The items of the instruments were found to be appropriate and relevant for the sampled population. The tools didn't have any question unsuitable to the tsunami affected population.
3. Respondents were approached mostly with prior appointments. Busy days (in the case of fishing [Quantitative interview] and meeting or other programmes [Qualitative interview] were avoided.
4. Similarities of the items in the instruments were reviewed by the researcher. The finer or slight differences in the emphasis in each

of these items were noted and explained to the respondents during the main study.

5. Respondents were allowed to take break for few minutes, if the need for the same was felt. This allowed breaking the monotony of the data collection exercise. Thus, the issues and concerns that were identified by the researcher in the pilot study phase of the data collection were addressed. The modifications eased the process of data collection in the main study phase.

Data Collection

The investigator obtained informed consent prior to the qualitative and quantitative interviews. The participants were asked to complete a brief demographic schedule which gathered information pertaining to their name, age, gender, ethnicity/caste, religion, education, occupation, income, and nature of loss. The quantitative data was collected using a questionnaire developed by the investigator for the study. The questionnaire contained questions pertaining to the availability of institutional mechanisms in the management of a disaster, people's awareness and perception about the role of local governments in the management of a disaster, and the level of community participation in dealing with a disaster. For the qualitative research, an interview guide was prepared by the investigator. The interview guide contained questions specifically related to the problems encountered by the people and significant others in managing the disaster situation. The qualitative interviews were conducted in Malayalam by the Principal Investigator and lasted for one to one-and-a-half hours. All the interviews were audio recorded and later transcribed for analysis.

Apart from primary level data collection, the researcher collected resources from secondary data such as books, journals, magazines, articles, news papers and related sources. The investigator also carried out field visits for data collection and conducted individual and group meetings or interaction with various stakeholders during the study period. The meetings were conducted in various places of Tamil nadu, Gujarat, Maharashtra and Andaman Nicobar Islands.

Data Analysis

The quantitative data collected was entered into Statistical Packages for Social Sciences (SPSS) for analysis. Initially, all the data were checked and analyzed for missing data. Subsequently, descriptive statistics were computed to identify frequencies and percentages for the study variables.

Correlation analysis was used to identify significant association between study variables. All the qualitative interviews were transcribed and analyzed using Axial coding method. Significant themes and subthemes were extracted during the coding process. All the themes and subthemes were later checked back to original data to ensure and verify their consistent occurrence in the qualitative data.

Ethical Issues

Informed consent of the respondents was obtained for the study. The respondents were detailed about the purpose of the study. The objectives of the study were made clear before the data collection, keeping in view that it will not raise any hope or expectation of help. Confidentiality was maintained with regard to the details enumerated from the respondents. The information gathered was be used only for the research and the academic purpose.

Justification of the Study

The research study revealed the nature of the participation of the local self government in the disaster management activities and the level of community participation obtained during and after the tsunami disaster which struck the coastal areas of Alappad in Kollam district. The findings of the study contributed to understand the enormous requirement of both local self government and local community in the management of the disasters. The study results will positively affect the various aspects of the disaster management programme in the country including disaster preparedness, planning, response, mitigation and post disaster recovery efforts.

The reference section of the study is included in the Appendices part while the notes of the research are included in the end of each chapter.

Chapter Scheme

I. Introduction

II. Disaster Management- A Conceptual Framework

III. Disaster Management at the Global Level

IV. Disaster Management in India

V. Disaster Management at the local level - Role of Local Self Government

VI. Community Participation and Disaster Management

VII. Findings & Recommendations

(1) Quantitative Analysis and Findings

(2) Qualitative Analysis and Findings

(3) Objective wise Analysis and Findings

VIII. Conclusion

References

Appendices

Notes

1. World Disasters Report 2012 focuses on forced migration and on the people forcibly displaced by conflict, political upheaval, violence, disasters, climate change and development projects, whose numbers are increasing inexorably each year. The enormous human costs of forced migration – destroyed homes and livelihoods, increased vulnerability, disempowered communities, and collapsed social networks and common bonds – demand urgent and decisive action by both humanitarian and development actors. The report analyses the complex causes of forced migration and its consequences and impacts on displaced populations, their hosts and humanitarian actors. It looks at the significant gaps in humanitarian protection for ever-increasing numbers of forced migrants who do not fit into conventional categories of protection, and the public health challenges caused by forced displacement, particularly for women, children and those with mental ill-health problems. It examines the 'urbanization' of forced migration, the role of climate change and environmental factors in forced displacement and how new communications, information and social networking technologies are reshaping the links between aid providers and migrants. It also tracks humanitarian funding for forcibly displaced populations, as well as the positive and negative economic impacts they have on host communities and countries. Published annually since 1993, the World Disasters Report brings together the latest trends, facts and analysis of contemporary crises and disasters, © International Federation of Red Cross and Red Crescent Societies, 2012, Editor: Roger Zetter, ISBN 978-92-9139-187-5, 2012.
2. The International Federation of Red Cross and Red Crescent Societies (IFRC) is the world's largest humanitarian network that reaches 150 million people in 187 National Societies through the work of over 13 million volunteers. As part of the International Red Cross and Red Crescent Movement, the agencies work is guided by seven fundamental principles; humanity, impartiality, neutrality, independence, voluntary service, unity and universality. The International Federation of Red Cross and Red Crescent Societies promote the humanitarian activities of National Societies among vulnerable people. By coordinating international disaster relief and encouraging development support it seeks to prevent and alleviate human suffering. The International Federation, the National Societies and the International Committee of the Red Cross together constitute the International Red Cross and Red Crescent Movement.

3. AmeriCares dispatched an Emergency Response Manager to Tokyo to direct efforts of their relief workers in Sendai. Their team is in direct contact with local officials, evacuation shelters and hospitals treating the injured in Miyagi, Fukushima and Iwate prefectures to determine health needs. They are preparing a shipment of basic hygiene items for urgent delivery to shelters in Miyagi and Iwate based on early assessments. Additionally, they are establishing an office in Tokyo to coordinate relief efforts. AmeriCares and its relief workers in Japan continue to work to deliver medicines and supplies to hospitals, shelters and health responders (AmeriCares, Mar 18, 2011).
4. The Centre for Research on the Epidemiology of Disasters (CRED) has been active for more than 35 years in the fields of international disaster and conflict health studies, with research and training activities linking relief, rehabilitation and development. It was established in Brussels in 1973 at the School of Public Health of the Catholic University of Louvain (UCL) as a non-profit institution with international status under Belgian law. In 1980, CRED became a World Health Organization (WHO) collaborating centre as part of WHO's Global Program for Emergency Preparedness and Response. Since then, CRED has increased its international network substantially and collaborates closely with numerous UN agencies, inter-governmental and governmental institutions, non–governmental organizations, research institutes and universities.
5. William S. Kern, The Economics of Natural and Unnatural Disasters (2010), W.E. Upjohn Institute, 10 - 143 pages presents a noted group of contributors who stand at the forefront of this increasingly important sub discipline of economics of disasters. The chapters they contribute cover a wide variety of events and delve into the human and economic impacts disasters impose on nations around the world. Several themes dominant in this literature are discussed. These include the ability of potential disaster victims to accurately assess the risks they face, the role of incentives in ensuring that mitigation efforts are undertaken, the adequacy of our evaluation of the impact of disasters on economies, and discussion of the effectiveness of current government policies toward disaster prevention and relief. These will in all likelihood continue to be topics of discussion in the future as well.
6. The book addresses the development of long-term interventions following disasters, emphasizing disadvantaged communities. Attention is given to the role of change agents, such as local and international non- governmental (NGOs) and psychosocial professionals, to ensure that the window of opportunity is realized, generating immediate help and sustained community development, University Press of America, ISBN 978-0-7618-5621-4 90000.
7. India Disasters Report- Toward's a Policy Initiate (2001), how does working in a natural disaster zone compare to working in other global health contexts? Dr. Unnikrishnan P.V, an expert, working as Disaster Response Coordinator, Plan International, United Kingdom and S.Parasuraman, currently Director, Tata Institute of Social Sciences, Mumbai explains in this book: Disasters devastate, leaving a long trail of mortality and morbidity. Hospital buildings collapse, case load increases, health workers get hit or busy taking care of their own neighbours and family members-it is like hell let loose. Add to that the stories of human suffering hour after hour you have to listen to-often you wish you were not

there. – India disasters report, Kluwer Academic Publishers. Printed in the Netherlands. 97. Book Review. S. Parsuraman and P. V. Unnikrishnan (eds).

8. UNDP as outlined in earlier sections, there were numerous constraints on local livelihoods, including conflict, poor government services, relations in the community and reliance on traditional money-lenders. The question of whether future livelihoods programmes aim merely for a 'recovery' of the pre-Tsunami situation, or for authentically sustainable livelihoods in Aceh". CIU/UNDP, 2005.

9. The Heritage Foundation is a Research and Educational Institution—a think tank—whose mission is to formulate and promote conservative public policies based on the principles of free enterprise, limited government, individual freedom, traditional American values, and a strong national defense. The vision is to build an America where freedom, opportunity, prosperity, and civil society flourish. As conservatives, the agency believes the values and ideas that motivated for the Founding Fathers are worth conserving. As policy entrepreneurs, The HF believes the most effective solutions are consistent with those ideas and values. The Great Eastern Japan Earthquake Assessing Disaster Response and Lessons for the U.S. written by James Jay Carafano, Ph.D., is Deputy Director of the Kathryn and Shelby Cullom Davis Institute for International Studies and Director of the Douglas and Sarah Allison Center for Foreign Policy Studies, a division of the Davis Institute, at The Heritage Foundation 2011.

10. The World Conference on Disaster Reduction was held from 18 to 22 January 2005 in Kobe, Hyogo, Japan, and adopted the present Framework for Action 2005-2015: Building the Resilience of Nations and Communities to Disasters (here after referred to as the "Framework for Action"). The Conference provided a unique opportunity to promote a strategic and systematic approach to reducing vulnerabilities and risks to hazards. It underscored the need for, and identified ways of, building the resilience of nations and communities to disasters.

11. The 'Kerala Model of Development', based on the development experience of the Southern Indian State of Kerala, refers to the state's achievement of significant improvements in material conditions of living, reflected in indicators of social development that are comparable to that of many developed countries, even though the state's per capita income is low in comparison to them. Achievements such as low levels of infant mortality and population growth, and high levels of literacy and life expectancy, along with the factors responsible for such achievements have been considered the constituting elements of the Kerala model.

12. At Risk: natural hazards, people's vulnerability and disasters, Wisner, Blaikie, Cannon and Davis: The book clearly highlights the various aspects pf the disaster risks and vulnerability. Analyzing disasters themselves also allows us to show why they should not be segregated from everyday living, and to show how the risks involved in disasters must be connected with the vulnerability created for many people through their normal existence. It seeks the connections between the risks people face and the reasons for their vulnerability to hazards. It is therefore trying to show how disasters can be perceived within the broader patterns of society, and indeed how analyzing them in this way may provide a much more fruitful way of building policies, that can help to reduce disasters and mitigate hazards, while at the same time improving living standards and opportunities more generally, Second edition, 2003, Copyright by Authors.

13. The Disaster Research Center, or DRC, was the first Social Science Research Center in the world devoted to the study of disasters. It was established at Ohio State University in 1963 and moved to the University of Delaware in 1985. The Center conducts field and survey research on group, organizational and community preparation for, response to, and recovery from natural and technological disasters and other community-wide crises. DRC researchers have carried out systematic studies on a broad range of disaster types, including hurricanes, earthquakes, tornadoes, hazardous chemical incidents, and plane crashes. DRC has also done research on civil disturbances and riots, including the 1992 Los Angeles unrest. Staffs have conducted nearly 600 field studies since the Center's inception, traveling to communities throughout the United States and to a number of foreign countries, including Mexico, Canada, Japan, Italy, and Turkey. Faculty members from the University's Sociology and Criminal Justice Department and Engineering Department direct DRC's projects. The staff also includes postdoctoral fellows, graduate students, undergraduates and research support personnel.
14. UNNATI - Organisation for Development Education is a voluntary non-profit organization registered under the Societies Registration Act (1860) in 1990 based at Ahmadabad, Gujarat. The aim of the agency is to promote social inclusion and democratic governance so that the vulnerable sections of society are empowered to effectively and decisively participate in mainstream development and decision making processes. After the 2001 Gujarat earthquake and 2002 communal riots, UNNATI was involved in disaster relief and rehabilitation. From 2001 to 2005 most of the energy was put on the rehabilitation work. Mr. Binoy Acharya, acting as the Director, Member Secretary of the organisation.

Chapter - 7

Findings and Recommendations

The chapter consists of two sections. The first section focuses on the findings of the quantitative research. The quantitative data collected was entered into Statistical Packages for Social Sciences (SPSS) for analysis. Initially, all the data were checked and analyzed for missing data. Subsequently, descriptive statistics were computed to identify frequencies and percentages for the study variables. Correlation analysis was used to identify significant association between study variables. In this section, I have initially presented the results of descriptive statistical analyses in order to provide a comprehensive view of the socio-demographic characteristics of the sample. Subsequently, I have presented the results of the various hypotheses tests I had conducted using correlation analyses. The second section of the chapter focuses on the major themes identified in the qualitative data collected through in-depth interviews.

(1) Quantitative Findings

1. **Socio Demographic Profile of the Respondents:** A total of 306 participants were surveyed for the quantitative section of the study.

   I. Table-7.1 illustrates the age wise distribution of study participants. As depicted in the table, 20.6% of the participants belonged to the age category of below 30 years. Another 38.2 % belonged to the category 31-40 years. Approximately 1/4th of the respondents (25.1%) were in the age category of 41-50 years. There were 16.1% respondents in the 51 years and above category.

   II. As shown in Table 7.2 below, 68.6% (n = 210) of the respondents were males and 31.4% (n = 96) were females.

Table 7.1. Age Wise Analysis of the Respondents

Age Category (Years)	*Number (N)*	*Percentage (%)*
Below 30	63	20.6
31-40	117	38.2
41-50	77	25.1
51 & above	49	16.1
TOTAL	306	100

Table 7.2. Gender of the Respondents

Gender	*Number (n)*	*Percentage (%)*
Male	210	68.6
Female	96	31.4
TOTAL	306	100

III. From Table 7.3, it is clear that majority (86.2%) of the respondents were married. Only 12.3% respondents were unmarried. There were 0.9% widows/widowers.

Table 7.3. Marital Status of the Respondents

Marital Status	*Number (N)*	*Percentage (%)*
Married	264	86.2
Unmarried	39	12.3
Others	3	0.9
TOTAL	306	100

IV. Table 7.4 shows that a little more than half of the respondents (53.2%) have studied up to high school level. There were 16.4% and 12.7% respondents who have studied up to primary and higher secondary levels respectively. The respondents who have studied at the college level were 5.8%.

Table 7.4. Education of the Respondents

Class of Study (Years)	*Number (N)*	*Percentage (%)*
Elementary	36	11.9
Primary	50	16.4
High school	163	53.2
Higher Secondary	39	12.7
College	18	5.8
TOTAL	306	100

V. Looking at the occupation of the respondents (see Table 7.5), it is clear that a little more than half of the respondents (52.8%) were working in the fishing and related sector. The other employment category (13.3%) included drivers, coolies, business men, teachers, painter, and shop keepers. The unemployed category comprising 33.9% included persons with disabilities, house wives, and students.

Table 7.5. Occupation of the Respondents

Occupation	*Number (N)*	*Percentage (%)*
Fishing & related	161	52.8
Other employment	41	13.3
Unemployed	104	33.9
TOTAL	306	100

VI. With regard to the religious attributes of the participants (see Table 7.6), a vast majority (95.8%) of the respondents were Hindus. A meager 2.6% were Christians and 1.6% were Muslims.

Table 7.6. Religion of the Respondents

Religion	*Number (n)*	*Percentage (%)*
Hindu	293	95.8
Christian	8	2.6
Muslim	5	1.6
TOTAL	306	100

VII. Table 7.7 illustrates the family type of the participants. A little more than 3/4th of the respondents (79.5%) belonged to nuclear families. Among the total respondents, 20.5% were from joint families.

Table 7.7. Type of Family of the Respondents

Type of Family	*Number (n)*	*Percentage (%)*
Nuclear	243	79.5
Joint	62	20.5
TOTAL	306	100

VIII. The table No: 7.8 shows that the categorical division of the type of loss which is listed below; The five categories are;

1. Loss of Family Members
2. Loss of House Hold Articles
3. Loss of House
4. Livelihood Loss
5. Physical Injuries/Psychosocial Issues etc

Table 7.8: Type of Loss Wise Respondents

Category	*Number*	*Percentage*
Severe Loss	75	24%
Very High Loss	183	60%
High level Loss	48	16%
Total	306	100%

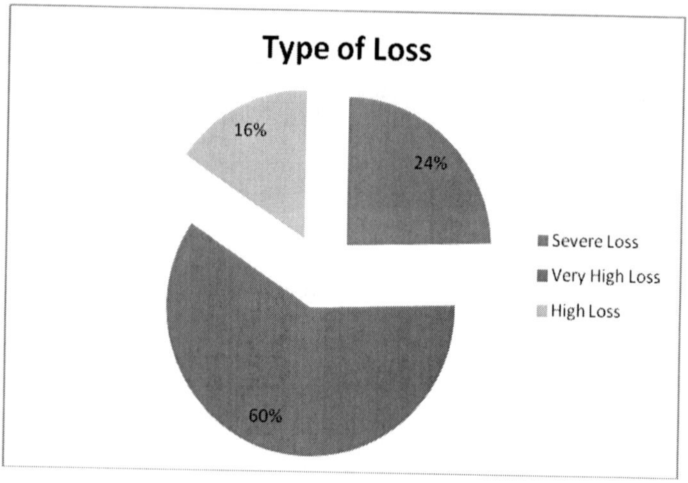

Diagrammatic Presentation

It is apparent that the majority of the respondents come under the category of Very High Loss. (ie. Loss of house or any other loss category except 1st category). Followed by the category of severe loss, (24%); which consists of the category No 1, ie, Loss of family members. 16% of the respondents fall under the third category including loss/damaged house hold articles or Livelihood loss.

Table 7.9: Means and Standard Deviations for All the Four Surveys Used in the Study

Item	*Mean (M)*	*Std. Deviation (SD)*	*N*
Disaster Management Effectiveness	23.4706	6.35564	306
Institutional Support	121.87	21.37	303
Family Support	30.4525	6.08859	305
Neighborhood Support	7.8203	2.04628	306
Support from Religious Groups	12.4020	2.63989	306

(Contd...)

NGO support	45.5148	9.08407	305
Support from LSG	10.5738	3.07825	305
Support from State and Central Government	11.2418	3.56858	306
Perception About Coordination Among Institutions	3.8987	2.57724	306
Awareness About the Role of LSG	120.96	18.01	304
Individual's Level of Participation	51.4375	16.02996	304

The reported mean scores of all the survey instruments for the participants in the present study are presented in Table 7.9. All the surveys were developed by the investigator and were pilot tested among the study population. The mean score of "people's perception about the effectiveness of disaster management" was 23.47 (SD = 6.35). The mean score of the Institutional Support scale was 121.87 (SD = 21.37).The mean and standard deviations for all the Institutional Support subscales were: Family support (M = 30.45, SD = 6.08); Neighborhood support (M = 7.82, SD = 2.04); Support from religious groups (M = 12.4, SD = 2.63); Support from NGOs (M = 45.51, SD = 9.08); Support from LSG (M = 10.57, SD = 3.07); Support from State and Central governments (M = 11.24, SD = 3.56); and perception about the effectiveness coordination among institutions (M =3.89, SD = 2.57).The mean score of the measure about the people's awareness about the role of local self government was 120.96 (SD = 18.01). The mean score on the self-report about the individual's level of participation in the disaster management activities was 51.43 (SD = 16.02).

Table No. 7.10, reveals the continuous variables in the current research study. The variables included for the correlation were Disaster Management Effectiveness (DME), Family Support (FS), Neighborhood Support (NS), Religious Support (RS), Non-Governmental Organization Support (NGO – S), Local Self Government Support (LSG – S), Coordination among institutions (CAI), Level of Participation (LOP), Institutional Support (IS). Pearson correlation (r) was computed for all the continuous variables in the study.

A significant positive correlation was found between the effectiveness of the disaster management with Institutional Support Total score ($r = 0.520$, $p < .01$) and its various subscales including family support ($r = 0.48$, $p<0.01$), Neighborhood Support ($r = 0.275$, $p<0.01$), Religious Support ($r = .406$, $p<0.01$), Non-Governmental Organization Support ($r = 0.384$, $p<0.01$), support from local self government ($r = 0.396$, $p<.01$), support from state

Table 7.10: Correlation among various continuous variables

	DME	FS	AWARENESS	NS	RS	NGO-S	LSG-S	SCG-S	CAI	LOP	IS
DME	1										
FS	.482(**)	1									
AWARENESS	.297(**)	.499(**)	1								
NS	.275(**)	.550(**)	.350(**)	1							
RS	.406(**)	.503(**)	.455(**)	.464(**)	1						
NGO-S	.384(**)	.558(**)	.481(**)	.428(**)	.647(**)	1					
LSG-S	.396(**)	.461(**)	.434(**)	.327(**)	.482(**)	.565(**)	1				
SCG-S	.400(**)	.285(**)	.330(**)	.278(**)	.384(**)	.420(**)	.451(**)	1			
CAI	.4(**)	.210(**)	.188(**)	.206(**)	.199(**)	.217(**)	.234(**)	.228(**)	1		
LOP	.046	.115(**)	.059(**)	.089(**)	.065(**)	.130(**)	.194(**)	.010	.064	1	
IS	.520(**)	.778(**)	.579(**)	.612(**)	.747(**)	.886(**)	.711(**)	.595(**)	.390(**)	.143(*)	1

* Correlation is significant at the 0.05 level;

** Correlation is significant at the 0.01 level; DME: Disaster Management Effectiveness; FS: Family Support; NS: Neighborhood Support; RS: Religious Support; NGO – S: Non-Governmental Organization Support; LSG – S: Local Self Government Support; CAI: Coordination among institutions; LOP: Level of Participation; IS: Institutional Support.

and central governments ($r = 0.400, p<.01$), and Coordination among institutions ($p<0.01$).

Hypotheses Tests

Hypothesis I: ***There is a direct relation between the level of individual participation and effectiveness of the disaster management***

There was no significant positive correlation between the study variables effectiveness of the disaster management and individual's level of participation ($r = 0.046, p>.05$) Therefore, the first hypothesis of the research, "there is a direct relation between the level of individual participation and effectiveness of the disaster management" was not supported.

Hypothesis II: ***There is a significant relationship between the level of local self government's involvement and effectiveness of the disaster management programme***

A significant positive correlation ($r = 0.396, p<0.01$) was found between the effectiveness of the disaster management and the level of local self government support. This finding supports the second hypothesis, "there is a significant relationship between the level of local self government's involvement and effectiveness of the disaster management programme". A significant positive correlation indicates that there is a direct positive relationship between people's perception about the level of local self government's involvement and their perception about the effectiveness of disaster management.

Hypothesis III: ***There is a direct relationship between the awareness of the role of local self government among community members and effectiveness of disaster management programme***

A significant positive correlation ($r = 0.297, p<0.01$) was seen between the effectiveness of disaster management and awareness of role of the local self government in disaster management. This finding supports the third hypothesis, "there is a direct relationship between the awareness of the role of local self government among community members and effectiveness of disaster management programmes". A significant positive association indicates that more people are aware of the role of local self government in disaster management, the more they perceive that disaster management is effective.

(2) Qualitative Findings

The present study investigated the community participation processes in disaster response and recovery in the light of 2004 tsunami. The study also focused on the major issues pertaining to relocation and ways to improve the disaster management activities. Qualitative approach was adopted in order to accurately capture the participants' perception about the role of local self government and community participation in managing a disaster situation. The universe of the study included tsunami disaster affected people from the Alappad Panchayat, the members from the Panchayat, Taluk and District, policy makers, representatives from non governmental agencies and the experts in the area of disaster management. The researcher used purposive sampling method to recruit the required number of respondents in the qualitative part of the research. The researcher also depended on secondary sources such as books, articles, journals, internet and other related documents for conducting this study. The researcher prepared an interview guide for conducting the study. The interview guide contained questions specifically related to the problems encountered by the people and significant others in managing the disaster situation. The qualitative interview was conducted in the local language and it lasted for one and a half hours. All the interviews were audio recorded and later transcribed for analysis. 'Axial coding' (*Axial coding is the disaggregation of core themes during qualitative data analysis)* was used to identify the core themes and subthemes pertaining to the major four research questions.

The researcher interviewed 10 participants including tsunami affected people, government officials who are related to the disaster management activities during tsunami, policy makers, field experts, disaster consultants, and local community leaders.

The following section briefly describes the results of qualitative data analysis identified through Axial Coding.

Research Questions

1. What are the problems and obstacles faced by local self government in effectively managing a disaster?
2. How best the local self government and the local community can be involved in managing a disaster situation?
3. What are some of the problems and challenges encountered by the families in the relocated villages?

Major Findings of the qualitative section of the Study

Part: A

Difficulties faced by local self government to manage rescue, recovery, and rehabilitation

Researcher identified the following major themes: lack of preparedness; lack of coordination among various actors; blaming the victims; identifying the deserving survivors; centralized disaster relief operations, early warning system, utilizing community resources etc.

1. **Lack of Preparedness:** A consistent theme that came up across participants' narratives is the lack of preparedness among local governments. Local governments were not prepared to face such a massive disaster because this event was one of the first of its kind. Nobody has ever dreamt of such an event happening in Alappad. In addition to delayed response from local government, public exaggeration and animosity made it difficult for local governments to provide a comprehensive relief and recovery service. Another important thing is that the Panchayat records were flawed which hindered the ability to make exact estimates of the houses lost and damages that occurred.
2. **Lack of Coordination among individual actors:** The disaster created a pandemonium in the affected places. All the political parties involved immediately came to conclude that disaster management programmes should include political parties, their youth federation, and trade unions who promptly rushed to the scene. Everyone thought they have the responsibility to intervene. However, each acted on his/her own with no clear vision of programme delivery. People, often the first responders, themselves started the rescue and immediate relief efforts. Even though not nourished by any guidelines, they went to other neighborhoods, dug out tapioca for the ones who were desperately in need of food. Youth groups forcefully opened medical shops and medicines were given to the victims as and when required. The volunteers even prepared ginger coffee for the displaced and local government supported the efforts. It was only after two days that other social service agencies poured in.
3. **Blaming the Victim:** The role of LSGs in emergencies such as these is countless, but because of the inadequacies of the system and the availability of limited resources their role was almost

confusing and reduced. Instead of showing empathy to local people in such situations, LSG's tried to provoke the people, attack them and in the process got self-provoked. This subsequently led to poor coordination and delayed delivery of relief services later. It would have been better if the relief agencies had worked with LSG's providing better services.

4. **Identifying the deserving survivors:** The situation in some of the wards was worse than in others. Instead of focusing on the worst affected 6 wards, the ward representatives tried to exaggerate the situation in the wards that they represented. The name of injured and disabled survivors' didn't appear in the original list which was created for relief distribution. These excluded survivors and their families had a hard time accessing relief resources and later receiving housing aid.
5. **Managing funeral and dead bodies:** Another major concern that was consistently expressed by the interviewees was the apparent difficulty faced by the community, NGOs, and government in managing the dead bodies. Alappad didn't have enough facilities to preserve dead bodies. Therefore, dead bodies had to be kept in different hospitals in Kollam district. Public had concerns regarding the preservation of corpses, the right time for burial, the level of assistance from government in finding the congenial place for a mass funeral, related expenses and financial assistance.
6. **Lack of Finance:** This was one of the major concerns expressed by Panchayat members and NGO workers. Members were not able to provide independent services because of lack of financial authority and mandate. Even though 33 relief centers had been opened subsequent to tsunami, transporting people to relief centers was problematic because of lack of funding. Even the representatives weren't able to move from site to site to address the concerns of their respective constituents.

Part B (1)

Ensuring the Participation of Local Self Government

1. **Delegate more power to local government authorities:** Local government is one among the first responders and is in close proximity to the disaster affected area. Study participants advocated for fundamental policy changes that give more power to local governments in dealing with the crisis. LSGs should have power in making decisions regarding local community's preparedness

needs, building local capacity, organizing immediate emergency relief operations, identifying beneficiaries and distributing benefits, planning short term and long term recovery goals, and coordinating the local, national, and international organizations engaged in relief operations.

2. **Clarification of LSG Role:** Local representatives are unclear about the role of local government and are very much apprehensive about the present patriarchal model top-down service delivery approach followed in the management of an emergency. Participants demanded change in the current approach where district authorities give directions to LSGs to manage relief operations and recovery efforts. According to them, district authorities are not in touch with ground realities unlike LSG and this cause unnecessary delay in processing relief applications and implementing relief efforts. In addition, participants argued that NDM Act need to specify the role of LSG's, and prepare them with periodical trainings to deal with any crisis.
3. **Increased Funding for LSG:** One of the major challenges experienced by the LSG was lack of funding. Funding was crucial in building shelters, building and maintaining the seawall, implementing early warning systems at the ward level, capacity building to ensure better preparedness, and supervise and evaluate recovery efforts. In addition, participants felt that funding was required to arrange for transportation, maintaining relief and recreation centers, and coordinating emergency response in the initial phase. The NDM act should set aside enough relief funds for disaster prone areas which would help speed up the relief and recovery operations subsequent to any crisis.

Part B (2):

How people's participation in disaster management can be ensured?

1. **Creating Information Centers:** Information centers need to be formed and must be equipped to provide early warning to the people, should provide guidance for evacuation, should provide consultation services in regard to relief aid and application process, and should maintain up-to-date data about resources and people in the community so that it can be the first point of contact with people and LSG.
2. **Active and collaborative role for LSG representatives:** Study participants felt that local government representatives such as

ward members need to reach out to the community after the disaster and should work in collaboration with the survivors. LSG members must be available when needed, should be trained to transmit knowledge and guidance to the public about accessing resources. Participants felt that district and state government authorities must work through LSG members to provide support and services to disaster affected community.

3. **Involving survivors in relief and recovery efforts:** People felt that they weren't part of the decision making process particularly in identifying the beneficiaries for relief benefits. Participants felt that many survivors were left out while determining housing benefits which resulted in several families languishing for a long-time in temporary shelters. They felt such omission have catastrophic consequences such as losing community trust which would hamper recovery efforts. In addition survivors can be involved in running relief centers, community kitchens, construction works, operating recreation centers, and routine preparedness training. They can also be involved in providing transportation services and emergency first-aid.
4. **Involving local agencies:** Participants felt that local community based organizations such as ward committees, Kudumbasree groups, temples, church, and other religious groups can play a significant role in relief and recovery efforts. Empowering local communities and promoting positive collaboration between LSGs and local agencies would speed up recovery process. Participants appreciated the services provided by Mata Amritanadamayi Math and several other local agencies. Participants also felt that these agencies could be empowered to address the basic concerns of the survivors such as meeting food, water, shelter etc, provide psychosocial support, communication and transportation services, first-aid, opening food pantries and community kitchens. Survivors can be actively involved in all these activities and it will be develop a sense of ownership among the survivors towards the recovery efforts and these all are very crucial for the effective community recovery

Part: C

Problems of Relocated villages

Participants in the study were concerned about the following problems in relocated villages:

1. **"Fish out of water":** Participants used the "fish out of water" metaphor to describe their situation at the relocated villages. In the relocated neighborhoods, clear division came to exist between families in the newly formed village. Some behaviors that were normal in their old neighborhood became kind of a concern for newly formed communities. For instance, in their old neighborhood it was perfectly alright for people to ample through the land, backyard or even front yard of their neighbours. It was culturally approved and had implicit community sanction. However, in the relocated villages this behavior was considered as trespassing and was very often a reason for conflict between neighbours. In addition, relocated families frequently got stopped by others while they went for fishing at night. Furthermore, families felt being strangers in the relocated places.
2. **Lack of cultural consideration while relocating:** Study participants felt that the relocation process was haphazardly planned and didn't take into consideration the cultural characteristics and employment prospects of the relocated individuals. Government officials didn't consult disaster survivors when they acquired the land for relocation. The acquired relocation land was far from the coastal areas making it difficult for fishermen to access the sea, particularly during night because of transportation issues. This has a negative impact on individuals and families as they depended solely on the income from fishing.
3. **Tsunami Colony:** People started labeling the newly formed communities as "tsunami colonies". People settled in the new communities were considered as refugees in need of special help and treatment by the neighbouring villages. People felt stigmatized and isolated in these colonies and this has been a growing concern for many of the families.
4. **Poor services at the relocated villages:** Families felt that there was poor water and sanitation services in the relocated villages were quite deplorable. In some cases, there wasn't even a desirable place to perform the funeral rites and many families were cramped together in a small area. The local politicians initially adopted a distant attitude towards the newcomers which escalated their problems. Participants felt that they had been involved in the relocation process and a more proactive role from the LSG would have helped to ameliorate some of their sufferings.

(3) Objective Wise Analysis/Findings

This section summarizes the significant findings in relation to some of the major objectives of the study. These findings were derived from the critical information collected from a detailed literature review, and an analysis of the formal and informal interactive sessions with the community leaders, NGO workers, and key officials in the government. The researcher has provided detailed information about this analysis in some of the chapters presented here.

First, in terms of the research objective aimed at analyzing the policy adopted by the Central and State government towards disaster management and with specific reference to the 2004 Indian Ocean Tsunami, the researcher has arrived at the following conclusion: In India, at the national level, National Disaster Management Authority (NDMA) is the responsible agency to lay down the policies, plans, and guidelines for disaster management. There is a complementary structure envisaged at the State and District level. The Authority aims to integrate disaster prevention and mitigation in development plans and projects and formulate projects and schemes for mitigation and has the responsibility to earmark funds. Enactment of Disaster Management Act (2005) confers legislative sanction to the institutional and coordination mechanisms to ensure holistic and coordinated disaster management measures. In addition to providing for institutional framework to cater to mitigation and preparedness efforts, the Act mandates constitution of the Disaster Response Fund and Disaster Mitigation Fund at the national, state and district levels and assigns an important role to urban local bodies and Panchayati Raj institutions.

The policy notes that state governments are primarily responsible for disaster management including prevention and mitigation, while the Government of India provides assistance where ever necessary as per the norms laid down from time to time and proposes that this overall framework may continue. However, since response to a disaster requires coordination of resources available across all the Departments of the Government, the policy mandates that the central government will, in conjunction with the state governments, seek to ensure that such a coordination mechanism is laid down through an appropriate chain of command so that mobilization of resources is facilitated.

Furthermore, the central government has successfully formulated a national disaster management policy in 2009. Subsequently, a large number of hazard-specific projects and programmes aimed at risk reduction have been initiated. Separate National Core Groups on Earthquake, Cyclone and

Landslides have been constituted to assist in risk assessment and mitigation planning, developing a techno-legal regime, and land-use zoning. Specific programmes for addressing earthquake and cyclone risk mitigation have been formulated along with training of engineers, architects and masons in hazard-resistant construction practices and inclusion of elements of earthquake engineering in undergraduate engineering and architectural courses. The role of national and state government authority is to make government ordinance appropriate to the phases of disaster such as relief, rehabilitation and reconstruction phases to help the community to recover from the disaster.

Second, in regard to the study objective of analyzing the policy adopted by the International Aid Organizations (INGO's) towards disaster management and with specific reference to the 2004 Indian Ocean Tsunami, the analysis of pertinent literature and data resulted in the ensuing conclusion. Immediately after the deadly tsunami, numerous international aid providers came to various disaster engulfed areas and provided immediate assistance to the long term recovery support programmes. In Kerala alone, around 33 INGO's were involved in the relief and rehabilitation activities. A larger number of families/individuals benefited from the support provided by these organizations. Each agency is guided by its own priorities and policies in helping the community.

Some of the agencies claim that they actively worked in engaging the communities in disaster relief and recovery. For instance, Oxfam International claims that the partnership between the aid providers and affected communities was in good physical shape *(Oxfam International, 2008)* subsequent to the tsunami. Another international player, CARE International emphasized risk prevention and mitigation through community participation with the objective of reducing the probability of life and property losses *(CARE International, 2009)*.

Even though the community felt that these INGOs did a commendable job in disaster relief operations, a critical analysis of their operations reveals some pitfalls in their approach to disaster service. First and foremost, in the entire disaster management activities carried out by the international relief agencies, it could be noted that a coordinated disaster management programme was not visible; almost all INGO's were trying to fulfill their agenda of extending support to the disaster victims but a mutual consensus and collaborative affinity were partially missing. Ultimately the receivers always demanded for something and that paved the way for complete dependency and eroded the feeling of community ownership. Second, many of these organizations literally disappeared from the community after providing immediate relief assistance. The overwhelming impression by the larger community is that local communities would have benefitted substantially, had these organizations stayed in the affected area for a longer time and phased out their activities gradually.

Third, in order to attain the goal of reviewing the profile of the organizations established by the Central and State government towards disaster management and with specific reference to the 2004 Indian Ocean Tsunami, the researcher collected information regarding all disaster related organization by doing a thorough literature review and contacting experts in the field. For instance, one of the major strategies the researcher used was to contact various government departments and disaster management project personnel involved in disaster management. Through the above mentioned methods, the following institutions/departments that have been involved in disaster management programmes in the country were identified: Orissa State Disaster Mitigation Authority (OSDMA); Gujarat State Disaster Management Authority (GSDMA); Natural Disaster Management Division of the Ministry of Home Affairs (MOHA).

In addition, the Ministries/Departments/Organizations concerned with the primary and secondary functions relating to the management of disasters include: India Meteorological Department, Central Water Commission, Ministry of Home Affairs, Ministry of Defense, Ministry of Finance, Ministry of Rural Development, Ministry of Urban Development, Department of Communications, Ministry of Health, Ministry of Water Resources, Ministry of Petroleum, Department of Agriculture & Cooperation. Ministry of Power, Department of Civil Supplies, Ministry of Railways, Ministry of Information and Broadcasting, Planning Commission, Cabinet Secretariat, Department of Surface Transport, Ministry of Social Justice, Department of Women and Child Development, Ministry of Environment and Forest, Department of Food. Each Ministry/ Department/Organization nominated their nodal officer to the Crisis Management Group chaired by Central Relief Commissioner. Other major organizations include: National Crisis Management Committee (NCMC); Crisis Management Group (CMG); and the National Disaster Management Authority (NDMA).

Fourth, in regard to the objective of understanding the programmes and projects implemented by the government in disaster management and with specific reference to the 2004 Indian Ocean Tsunami, the investigator relied on literature review, his own field experience, and interviews with key players in the field of disaster management in India. In Connection with the 2004 Tsunami, the Government of India initiated and implemented a number of projects including both short term and long term programmes for extending support to the disaster affected community. The programmes like CBDP programmes, Early Warning /Communication Projects, TEAP (Coastal Region Development Project) Projects, Disaster Risk Reduction Projects and Capacity development programmes/ training are some of the few projects initiated by the Government of India in almost all states of the country with the technical and financial support of UNDP.

In Kerala, DEEDS, national level non- profit organization with the technical support of NIMHANS, and MALTESER (International Agency) implemented a three year long psychosocial care and rehabilitation programme with the objective of supporting the tsunami affected population. The major activities were continuous intensive and extensive way of interaction with the affected people, providing timely psychosocial relief, addressing social issues, Liaising with local self government, providing medical support, addressing compensation issues of the tsunami affected people, imparting capacity development exercises/training programmes to the psychosocial workers/volunteers to equip them to handle disaster and emergency or crisis situations. The project also aimed at offering skill development training and support for starting income generation programme for few selected, most vulnerable women. And briefly the project carried out providing psychosocial support to specific groups of population such as aged/ senior citizens, women and children, setting up a drop-in-cum field office, counseling service, referral services, strengthening the Community Based Organization, orientation on health and hygiene, promotion, coordination and monitoring of micro-enterprises, recreation activities for children and youth, skill development training for youth and women, second phase of life skills education programmes to children and adolescence, networking and linkage with other agencies, awareness generation programmes on minor mental morbidity, women's day celebration, data collection, training on family dynamics, street play on the ill effects of alcoholism and drug abuse *(DEEDS- NIMHANS- MALTESER Reports, 2007).*

Action Aid, an international agency extended help to the tsunami affected people in the country. By giving material support, psychological care and legal advice, Action Aid has helped ensure that survivors stand up for their rights to a home, an education, a livelihood and life free from discrimination and violence. As a result, some of the most marginalized groups, including stateless boat people, women displaced by war as well as the tsunami, landless tribal communities, Dalits facing decades of discrimination, female fish workers and children out of school now have a stronger voice and a more secure future than they did before the disaster. They are better equipped to deal with the challenges ahead. In Tamilnadu, Action Aid, actively engaged in relief and rehabilitation activities and initiated alternative livelihood programmes, micro enterprises for the disaster victims, provided training programmes to various target groups, facilitated disaster preparedness programmes etc.

During the post Tsunami relief work in Andaman and Nicobar Island's Mata Amritanadamayi Math, an International Organization based in Kerala, had deployed volunteers to distribute relief materials such as clothes, medicines, food supplies, etc. in Little Andaman's (Hut Bay) and Port Blair. With many people stranded without shelter, their homes having been destroyed by the Tsunami, the Math's centre at Shadipur, Port Blair served as the nucleus for Tsunami IDP's rehabilitation for several weeks. Following the immediate relief work, the Math also took up the massive task of constructing 200 houses as per CPWD specifications in Bambooflat and other areas in Port Blair. The researcher had an exposure visit to the island and deeply engaged in understanding the Care India- Amrita SREE partnership project in Andaman Island. The project activities includes promotion of SHGs, regular visits to the SHGs, providing SHG level trainings, maintaining Management Information System, assistance in initiating Micro Enterprises and also in setting up units, networking with governmental and non governmental agencies to organize trainings and to avail schemes and privileges for the SHG's.

The researcher found out that the vast areas affected by the tsunami in the island have undergone enormous changes and the survivors are so helpless in all respects that it needs a serious and prolonged intervention on the part of the government and well-meaning organizations. But the measures taken so far are not sufficient in face of the mounting problems. We can promise on our part that we are ready to go anywhere with our service if the logistic and other support could be provided.

Fifth and last, in terms of analyzing the process of community responses to disasters, with specific reference to the 2004 Indian Ocean Tsunami, the researcher depended on his field experience, the in-depth interviews conducted with disaster experts, and the quantitative data collected. Apart from the quantitative survey and qualitative interviews carried out by the researcher, a number of informal discussions with the disaster survivors were carried out during the period of relief, rehabilitation, and recovery efforts in Kerala and Tamilnadu. In the initial days, the shattered communities were so disappointed and annoyed with the approach of the government towards the victims in terms of meeting basic needs to the affected communities. The delay in providing food, clothing, and shelter to the victims, improper, and in some cases, lack of communication and clear direction, created discomforts among the disaster victims. Survivors were not well-informed about the legalities of compensation, relocation and employment benefits. They were not sure who to approach for help as numerous players were active in the field providing relief services. At a later stage, community members, along with the support from NGOs and other aid providers, chartered programmes which helped in extending support and care to the disaster affected people. One of the take home messages is that community members expressed their dissatisfaction at relief providers for not letting them involve in the recovery process right from the beginning.

Recommendations

1. **Capacity Building/ Training local youth:** It is a weathered fact; that the local communities' role in a disaster situation is crucial in saving lives and other aspects. Therefore, it is essential to train the local youth in basic emergency response be it paramedical, forming communication links or responding to emergencies. Community Based Disaster Management Plans and mock drills will be undertaken to ensure better preparedness. Efforts will be made to minimize vulnerability of disadvantaged groups like women, children, elders, physically and mentally challenged, and other marginalized groups. Aspects of reducing/minimizing long-term impact of various disasters on these vulnerable sections will be an integral part of the strategic plan.
2. **Emergency Medical team:** The public health system is woefully inadequate in India. The country is way too vast and poverty-ridden. Having a reserve emergency medical team district-wise on alert 24×7 may be helpful. Personnel can be put on duty on a rotational basis.
3. **Resource data base:** Lessons should be learnt from past disasters within and outside the country. Whole papers and extensive research base should be built up. A comprehensive directory of experts in every field should be amassed and made available.
4. **Linking Traditional knowledge & Technology:** The disaster management authorities need to ensure that early warning systems

(to be used in disaster prone areas), dissemination of warning and plans for risk avoidance actions are people-centered, i.e., they are tailored for local use and they incorporate the traditional knowledge of the local communities with regard to coping with natural disasters. The disaster management apparatus needs to catch early warnings from the disaster-prone areas and take prompt action subsequently. Another important recommendation was with regard to- development of effective communication systems in the country, public awareness and education on disaster management, application of latest technology for disaster preparedness (like, Geographic Information System, Remote Sensing, Communication Satellites, etc.), and promotion of risk transfer options like insurance.

5. **Role of Public Health Institutions:** The Government must take strong initiatives for expanding the network of public healthcare institutions, especially in the rural areas, improving their manpower and infrastructure and for giving proper guidelines regarding their role in the wake of a disaster. In the post disaster some of the agencies expressed similar kind of suggestions on various platforms. In Tamilnadu and Kerala many of the leading international agencies including UN bodies were keen in teaching the community or specific targeted groups to understand and practice various technologies in connection with the disaster preparedness programme. In Kerala where Health systems are comparatively well established when compared to other States, it would be a possible venture to integrate disaster management programmes through PHCs and CHCs. The change should come within the self, group and the community itself. Therefore, Government should organize and facilitate such kind off activities in the coming days to ensure people's participation and coordination in the pre and post disaster and emergency context. In this context, it is very important to strengthen the primary healthcare institutions, which must be accessible to a widely divergent population. Healthcare institutions at different levels- primary, secondary, and tertiary, should be given well-defined and mutually supportive roles vis-à-vis disaster management. At the village level, emergency healthcare providers, with proper training in life-saving skills, need to be deployed so that they can provide the essential service to local communities during disasters.

6. **Decentralizing Disaster Management:** There should be decentralization of disaster management efforts- in terms of involving the village Panchayats and other local bodies in both planning and implementation of disaster preparedness measures specific to their areas. As we have already noted, the processes of dissemination of warning and risk avoidance action necessarily depend on the active participation of local people in a disaster-prone area, hence, the Panchayats and other local bodies should have substantial roles to play in these activities. In fact, the planning towards management of natural disasters has to combine both the 'top down' approach and the 'bottom up' approach. Among the various measures for disaster mitigation mentioned above, ensuring that development plans incorporate disaster mitigation norms, catching early warnings, prediction of natural disasters in time, issue of warnings from the disaster management authorities, availability of necessary hardware (such as, search and rescue equipments, high wind-proof radio masts, emergency communication infrastructure, etc.), having an emergency response plan, activating the emergency response plan promptly during a disaster, and providing comprehensive as well as effective relief and rehabilitation to the people affected- could be undertaken with a top down planning approach. However, several important activities, such as, creating awareness among people, promotion of disaster mitigation and preparedness measures among the local communities, dissemination of warning among people in the affected areas, evacuation of people to safer places in the event of a disaster, and taking precautionary measures in the post-disaster situation (such as against epidemics), etc. need to be undertaken with a bottom up planning approach. The local self-government bodies must have a major say in the latter.
7. **Integrating Disaster Management with Development Planning:** All aspects of disaster management need to integrate with the normal development planning at all levels. Additionally, relevant departments should earmark a certain portion of the plan budget to undertake preparedness and prevention measures. Disaster Risk reduction activities needs to strengthen in the country.
8. **Preparedness Needs:** Locally appropriate prevention measures such as bio-shields, sea walls and other measures must be erected to prevent further erosion and disasters; A Disaster Preparedness Plan must be drawn up for action at various levels and must be

part of the Annual Development Plan; There must be Regular Disaster Preparedness Drill at community and institutional levels (Orissa Model) on fixed dates to prepare local communities in disaster preparedness; Government officials must be easily accessible and available on all days (even on holidays) in times of Emergency, as in the days following December 26, 2004.

9. **Attitudinal Change among government officials:** A major factor that has obstructed proper management of natural disasters in India in the past is that the Government authorities have been treating disaster management only as an emergency responsibility. This attitude needs to be changed and the authorities must learn to tackle natural disasters as a regular phenomenon. A sizable chunk of the officials, drawn from all the relevant branches of the Government, and serving at different tiers of Government, need to be given adequate training as well as regular practice in handling natural disasters.

10. **Empowering the local community:** Disasters can be mitigated if local communities and Government are adequately equipped to handle them. While appreciating the overwhelming solidarity with the victims of Tsunami, the participants asserted that local communities must be made capable to spearhead any relief and rehabilitation operation in the wake of a disaster in a participatory manner. What is needed is the creation of "hazard-resilient bio-regional communities" with emergency reshuffle plans handled by fully-equipped and well-prepared Disaster Prevention and Preparedness Committees of village clusters. He also said that it is not out of place for each Panchayat Raj to create some kind of emergency corpus funds so that people can have immediate access to relief. This would enhance their self-esteem make them proactive in times of disaster. In addition, identify the immediate needs to combat any further deterioration in disaster management and effective reconstruction as the installation of early warning systems; streamlining of relief distribution system; launching public awareness campaigns; and issuing guidelines to relief workers.

11. **Integrating psychosocial care and development efforts:** Psychosocial care should be integrated into the development planning and processes as much as gender and environment concerns have been.

12. **Improved coordination among relief organizations:** One of the major problematic areas during the relief work period was lack of coordination among NGOs and interference of local political party bosses. The latter has forced many deserving fishermen from being assisted by NGOs and they used the tragedy to enhance their political clout in the area. This dividing of the community prevented meaningful participation of the people as a whole in reconstructing their livelihoods. Lack of alternative sources of income for the women in the fishing community is also seen as a major concern.
13. **Disaster Management in Educational Curriculum:** To inculcate a culture of preparedness and prevention, disaster management will be incorporated in the education system and curricula at all levels. The students should be exposed to mock drills to develop requisite intuitive skills.
14. **Higher degree role of local self-government:** Being closest to the people, the role of the local self-government institutions assumes greater importance in disaster management. They will be the first responders in emergencies. Emphasis will be given to strengthen and empower these institutions and their functionaries, to effectively discharge their functions.
15. **Crucial Community participation:** The Government will actively promote, through its own agencies, NGOs and other stakeholders, active community participation in risk assessment, vulnerability analysis, mitigation, planning and implementation of response and rehabilitation activities. Since the communities face the brunt of any hazard, strengthening their coping mechanism will receive the highest priority.
16. **Create a Rapid Action Force for quick Relief and Rehabilitation efforts:** Formation of Specialized Action Group(s) will be an essential and adequate training and provision of using equipments to enable them to carry out search and rescue work, establish communications, provide emergency medical services, set up temporary shelters, maintain law and order, etc. These units, under designated commands, will automatically swing into action during disasters. The task group can be classified in to various areas on the basis of the requirement such as rescue group, water and food, shelter management, sanitation, first aid, financial resource groups, capacity building, information sharing, security, rapid damage assessment, rehabilitation and reconstruction

team, resource mobilization team, environmental protection groups, psychosocial team, research and documentation.

17. **Revision and Updation of the Policy:** The government should revise and update the disaster and emergency related policies as and when required.

Conclusion

The qualitative study revealed some of the major concerns of the disaster survivors and policy makers. The absence of effective community participation for rebuilding the lives of the people and the community is delaying the recovery process even several years after the tsunami. The towering role of the local self governments is of utmost importance in this context and calls for a supportive, facilitative and cooperative effort between LSGs, Community based organizations, and disaster survivors to build up community resilience and long term development.

In brief, it is well evident that the disaster management is not a stand-alone activity, a well structured people centric, coordinated and integrated effort is the need of the hour to deal with disaster and emergency situations in the country. The work should start form the bottom to the top, the community should take up the ownership of the activity, they can act immediately in a, cohesive and efficient manner, if they were well trained, and their capacities would have boosted up, had they been recognized. The role of the local self government in managing natural disasters is of paramount importance and the effective, technical and practical oriented capacity development exercises need to be provided to the PRI's throughout the country as India is considered the "theatre of disasters". Undoubtedly, we can say that team effort with "effective" participation of the Government and the Community in place, disaster management programmes could make a difference. Effective management is possible only if a comprehensive plan and implementation mechanism programmes are chartered out. The post tsunami scenario gives us a grave lesson to learn concerning the do's and don'ts that should be practiced, activities that need to be employed, the role and responsibilities of each and every person who are directly or indirectly affected by the disaster and so on. Such a study, analysis and implementation could help contribute in reducing or eliminating the consequences arising in the wake of a disaster or any kind of emergencies which shake the entire fabric of the community or the lives of the people.

Chapter - 8

Conclusion

Natural disasters alone account for nearly 80 percent of all disaster-affected people, world-wide. The insurance industry estimates that natural disasters represent 85% of insured catastrophe losses globally *(UNEP, 1997)*. As of the year 2000, it was estimated that at least 75% of the world's population lived in areas at risk from a major disaster (*UNDP, 2004)*. Also, between 1980 and 2000, 53% of the deaths attributable to disasters occurred in countries with low human development ratings, although these countries accounted for only 11% of the world's "at-risk" population *(UNDP, 2004)*. In fact, on average, 65% of disaster-related injuries and deaths are sustained in countries with per-capita income levels that are below $760 per year *(UNEP, 2001)*.

India is one of the world's major theatres of disasters. Coastal states, particularly in the East Coast and Gujarat, are vulnerable to cyclones, 4 crore hectare land mass is vulnerable to floods, 68 per cent of net sown area is vulnerable to drought, 55 per cent of total area is in Seismic Zones III-V and vulnerable to earthquakes and Sub-Himalayan/ Western Ghat is vulnerable to landslides (*Planning Commission, 2002*). The impact of these disasters has been devastating. Between 1988 and 1997, disasters killed on an average 5,116 people and affected 24.79 million people in the country every year *(UNDP and National Disaster Management Division, 2002)*. The death toll due to natural disasters has gone up, with about 10,000 people killed in the super cyclone of 1999, about 20,000 killed in the earthquake of 2001, and more than 11,000 in the Tsunami of 2004 *(Das, 2005)*.

In the recent history, the deadliest disaster which shook the entire nation was the 2004 Sumatra-Andaman earthquake and the subsequent tsunami. The massive undersea earthquake north-west of Sumatra, Indonesia, with a Richter-scale magnitude of 9.3, caused a giant ocean shockwave or tsunami that devastated the shorelines of Indonesia, India, Thailand and many other countries *(USAID, 2005)*. The death toll in India was 12,405. Another 5,640 people went missing and 647,599 people were totally displaced. Among the victims, 75% were women and children; while 787 women became widows and 480 children were orphaned. The state of Tamil Nadu has been the worst affected on the mainland, with a death toll of 7,793. Nagapattinam district has had 5,525 casualties, with entire villages having been destroyed. Kanyakumari district has had 808 deaths, Kadalur district 599, the state capital Chennai 206 and Kanchipuram district 124 *(Mohanty, 2010)*.

In this context, the current study aimed at studying the impact of psychosocial care on the survivors of disaster by community level workers with the major objectives of: (1) Analyzing the formal and informal institutional arrangements that exists towards disaster management in Kerala; (2) Studying the nature of local self-governance in disaster management with specific reference to the 2004 Indian Ocean Tsunami; and (3), Analyzing the nature of community participation in disaster management with specific reference to the 2004 Indian Ocean Tsunami.

To achieve the aims and objectives of the study, the researcher used a combination of three different methods: (a) conducting a detailed literature review; (b) quantitative data collection and analysis; and (c), qualitative data collection and analysis. In the literature review, researcher examined and critically analyzed the available research on local, national, and international disaster management. In quantitative data collection and analysis, the researcher developed and administered four questionnaires and a socio-demographic profile for 306 participants. In qualitative data collection and analysis, the investigator developed an interview guide and conducted in-depth interviews with 10 participants. In addition, the investigator visited the disaster devastated places such as Andaman Islands, tsunami affected places of Tamilnadu (Kanyakumari, Kadalur, Tirunelveli, and Chennai), Kollam and other tsunami affected districts of Kerala in order to collect more reliable information. Furthermore, the researcher had informal interviews with international and national experts in the field of disaster management including officials from Action Aid International, Oxfam International, Plan International, and UN officials.

The quantitative analysis of the data revealed that there were significant positive correlation between the effectiveness of the disaster management with Family Support, Neighborhood Support, Religious Support, Non-Governmental Organization Support, Coordination among institutions, Institutional Support, level of Local Self Government Support, and the awareness of the people about the role of the local self government in disaster management. The qualitative data analysis revealed the following major themes: Difficulties faced by local self government to manage rescue, recovery, and rehabilitation; Ensuring the participation of Local Self Government; Ensuring people's participation in disaster management; Problems of Relocated villages; and recommendations to improve disaster management services.

Future Directions

Based on the study findings, the researcher recommends the following strategies in order to improve disaster management programme in India.

1. The current consensus on disaster management calls for an integrated approach that combines relief with developmental concerns. However, it is to be remembered that a crucial aspect of any long-term developmental approach towards disaster management should be possible only with the active participation of the community and the effective implementation by the local bodies.
2. A well -aware community will be always prepared physically and mentally to face the realities of any disaster and will contribute to the disaster management efforts to a considerable degree. Increasing awareness levels would also succeed in freeing the community from unrealistic myths that bind them and are counterproductive in the context of proper pre-disaster mitigation efforts.
3. The most obvious, visible effort that results from community involvement in disaster management are: reduction in the number of causalities, compliance with warnings and government instruction used, ease in distribution of relief material and quick (under the circumstances) resumption of normal life. It also prevents the rising of a 'panic situation' which often results in needless deaths and injuries. Once every one knows what to do and when to do it, they can make decisions in a calm and rational manner, reducing losses considerably. Therefore, the community must have a voice in identifying site- specific solutions and assessing the efficacy of proposed measures. Enhanced community awareness is very essential.
4. Decentralization of decision making is important in the strengthening of organizations for disaster preparedness, prevention and mitigation, particularly because of the need for rapid and localized resources in the face of swiftly occurring catastrophes.

5. One crucial factor that has to be accounted for, is people's ignorance of risk. Widespread dissemination of accurate and vital information is, therefore, essential. Improved warning and mitigation have reduced significantly the number of lives lost in the developed world. Improvements in institutional arrangements such as better urban management also critical.
6. The lessons learned from one phase of disaster management can be extended for use in other phases as well as from one country to another and from past disasters to face the future ones. Lessons should also be learnt from past disasters within and outside the country. Whole papers and extensive research base should be built up. A comprehensive directory of experts in every field should be amassed and made available.
7. The present period is witnessing a shift from post disaster assistance to pre disaster preparedness, from readiness to mitigation, from individual aid to restoration of community services, and from relief to rehabilitation. A community based approach is considered appropriate in not only responding to disasters but also in addressing all disaster management facets of preparedness, recovery and reconstruction. This call for adoption of multipronged strategies involving community based organizations, nongovernmental organizations, inter- community groups, local government representatives at the grass roots level, and strengthening their capacities and support system.
8. It is a very clear fact that the local communities' role in a disaster situation is crucial in saving lives and in recovery and rebuilding of the community. Therefore, it is essential to train the youth in the community in basic emergency response be it paramedical, forming communication links or responding to emergencies.
9. The public health system is woefully inadequate in India. The country is way too vast and poverty-ridden. Having a reserve emergency medical team on alert all times district-wise may be helpful. Personnel can be put on duty on a rotational basis.
10. Recommendations for meaningful community participation in disaster response and recovery include extending planning timeframes to allow community input in the planning and implementation of response and recovery projects. Community members should be involved very early in disaster response and recovery since they will best know community's needs and build trust and partnership between the community and the relief

providers. Relief organizations and/or government need to step back and enable the affected communities to drive their own disaster recovery project. Lastly, regular meetings and discussion among the victims as well as with the aid providers is a therapeutic way of dealing with grief and sorrow. The meetings and discussions are also an opportunity to rebuild community ties and networks which may have been lost due to the disaster.

11. The overall aim should be to work with the communities and not just for them. The areas of interaction between the government, non- government and community based bodies must include pooling of resources, forming emergency response realms, problem solving, monitoring and assessment, education and training, information sharing, resource mapping and capacity building. The ideal solution should combine the risk reduction programmes with the ongoing development programmes. Only when disaster preparedness and prevention projects are built into a wider development strategy or when mitigation efforts go beyond the individual action of a single department, can there be any lasting impact on the lives of the affected. There is a growing need to tap professional abilities and to share resources for addressing the hazards and risk factors with in a common social or economic environment. All practitioner's in the potential risk community should realize their own possible contributions and ensure that broader context of disaster risk management becomes more widely understood and formulated in practical terms.

The present study tries to an attempt to understand, analyze the disaster management activities carried out in the aftermath of the tsunami natural disaster in 2004. The particular study is concluded with emphasizing that the effective participation of both local self government and the affected community in all levels of disaster management activities including pre-disaster management, during the disaster period, post disaster phase is not only a requirement but also a vital one to ensure better and coherent disaster response and recovery efforts. Nevertheless to say, a joint systematic, scientific and collaborated effort with the active involvement of all stakeholders is crucial for an effective disaster management programme. Again a bottom to top level approach- local community and local self government to the higher bodies is the need of the hour to effectively execute disaster management programme in the country.

List of Acronyms

AAI	:	Action Aid International
ACEP	:	American College of Emergency Physicians
ADPC	:	Asian Disaster Preparedness Center
ADRC	:	Asian Disaster Reduction Center
ADRRN	:	Asian Disaster Reduction & Response Network
AEM	:	Australian Emergency Management
CDMP	:	Comprehensive Disaster Management Programme
CMG	:	Crisis Management Group (CMG):
CRC	:	Central Relief Commissioner
CRED	:	Centre for Research on the Epidemiology of Disasters
CVAM	:	Capacity and Vulnerability Analysis Matrix
DMC	:	Disaster Management Centre
DMC	:	Disaster Management Cycle
DMIC	:	Disaster Management Information Centre
DRC	:	Disaster Research Center
EM-DAT	:	Emergency Events Database
ERM	:	Emergency Response Manager
FEMA	:	Federal Emergency Management Agency (FEMA)
GDA	:	Global Disaster Authority
GDW	:	Global Disasters Watch
GIS	:	Geographic information system
GSDMA	:	Gujarat State Disaster Management Authority
HPCDM	:	High Powered Committee [HPC] on Disaster Management
IDM	:	International Disaster Management
IDMP	:	International Disaster Management Plans
IDNDR	:	International Decade for Natural Disaster Reduction
IDRiM	:	Journal of Integrated Disaster Risk Management

IFRC	:	International Federation of Red Cross and Red Crescent
IMD	:	India Meteorological Department
IPID	:	Institute for Participatory Interaction in Development
KSDMA	:	Kerala State Disaster Management Authority
MDI	:	Meteorological Department of India,
NCMC	:	National Crisis Management Committee (NCMC):
NDMA	:	National Disaster Management Authority
NIDM	:	National Institute of Disaster Management
NIMHANS	:	National Institute of Mental Health and Neuro Sciences
OSDMA	:	Orissa State Disaster Mitigation Authority
PRI's	:	Panchayati Raj Institutions
PVC	:	ProVention Consortium
SPHERE Project	:	Humanitarian Charter & Minimum Standards in Disaster Response
TVSG	:	Trust for Village Self Governance, Tamilnadu
UNCRD	:	United Nations Centre for Regional Development
UNDP	:	United Nations Development Programme
USAID	:	United States Agency for International Development
WCDR	:	World Conference on Disaster Reduction
WDR	:	World Disaster Report
WHO	:	World Health Organization

Reference

A.C.Jena. (2009). *Empowering Panchayats and Community for disaster preparedness and mitigation: an Institution Building Perspective*. A.P.H. Publishing Corporation, New Delhi, (189-215).

Action Aid India. (2007). *Tsunami Rehabilitation Programme Reports* Kanyakumari, Tamilnadu, India.

Action Aid International. (2007). *Building Comprehensive Resilience and facilitating women's leadership: Critical Success factors for Disaster Risk Reduction and Climate Change Adaptation*, South Africa.

Action Aid International. (2007). *What we do: Emergencies: Tsunami disaster: Disaster Risk Reduction in the Post- Tsunami Context*, Action Aid Publication, South Africa.

ADPC. (2004). Program Completion Report: Asian Urban Disaster Mitigation Program. Asian Disaster Preparedness Center (ADPC). Bangkok, Thailand.

ADPC. (2004). *Report of the 4th Meeting of the ADPC Regional Consultative, Committee on Disaster Management*. Dhaka, Bangladesh, March 2004. Bangkok, Asian Disaster Preparedness Center (ADPC).

Alexander, David. (2002). "*Confronting Catastrophe: New Perspectives on Natural Disasters*", NY: Oxford University Press, New York.

All India Disaster Mitigation Institute, Disaster management articles, Gujarat, India.

Amrita Sree. (2010). Microfinance and Livelihood Projects in Andaman Island: Programme *reports*, Andaman Nicobar Island.

Anderson. (1997). *Community Participation in Disaster Rehabilitation and Recovery, Information Manuel*, Published by Governance and Social Development Resource Centre (GSDRC).

Andrew S. Mener. (2007). *Disaster Response in the United States of America: An Analysis of the Bureaucratic and Political History of a Failing System*, University of Pennsylvania, CUREJ - College Undergraduate Research Electronic Journal, 2-28.

Arun Kumar Talwar and Satish Juneja. (2009). *Earthquake disaster management*, Commonwealth Publications, New Delhi, 28-49.

Arun Kumar. (2008). *Global disaster management*, SBS publishers, New Delhi, 16-84, 112-164.

Arvind Kumar. (2006). *Disaster Management- Recent Approaches*, Institute for Sustainable Development, Lucknow, Anmol Publications, New Delhi, 23-47.

Asian Disaster Reduction and Response Network *Reports* (ADDRN). (2007). Malesia.

Asim Kumar Mukhopadhya. (2005). *Crisis and disaster Management Turbulence and Aftermath*, New Age International (P) Ltd, Publishers, New Delhi, 29-36.

Augustine J & Vivek C Kokkamadathil. (2011). *Crisis as an Opportunity-Organizational and Community Responses to disasters*, University Press of America, United States.

Behera Aurobindo. (2002). "Government - *NGO Collaboration for Disaster Reduction and Response: The India (Orissa) Experience*", paper presented at the Regional Workshop on Networking and Collaboration among NGOs of Asian Countries in Disaster Reduction and Response.

Binoy Acharya. (2005). UNNATI, *Earthquake in Gujarat and Role of Panchayats.*

Birkmann John. (2006). *Measuring Vulnerability to Natural Hazards*, edited by TERI Press, New Delhi, India, 34-95.

Bishnu Pandey and Kenji Okazaki. (2007). *Community Based Disaster Management: Empowering Communities to Cope with Disaster Risks,* United Nations Centre for Regional Development, Japan, 2-7.

Biswas et.al, (1997), Article *on Disaster Management.*

Blaikie, P., Cannon, T., Davis, I., & Wisner, B. 1994. *At Risk, Natural hazards, People's vulnerability and disasters*. London: Routledge Buchanan-Smith and Christopolos. (2004). 'Natural disasters amid complex political emergencies', Humanitarian Exchange (27), Humanitarian Practice Network, London:ODI, p. 3.

Brennan, M.A., C. Flint, and R. Barnett. 2005. *Community Volunteers: The Front Line of Disaster Response*. Journal of Volunteer Administration. 23(4): 52-56.

Building and Enabling Disaster Resilience of Coastal Communities (BEDROC), Reports, and Humanitarian field studies. 2004. Annie George, Nagapattinam, South India.

Carter.W.Nick. (1991). Disaster Management: A Disaster Manager's Handbook, Manila, ACB. p. xxiii.

Center for Research on the Epidemiology of Disasters. (CRED, 2011). EM-DAT, The International Disaster Data Base, Supported by USAID.

Charlotte Benson and John Twigg with Tiziana Rossetto. (2007). *Tools for Mainstreaming Disaster Risk Reduction: Guidance Notes for Development Organisations*, by the International Federation of Red Cross and Red Crescent Societies / the ProVention Consortium, Geneva, Switzerland.

Charveriat. (2000). Charveriat, Celine, "*Natural Disasters in Latin America and the Caribbean: An Overview of Risk*", Working Paper No. 434. Washington, D.C. Research Department, Inter-American Development Bank.

Chawla.P.S.(2008), *Emergency and Disaster Management*, Perl Books, New Delhi.

Chris, Thyagarajan et.al. (2006*). DEEDS, Tsunami Psychosocial care programme, reports*, Kerala

Comfort, L. K., Ko, K., & Zagorecki, A. (2004). *Coordination in rapidly evolving disaster response systems: The role of information*. American Behavioral Scientist, 48(3), 295-313.

Community Participation in Post-disaster Reconstruction: Lessons Learned from the Maharashtra Emergency Earthquake Rehabilitation Program [MEERP]. (1999).

CRED. (2009). *Disaster Category Classification and Peril Terminology for Operational Purposes*: Brussels, MunichRe: Munich.

Crook and Manor. (1998). Crook, R. C., and J. Manor, "*Democracy and Decentralization in South-East Asia and West Africa: Participation, Accountability and Performance*", Cambridge: Cambridge University Press.

Cuny FC: *Introduction to disaster management*. Lesson 1: The scope of disaster management. Prehosp Disast Med. (1992). 7(4):400–405.

Damon Coppola, (2007) *Introduction to International Disaster Management*, Publisher: Butterworth-Heinemann Edition: 2 (English), 26-82.

David E. Hogan, Jonathan L. Burstein. (2007). *Disaster Medicine*, Published by Lippincott Williams & Wilkins, Printed in USA.

Davidson, C. H. et al. (2006). *Truths and Myths about Community Participation in Post-Disaster Context.*

Denis McClean, eds. (2010). *World Disasters Report- focuses on urban risk, (International Federation of Red Cross and Red Crescent Societies*, Printed by Imprimerie Chirat, Lyons, France.

Development Initiatives. (2003). *Global Humanitarian Assistance*: 2003, Somerset: Development Initiatives, p.8

DFID. (2005). *Disaster Risk Reduction: A Development Concern*. Department for International Development. London, http://www.dfid.gov.uk/pubs/files/disaster-risk-reduction.pdf

Dhruba Raj Gautam. (2009).*Community-Based Disaster Risk Reduction- Good Practice Design and Printing:* Mind Share Communications Pvt. Ltd. Published by: Mercy Corps Nepal, Lalitpur, Nepal.

Disaster Management (CBDM) practices in Asia, *A Users guide,* Kobe Japan,

Disaster Management in India - *A Status Report, Ministry of Home Affairs, National Disaster Management Division.* (2004). 2- 32, 35-75.

Disasters Emergency Committee Disaster Risk Reduction ;A review of DRR work by DEC Member Agencies in response to the 2004 Tsunami, All India Disaster Management Institute, and Humanitarian Activities (UK). (2010).

Disasters, proceedings on international workshop on earthquake safer world in the 21st century, Kobe, Japan, February. (2003).

Dr. Sheonandan Pandey. (2008). CHINA: *Wenchuan Earthquake Management - Ground Realities*, Published by South Asia Analysis Group (SAAG), Noida, India.

Dreze, J. and A. K. Sen. (1988). "*Public Action for Social Security: Foundation and Strategy*", paper presented for STICERD/WIDER Workshop on Social Security in Developing Countries, London: London School of Economics.

ECLAC. (20020. *United Nations Economic Commission for Latin America and the Caribbean, "Handbook for Estimating the Socio-Economic and Environmental Effects of Disasters*", report LC/MEX/L.519, Mexico, D.F.

EM-DAT, OFDA/CRED *International Disaster Database,* Université Catholique de Louvain, Brussels, Belgium, http://www.em-dat.net.

Eranen & Liebkind. (1993). *Future of CBDM*, UNCRD tapestry, Kobe Japan,

Federal Emergency Management Agency (FEMA). (2003). *Disaster declarations and Emergency Assistance*, Dept of Homeland Security, Unites States

Frederick C. Cuny. (1944-1995). *Disaster Management*, Published in Prehospital and Disaster Medicine, - U.S.

Friedrich Ebert Stiftung (FES). (1992). *Women in Politics: Forms and Processes.*

G. Placid. (2005-07). SAHAYI, *Integrated Tsunami Relief and Rehabilitation Programme*, Kerala.

Global Humanitarian Assistance Update. (2004-05). *Development Initiatives.* Designed and typeset by Discript Ltd, London WC2N 4BN Printed in Scotland by Bell & Bain Ltd, Glasgow

Goel, S L. (2006). Encyclopedia of disaster management - vol. 3: Management of man-made disasters, Deep and Deep, New Delhi Green Paper on Disaster Management,(1998) Pretoria: Government of South Africa, *Green Paper Secretariat for Disaster Management*, South Africa.

Goel.S.L.. (2010). *Disaster Management- -Policy and Administration*, Daya Publications, 25-75.

GOI (2001) *High Powered Committee on Disaster Management: Report*, Department of Agriculture and Co-operation, Ministry of Agriculture, Government of India, New Delhi.

GOI (2004) *Disaster Management in India: A Status Report*, Natural disaster Management Division, Ministry of Home Affairs, Government of India, new Delhi.

Golandaz, H. M. and B. Mohanty (ed.), *Empowerment of Urban Local Government in India (with Special Reference to the Seventy-Third Constitutional Amendment Bill of 1991), in: Urbanization in Developing Countries*; Basic Services and Community Participation, pp. 376-388, Indian Institute of Social Sciences and Concept Publishing Company, New Delhi, 1993.

Government of Gujarat. (2003). *The Gujarat Disaster Management Act, 2003.* Gandhinagar: Government of Gujarat.

Guha-Sapir, D. Hargitt and P. Hoyois. (2004). *Thirty Years of Natural Disasters 1974-2003*: The Numbers, Presses Universitaires de Louvain: Louvain-la-Neuve.

Gujarat Earthquake Recovery Program Assessment Report. (2001). A Joint Report by the World Bank and the Asian Development Bank to the Governments of Gujarat and India.

Guzman. (2002). Manny de Guzman, "*The Total Disaster Risk Management Approach: An Introduction", paper presented at the Regional Workshop on Networking and Collaboration among NGOs of Asian Countries in Disaster Reduction and Response*, 20-22 February 2002, Kobe, Japan.

Guzman and Dixit. (2002). Manny de Guzman and Amod Mani Dixit, "*Profiling NGOs of Asian Countries: Commonalities and Rationale for Networking in Disaster Reduction and Response*", paper presented at the Regional Workshop on Networking and Collaboration among NGOs of Asian Countries in Disaster Reduction and Response, 20-22 February 2002, Kobe, Japan.

Habitat. (1996). Habitat Agenda, "*Istanbul Declaration on Human Settlements", United Nations Conference on Human Settlements* (Habitat II), Istanbul, 3-14

June 1996; Chapter 11: Disaster prevention, mitigation and preparedness, and post-disaster rehabilitation capabilities. Habitat, Housing Projects, Vol. 31, Issue 1, pp. 100-115.

Hangzhou Lai. Dr, Ms. Yanna Sun. (2005). *Recovery and Reconstruction management office of, National Disaster Reduction Center of China*, funded by Provention Consortium, guided by Asian Disaster Preparedness Center, Bangkok.

Hanumantha Rao, K and Srinivas Subba Rao. (2008). *Disaster Management*, Serials Publications, New Delhi.

Harsh K Gupta, ed. (2003). *Disaster management.-Universities* Press, Hyderabad, India.

High Power Committee on Disaster Management. (2001). *Report of the High Power Committee on Disaster Management*. New Delhi: National Center of Disaster Management.

Hoyois Ph.Debarati Guha Sapir. *(2008). Disasters in India: Policy overview of vulnerability, risks and human impact, "Recovering from earthquakes: Response, Reconstruction and Impact Mitigation in India"* (ed. Shirish B. Patel, Aromar Revi), Routledge; pp. 14-38.

ICT for Disaster Management/Disaster Management. (2008).

IFRC. (2003). "*Annual Report 2003*", The International Committee of Red Cross and Red Crescent Societies, Geneva.

Inter-Agency Secretariat of the International Strategy for Disaster Reduction (UN/ ISDR). (2004). Living with Risk: A global review of disaster reduction initiatives, Geneva, UN/ISDR, p. 3.

ISDR. (2007). "*Disaster risk reduction: 2007 global review*", consultation edition, prepared for the Global Platform for Disaster Risk Reduction, first session, Geneva, Switzerland, 5-7 June 2007, ISDR/GP/2007/3.

Jagbir Singh, ed. (2007*). Disaster management: future challenges and opportunities*, I.K.International, New Delhi.

Jain & Polman. (2003). *The Panchayati Raj model in India*, FAO Regional Office for Asia and the Pacific, Bangkok, Thailand.

Jain, A.K. (2008.) *Practical guide to disaster management.*— Pragun Publication.

Japan Earthquake Report. (2011). Disaster Watch, International Article on Disaster Management.

Jha, Gangadhar and B. Mohanty, (ed.), *Strengthening of Municipal Government in India;* Options for Reform, in: Urbanization in Developing Countries, Basic Services and Community Participation, pp. 361-375, Indian Institute of Social Sciences and Concept Publishing Company, New Delhi. (1993).

Joseph F. Gustin. (2010). *Webster's New World Dictionary of The American Language, United States.*

Journal of Integrated Disaster Risk Management (IDRiM). (2012). *Disaster Prevention Research* Institute of Kyoto University, Kyoto, Japan, ISSN: 2185-8322.

Kamal Taori, *Disaster Management through Panchayth Raj*. (2005., Concept Publishing Company, New Delhi.

Kanwar, Rakesh. (2001). *Disaster Management, The Administrator*, Vol. XLIV, December, pp. 96-110.

Kelman, I. (2005). "*Tsunami Diplomacy: Will the 26 December, 2004 Tsunami Bring Peace to the Affected Countries?*". Sociological Research Online, vol. 10, issue 1, http://www. socresonline.org.uk/10/1/kelman.html.

Kelman, I. and T. Koukis (eds). (2000). *'Disaster Diplomacy', special section in Cambridge Review of International Affairs (edited by Charlotte Lindberg Clausen)*, vol. XIV, no. 1, pp. 214-294.

L.W.Sunil Edward (2008), www.oxfamamerica.org/articles/the-perfect-knowledge-for-survival, Diviyagala, Sri Lanka.

Laurence C. C. Breaker. et.al. (2011), *the response of Monterey bay to the 2010 Chilean earthquake, science of tsunami hazards*, Journal of Tsunami Society International, Vol. 30, No. 1, page 23, Ottawa, Canada.

Lopez-Ibor, JJ., Christodoulou,G., Maj, M., Sartorius, N., & Okasha, A. (2005). *Disasters and Mental Health*. England, John Wiley & Sons Ltd.

Luis Flores Ballesteros. "Who's getting the worst of natural disasters?" 54 Pesos May. (2010).:54 Pesos 04 Oct 2008, http://54pesos.org/2008/10/04/who%e2%80%99s-getting-the-worst-of-natural-disasters

Madhava Rao V, and Hermon, R.R. (2004). *Management of Disasters, India.*

Maiya Kadel. (2011). *A comparative Study of Nepal and Japan" Community Participation in Disaster Preparedness Planning:* Asian Disaster Reduction Center, Nepal.

Mallika Samaranayake/Atul Loke/Panos. (2009). Oxfam America.

Marwaan Macan-Markar. (2011), *Tsunami impact-Communities Play Vital Role in Disaster Mitigation Analysis* –Inter Press Service News Agency Bangkok.

Maskrey. (1989). Maskrey, Andrew, "Disaster Mitigation - A Community Based Approach", Development Guidelines No 3, Oxfam, Oxford, UK.

Medina. (1994). Medina, Juvenal, "Experiencias de Mitigación de Desastres con Participación Comunal," www.desenredando.org.

Miskel. (2007). *Disaster Response and Homeland Security*, United States, 41- 44.

Moving towards Harmonization of Disaster Data. (2010). A Study of Six Asian Databases CRED.

Murthy, D B N. (2007). *Disaster Management: text and case studies*.-Deep & Deep, New Delhi.

Narayan, B. (2000). Disaster Management, A.P.H.Publishing Corporation, New Delhi.

National Disaster Management Authority. (2009). Policy and Guidelines. New Delhi: National Disaster Management Authority, Government of India. Accessed at http://ndma.gov.in on April 27, 2005.

National Disaster Management Division. (2004). *Disaster Management in India: A Status Report*. New Delhi: National Disaster Management Division, Ministry of Home Affairs, Government of India.

Norris, F.H., Galea, S., Friedman, M.J., & Watson, P.J. (2006). *Methods for Disaster Mental Health Research*. New York, The Guilford Press.

Oxfam International. (2008). *Humanitarian field studies, Tsunami response: Sheltering People after disasters: Lessons from the tsunami.*

Oxfam International. (2006). Oxfam Humanitarian *Field Studies, Disaster Management Policy & Practice: Lessons for Government, Civil Society, & the Private Sector in Sri Lanka.*

Palanithurai, G. (2009). Panchayats in Disaster Preparedness and Management. 22-90.

Pandey and Okazaki, UNCRD, 2010, Publications.

Parasuraman S & Unnikrishnan P. V. eds. (2001). *Disaster Response in India-an Overview , India Disasters Report- towards a policy initiative*, Oxford University Press, New Delhi.

Pearce L. (2003). Disaster Management and Community Planning, and Public Participation: How to Achieve Sustainable Hazard Mitigation, Natural Hazards, 28, 211-228.

Pearce, Laurie. (2001). An Integrated Approach for Community Hazard, Impact, Risk and Vulnerability Analysis: HIRV. Vancouver, BC: University of British Columbia.

Perez and Thompson. (2002), Natural Disasters, Series.

Pradeepkumar, A.K. (2010), Disaster Risk Vulnerability Conference, Mahatma Ghandi University, Kottayam, Kerala.

Prasad, S. (2007), Natural disaster management: destruction, safety and precautions. — Delhi: Manglam Publishers.

Prasad.S. (2009). Planning For Human settlements in Disaster prone Areas.

Probo Sudarmo, World Bank. (2009). personal communication; and World Bank, 2007, *Community-Based Settlement Rehabilitation and Reconstruction Project for Central and West Java and Yogyakarta Special Region, project documents*, http://web.worldbank.org.

Quarantelli. (1998). Quarantelli, E. L., "*Major Criteria for Judging Disaster Planning and Managing and their Applicability in Developing Societies*", Disaster Research Center, University of Delaware, Newark, USA.

R.K.Sharma, Gagandeep Sharma eds. (2009). *Natural Disaster: Institutional Building for Mitigating the impact on Vulnerable Sections*: A.P.H.Publishing Corporation, New Delhi.

Rajdeep Dasgupta. (2007). *Disaster Management and Rehabilitation*: Mittal Publications, New Delhi.

Rajib Shaw, ed. and Krishnamurthy, R R, ed. (2009). *Disaster management: global challenges and local solutions.:* Universities Press, Hyderabad R. Shaw, N Britton, M Gupta (eds); PNY: Towards Sustainable Community Recovery.

Ramakant Gaur. (2008). *Disaster management: strictly on the basis of prescribed syllabus with modern trends.*: GNOSIS, New Delhi.

Ramana Murthy, K. (2004). *Disaster Management*, Dominant Publishers, New Delhi.

Reports. (2007). Disaster Information's, Govt of Kerala.

Rhoda Margesson, Maureen Taft-Morales. (2010). H*aiti earthquake: Crisis and Response*, Congressional Research Service, 7-5700, www.crs.gov, R41023, United States.

Ribot. (1999). Ribot, Jesse C., "*Accountable Representation and Power in Participatory and Decentralized Environmental Management*", World Resources Institute, Washington, DC.

Richard W. Franke, (1999). *Kerala Model of Development*, Report.

Robert T. Stafford *Disaster Relief and Emergency Assistance Act.*

Rohit Jigyasu. (2002). "*Reducing Disaster Vulnerability through Local Knowledge and Capacity*" (PhD thesis, Trondheim: Norwegian University of Science and Technology),http://ntnu.divaportal. org/smash/record.jsf?searchId=1&pid= diva2:12384.

Ronald.W .Perry, E.L.Quarantelli.eds. (2005). "*What is Disaster"? by International Disaster Committee on disasters*, United States of America.

Rubin. (2006). 'The humanitarian-development debate and chronic vulnerability: lessons from Niger', Humanitarian Exchange, Number 33, March 2006, London: ODI.

S.P. Jain Wim Polman. (2003). A Handbook for Trainers on Participatory Local Development: The Panchayati Raj model in India, RAP publication 2003/07 FAO Regional Office for Asia and the Pacific, Bangkok, Thailand August 2003.

Satish Modh. (2006). Citizen's guide to disaster management: how to save your own life and help others, Macmillan Publications, New Delhi.

SDMA. (2005). State Disaster Management Authority, Govt of Kerala.

Sekar.et.al. (2005). Facilitation Manual for Trainers of Trainees in Natural Disasters, NIMHANS, Bangalore.

Shah, Anup. (2011). "Natural Disasters." Global Issues. 2011.

Sharma, Vinod K. (2003). Disaster Management - Approach and Emerging Strategies in India, VISION : The Journal of Business Perspective, January - June, 2003.

Shesh Kanta Kae and Zubair Murshed. (2006). Community-based Disaster Risk Management for Local Authorities, (2006) Published by the Asian Disaster Preparedness Center through its Partnerships for Disaster Reduction - Southeast Asia Phase 3 (PDRSEA3) Project jointly implemented by ADPC and UNESCAP with funding support from DIPECHO, Bangkok, Thailand.

Singh & Ballabh,. (2004). Disaster Management information's.

Singh, Katar and V. Ballabh. (2002). Incidence, Impacts, and Management of Droughts in India: An Overview, Paper presented in a workshop on "Sustainable Livelihood and Drought Management in South Asia: Issues, Alternatives.

Singh, R.B. (Ed.). (2000). Disaster Management, Rawat Publications, Jaipur and New Delhi.

Social Work Chronicle. (2012). Dr. Meena Galliara, Ananya Prabhawalkar, Disaster Management and Role of Academic Institutions, India, Publishing India, Volume 1 Issue 1, PISSN Number: 2277-1395, 1-29.

Soumitra Roy. (2004). Natural Disaster Management: A Case Study of Tornado, (New Delhi, Abhijeet Publications, 2004), p. 32.

SPHERE Project. (2010). The SPHERE Project, Accessed 15.

Subbiah, A.R. (2004). Natural Disaster Management, Vol. 21, State of the Indian Farmer: A Millennium Study, Academic Foundation, New Delhi for the

Department of Agriculture and Cooperation, Ministry of Agriculture, Government of India, New Delhi.

Sundar.I, Sezhiyan.. (2007). Disaster management, published by Sarup & Sons, New Delhi.

Supe AN. (2004). Disaster management—are we ready? Dept of Surgery, Seth G S Medical College and KEM Hospital, Parel, Bombay, Maharashtra.

Swiss Reinsurance Company Limited. (2009). Natural Catastrophe, and Man-made Disasters in 2008: North America & Asia.

The Asian Disaster Reduction & Response Network (ADRRN). (2007).

The Heritage Foundation, Reports. (2011).

Twigg, J. et al. (2000). NGO Natural Disaster Mitigation and Preparedness Projects: A Study of International Development and Relief NGOs Based in the UK. (London: British Red Cross Society), pp. 76–78. Case Study 18.1.

UNCRD, Kobe Japan. (2011). UNCRD Disaster Management planning Hyogo office; Defining the past and Building the Maiya Kadel, Asian Disaster Reduction Center, Ministry of Home Affairs, Nepal.

UNDP. (2004). Reducing Disaster Risk: A Challenge for Development, UNDP/ org.bcpr/disred/English/publications.htm.NewYork, USA.

UNDP.(2005). Reducing disaster risk: A challenge for development, New York, UNDP, p. 136.

UNDP. (1992). An Overview of Disaster Management, UNDP- UNDRO Disaster Management Training Programme Manuel, 2nd Edition.

UNDP. (1992). An Overview of Disaster Management, UNDP- UNDRO Disaster Management Training Programme Manuel.

UNEP 2001 GEO 3 Report, UNEP Nairobi, Kenya.

UNISDR. (2005). Building the Resilience of Nations and Communities to Disasters: Hyogo Framework for Action 2005-2015. World Conference on Disaster Reduction, held in Kobe, Japan. Geneva: United Nations International Strategy for Disaster Reduction.

United Nations Economic and Social Commission for Asia and the Pacific (UN ESCAP), Local Government in Asia and the Pacific: A Comparative Study. (1993). New Delhi.

Universal Law Publishing, Delhi. (2005). The disaster management act, 2005 (53 of 2005), Universal Law Publishing. New Delhi.

Urasano & Blumenfield. (2005). Disaster Management article.

Vaidyanathan, S. (2011). An introduction to disaster management: natural disasters and manmade hazards.-Ikon Books, New Delhi.

Vivek R, Rajendra D, & Dharmesh J. (2006).

Vogt, F.Debarati Guha Sapir, Cyclone Nargis in Myanmar: Lessons for public health preparedness for cyclones, American Journal of Disaster Medicine 4 (5): 273-278.

Vulnerability Atlas, GOI. (2007).

Wannasorn (2008). Community Participation in Tsunami Disaster Response and Recovery in Thailand, Natural Resources Institute, University of Manitoba, Canada R3T 2N2, September 26, 2008, 6-23.

WFP. (1998). World Food Programme, "Prevention and Preparedness: Mitigating the Effects of Natural Disasters", Strategy and Policy Division, Rome.

Wisner, Blaikie, Cannon and Davis. (2004). At Risk: Natural hazards, people's vulnerability and disasters (2nd edn.), London,Routledge, p. 27.

World Bank. (2002).. "The Last Straw: Integrating Natural Disaster Mitigation with Environmental Management", prepared by Maarten van Aalst and Ian Burton, Disaster Management Facility, Working Paper Series No. 5.

World Conference on Disaster Reduction. (WCDR, 2005).

World Disasters Report. (2009). Focus on early warning, early action: International Federation of Red Cross and Red Crescent Societies Printed by ATAR Roto Presse, Satigny/Vernier, Switzerland.

World Disasters Report. (2012). Focus on forced migration and displacement.

Wright et al. (1999). Wright, Graham A.N., Deborah Kasente, Germina Semogerere and Leonard Mutesasira, "Vulnerability, Risks, Assets and Empowerment - The Impact of Microfinance in Poverty Alleviation", Kampala, Uganda: Micro-Safe Africa and Uganda Women's Finance Trust.

Yongong et al. (1999). The Role of local institutions and their interaction in disaster risk, Produced by: Economic and Social Development Department.

Appendices

Appendix - I

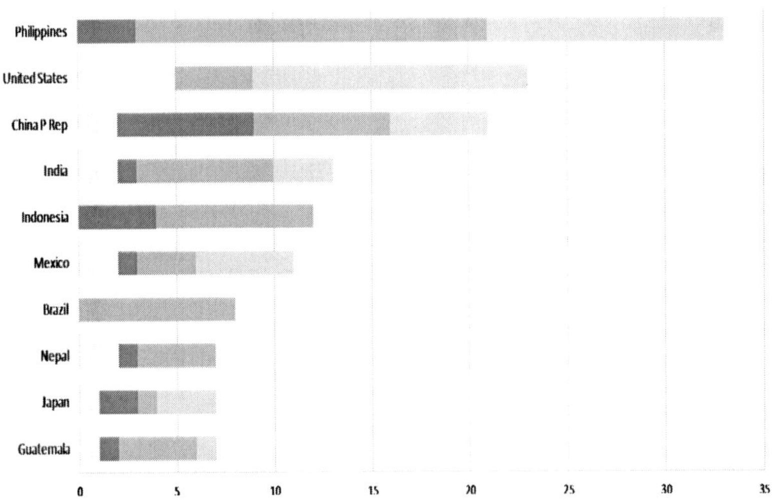

	Philippines	United States	China P Rep	India	Indonesia	Mexico	Brazil	Guatemala	Japan	Nepal	Total
Climatological	0	5	2	2	0	2	0	1	1	2	14
Geophysical	3	0	7	1	4	1	0	1	2	1	20
Hydrological	18	4	7	7	8	3	8	4	1	4	64
Meteorological	12	14	5	3	0	5	0	1	3	0	43
Total	33	23	21	13	12	11	8	7	7	7	141

Fig. 1: Top 10 countries by number of reported events in 2011

Country	Disaster distribution	No. of deaths	Country	Disaster distribution	Deaths per 100 000
Japan		19 975	Japan		15.7
Philippines		1933	Namibia		4.7
Brazil		978	New Zealand		4.2
Thailand		896	Cambodia		2.2
India		852	Philippines		2.1
United States		809	Thailand		1.3
China P Rep		746	Lesotho		1.2
Turkey		655	Turkey		0.9
Pakistan		511	Lao P Dem Rep		0.8
Colombia		313	Angola		0.7

Fig. 2: Top 10 countries in items of disaster mortality in 2011 and distributed by disaster type

Country	Disaster distribution	No.victims (millions)	Country	Disaster distribution	Victims/ pop. (%)
China P Rep		159.3	Somalia		42.9
India		12.8	Lesotho		23.9
Philippines		11.7	Cambodia		23.2
Thailand		11.2	Djibouti		22.5
Pakistan		5.4	Namibia		21.9
Ethiopia		4.8	Niger		19.6
Kenya		4.4	Thailand		16.2
Somalia		4.0	Philippines		12.6
Brazil		3.7	Burkina Faso		12.1
Mexico		3.7	China P Rep		11.9

Climatological ■ Geophysical ■ Hydrological ■ Meteorological

Fig. 3: Top 10 countried by victims in 2011 and distributed by disaster type.

Table 2 – Top 10 natural disasters by number of deaths

Event	Country	No. of deaths
Earthquake/Tsunami, March	Japan, Indonesia*	19 847
Tropical cyclone 'Washi' (Sendong), December	Philippines	1 439
Flood, January	Brazil	900
Flood, August-December	Thailand	813
Earthquake, October	Turkey	604
Flood, August-November	Pakistan	509
Flood, June	China P Rep	467
Storm, April	United States	354
Flood, August-November	Cambodia	247
Flood, August-October	India	204
	Total	25 584

*Japan (19 846), Indonesia (1).

Table 3 – Top 10 natural disasters by number of victims

Event	Country	Victims (in millions)
Flood, June	China P Rep	67.9
Drought, January-May	China P Rep	35.0
Storm, April	China P Rep	22.0
Flood, September	China P Rep	20.0
Drought	Burundi, Djibouti, Ethiopia, Kenya, Somalia, Uganda*	14.0
Flood, August-December	Thailand	9.5
Flood, August-October	India	5.5
Flood, August-November	Pakistan	5.4
Cold Wave, January	China P Rep	4.0
Flood, August-September	China P Rep	3.8
	Total	187.2

*Ethiopia (4.8 million), Kenya (4.3 million), Somalia (4.0 million), Uganda (0.7 million), Djibouti (0.2 million), Burundi (0).

Table 4 – Top 10 natural disasters by economic damages

Event	Country	Damages (in 2011 US$ bn.)
Earthquake/Tsunami, March	Japan, Indonesia*	210.0
Flood, August-December	Thailand	40.0
Earthquake, February	New Zealand	15.0
Storm, May	United States	14.0
Storm, April	United States	11.0
Drought, January-December	United States, Mexico**	8.0
Hurricane 'Irene', August-September	United States, Puerto Rico, Bahamas, Dominican Rep, Haiti, Canada***	7.9
Flood, June	China P Rep	6.4
Flood, April-May	United States	4.6
Flood, September	China P Rep	4.3
	Total	321.1

*Japan (210.0 billion), Indonesia (0).

**United States (8.0 billion), Mexico (0).

***United States (7.3 billion), Puerto Rico (0.5 billion), Bahamas (0.04 billion), Dominican Rep (0.03 billion), Haiti (0), Canada (0).

Appendix - II

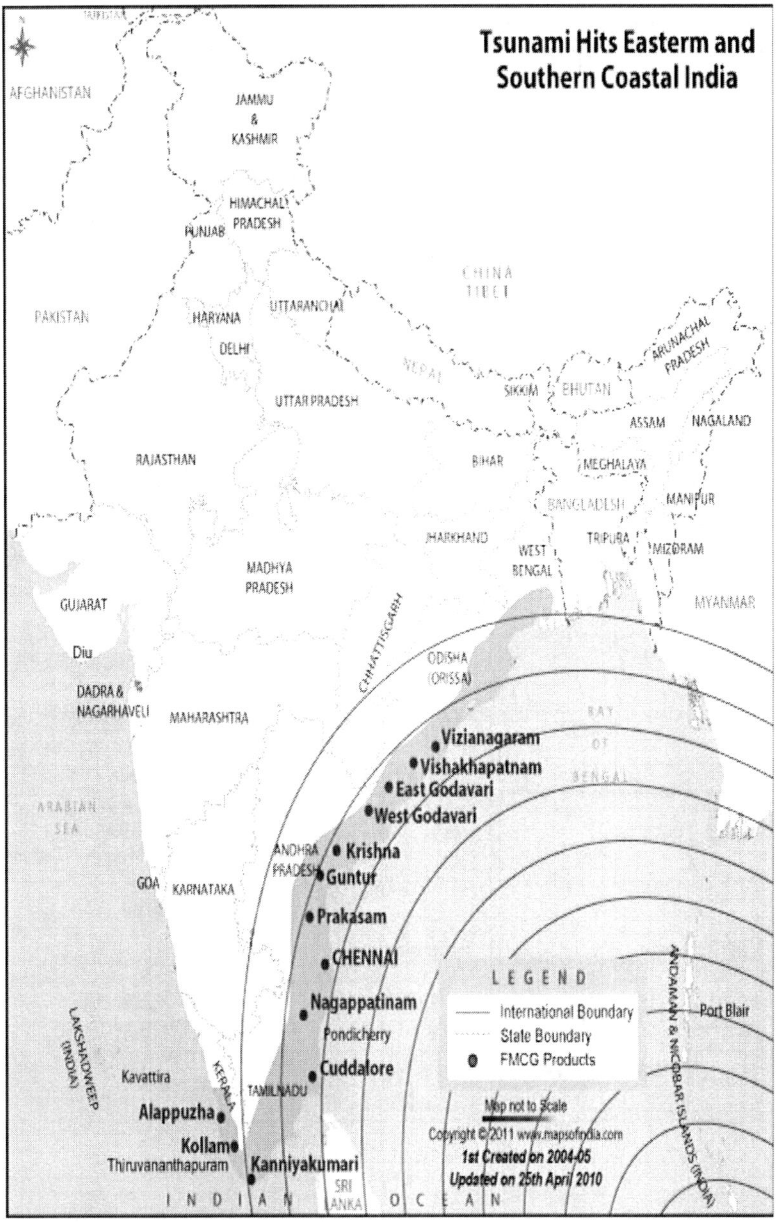

Tsunami Hits Easterm and Southern Coastal India
AFGHANISTAN
JAMMU & KASHMIR
HIMACHAL PRADESH
PUNJAB
CHINA TIBET
PAKISTAN
HARYANA
UTTARANCHAL
DELHI
ARUNACHAL PRADESH
NEPAL
SIKKIM
BHUTAN
UTTAR PRADESH
ASSAM
NAGALAND
RAJASTHAN
BIHAR
MEGHALAYA
BANGLADESH
MANIPUR
JHARKHAND
WEST BENGAL
TRIPURA
MIZORAM
MADHYA PRADESH
GUJARAT
CHHATTISGARH
MYANMAR
Diu
ODISHA (ORISSA)
DADRA & NAGARHAVELI
MAHARASHTRA
BAY OF BENGAL
Vizianagaram
Vishakhapatnam
East Godavari
West Godavari
ARABIAN SEA
ANDHRA PRADESH
Krishna
Guntur
GOA
KARNATAKA
Prakasam
CHENNAI
LEGEND
Nagappatinam
International Boundary
Port Blair
State Boundary
Pondicherry
FMCG Products
LAKSHADWEEP (INDIA)
Kavattira
KERALA
Cuddalore
TAMILNADU
ANDAMAN & NICOBAR ISLANDS (INDIA)
Map not to Scale
Alappuzha
Copyright © 2011 www.mapsofindia.com
Kollam
1st Created on 2004-05
Thiruvananthapuram
Kanniyakumari
Updated on 25th April 2010
SRI LANKA
INDIAN OCEAN

Appendix - III

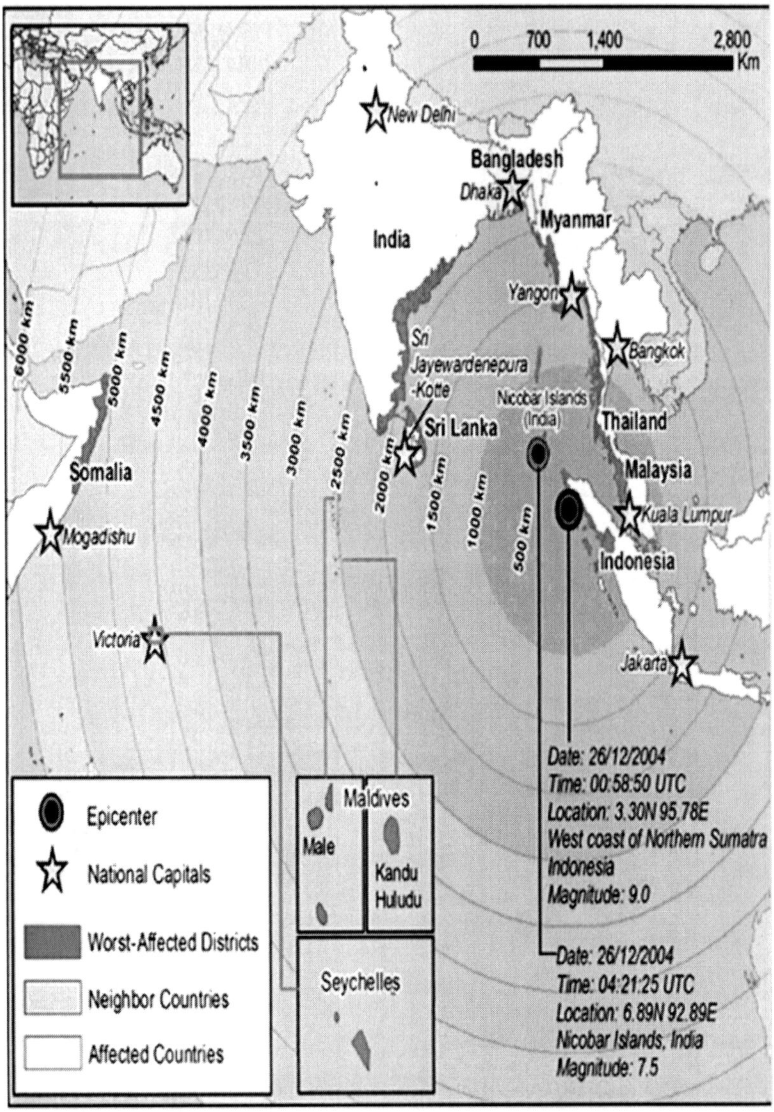

FIGURE Areas affected by the December 26, 2004, Indian Ocean tsunami. (*Source:* usgs.gov.)

Index

C

J

K

L

M